FULFILLING POTENTIAL, CREATING SUCCESS

Perspectives on Human Capital Development

FULFILLING POTENTIAL, CREATING SUCCESS

Perspectives on Human Capital Development

Edited by
Garnett Picot, Ron Saunders,
Arthur Sweetman

School of Policy Studies, Queen's University
McGill-Queen's University Press
Montreal & Kingston • London • Ithaca

Library and Archives Canada Cataloguing in Publication

Fulfilling potential, creating success : perspectives on human capital development / edited by Garnett Picot, Ron Saunders, Arthur Sweetman.

Includes bibliographical references.
ISBN-13: 978-1-55339-128-9 (bound)
ISBN-13: 978-1-55339-127-2 (pbk.)
ISBN-10: 1-55339-128-4 (bound)
ISBN-10: 1-55339-127-6 (pbk.)

1. Human capital. I. Picot, W. G. II. Saunders, Ron (Ronald S.)
III. Sweetman, Arthur IV. Queen's University. School of Policy Studies

HD4904.7.F84 2007   658.3   C2006-906761-9

Contents

Acknowledgements

This book follows from a research program managed by the Canadian Policy Research Networks (CPRN), the School of Policy Studies at Queen's University, and Statistics Canada. Financial support for the project was provided by Human Resources and Skills Development Canada; the Canadian Council on Learning; Alberta Human Resources and Employment; the Ontario Ministry of Training, Colleges and Universities; and the Canada Millennium Scholarship Foundation. The opinions expressed in this book are those of the authors and do not necessarily reflect the opinions of the organizations that funded the research program. The original papers, with one addition not in the original set, were all peer-reviewed and revised for incorporation into the present volume. The editors extend their gratitude to all the people who worked on the project and made this volume possible.

Special thanks go to Marilyn Banting for copy-editing the final essays; Val Jarus and Mark Howes who prepared the final manuscripts; Craig Jones for managing the revision process; Keith Banting, Patrice de Broucker, David Hay, Mary Pat MacKinnon, Tom McIntosh, François Nault, and Lynn Barr-Telford who all helped to plan and oversee the original program of research; and Trish Adams, Heather Fulsom, and Gisèle Lacelle who looked after the administrative aspects of that project.

We hope that this volume contributes to increased interactions between researchers and policymakers from different backgrounds and disciplines in their ongoing efforts to improve Canada's policies for, and management of, human capital development.

Garnett Picot, Director General
Business and Labour Market Analysis
Statistics Canada

Ron Saunders, Director, Work Network
Canadian Policy Research Networks

Arthur Sweetman, Director
School of Policy Studies
Queen's University

1

Introduction: Integrating Diverse Perspectives on Human Capital Development

GARNETT PICOT, RON SAUNDERS
AND ARTHUR SWEETMAN

Human capital, such as that derived from education and training, has widespread importance that is rarely disputed. It benefits individuals and society not only through improved economic and health outcomes, but also, for example, by increasing levels of civic engagement and by reducing levels of crime and other detrimental and costly behaviours. Increasing the benefits accruing to both individuals and society requires pursuing effective human capital development strategies. To be most efficient, these strategies should be both comprehensive and based on the most up-to-date research regarding the determinants, benefits and causal mechanisms of human capital acquisition. Unfortunately, much discussion of such strategies occurs in "silos," with information from one discipline or area not being promulgated more broadly. Further, knowledge is accumulating rapidly, so there is a need to identify new findings and put them into context.

This collection aims to break down the barriers between various areas of research and bring us to the frontier of knowledge regarding human capital development. Its strength is that leading researchers in various academic disciplines provide their take on what we know and just as importantly what we do not know about human capital development. We conceptualize human capital as the skills and knowledge that can be drawn upon (like any asset) to generate market outputs such as earnings and productivity, as well as valuable non-market-based outcomes such as civic engagement, citizenship skills and reduced crime rates.

The papers in this book arise from a research program managed by Canadian Policy Research Networks (CPRN), the School of Policy Studies at Queen's University and Statistics Canada. The volume's contribution is unique in that it takes the unusual step of providing syntheses of recent research on human capital development from a variety of academic disciplines including public health, economics, sociology, psychology, political science and education. As a result, the reader is treated to a very broad review of the relevant issues. The papers, as a group, investigate what existing research in each discipline tells us about:

- the determinants of human capital development, including the extent to which causal connections have been well-established and where such connections are more speculative;
- the effects of human capital acquisition on individual and societal outcomes;
- the potential policy implications of these streams of research; and
- key questions that are *not* being answered (or asked) and new ways of framing the issues that might be worth exploring.

Questions are examined not only across different disciplinary perspectives, but also across different phases of the life course, including prenatal development, early childhood, the years of formal schooling and adulthood.

The first paper looks at how child health affects later human capital development. In their paper, "The Effects of Deficits in Health Status in Childhood and Adolescence on Human Capital Development in Early Adulthood," Cameron Mustard, Emile Tompa and Jacob Etches note that children with poor physical or mental health commonly find it difficult to fully benefit from primary and secondary schooling, and frequently have lower expectations for postsecondary educational attainment.

They review evidence of the effects on human capital acquisition of a selected range of child and youth health conditions: fetal alcohol exposure, lead exposure, low birth weight, delayed growth, childhood behavioural disorders and childhood functional limitations. Fetal alcohol exposure, even at "social drinking levels," can lead to reduced academic and social functioning during the preschool and school years, and even as adults through symptoms such as increased inattention, lack of persistence and developmental delay. Lead exposure, at any level, is associated with lowered IQ, impaired neuropsychological functioning and impaired academic achievement. Unusually low birth weight is associated with impaired cognitive ability, independent of subsequent body size. Childhood and adolescent cognitive ability associated with the length of breast feeding is also discussed. Hyperactivity at ages 4 to 16 is shown to be associated with reduced upward occupational mobility in young adulthood for boys and decreased upward educational mobility for boys and girls. The authors suggest that other childhood conditions, such as traumatic injury, asthma and depression, likely also affect human capital attainment.

While none of these conditions has a high prevalence, Mustard, Tompa and Etches state that "the cumulative prevalence of all childhood disorders that may have at least some degree of consequences for human capital attainment will be in the range of 15 to 25 percent of the population of children." Aside from the health imperatives associated with these disorders, which have prompted government responses in some cases, the human capital development evidence presents an additional case for intervention to reduce the incidence of these disorders. The authors argue that the policy response must cut across traditional institutional boundaries and that it should be targeted to the most vulnerable households and children.

While Mustard, Tompa and Etches touch upon the evidence of an inverse relationship between health status and socio-economic status (SES), Lori Curtis, in her paper, "Socio-Economic Status and Human Capital: Recent Canadian Evidence," focuses on the relationships between SES and both health status and educational attainment. Curtis points to evidence that maternal education and lone-mother status are strongly associated with child health outcomes, more so than is family income. She notes that many studies show a strong relationship between SES (as measured by parental education, parental income and lone-parent status) and attainment of postsecondary education. There is some disagreement in the literature as to whether the SES gradient in postsecondary participation strengthened as tuition fees rose over the 1990s and early 2000s, but the majority of the studies indicate little change, perhaps because of off-setting government programs.

Explanations for the SES gradients in health status and educational attainment have included "income constraints, imperfect capital markets, imperfect knowledge, learned values and behaviours, or stress resulting from poor economic and social circumstances." Curtis cites recent research indicating that income constraints affecting educational access explain only a small part of the gradient in postsecondary participation. Earlier influences, such as child health and the readiness of young children to learn are more important, leading some researchers to call for a strengthening of early childhood development programs, including the targeting of government support to low-SES families. But such investments take a generation to yield results, and Curtis cites Keith Banting's conclusion that because of this long time lag and the fact that inequality in human capital development cannot be divorced from poverty issues, income redistributive measures are needed in the present in light of the current SES gradient in human capital among adults.

Craig Riddell's study, "The Impact of Education on Economic and Social Outcomes: An Overview of Recent Advances in Economics," highlights how "natural experiments" (such as increases in the age of compulsory schooling) have improved our understanding of the causal relationship between educational attainment and labour market outcomes. Recent studies oriented toward establishing causal, not just associative or correlational, relationships indicate that the effect of increased educational attainment on earnings is even larger than previously believed, especially for those with relatively low levels of education.

Riddell also points to recent causal evidence of the social benefits of education beyond the labour market outcomes of the individual. These include improving health, fostering innovation, enhancing the productivity of those with whom the highly educated interact and work, reducing crime and fostering civic participation. While supported by less research than that for the private/personal returns to education and training, the social returns appear to be substantial. However, there is considerable uncertainty regarding the exact magnitude of the effects, and the evidence is mainly from the United States and a few international studies since, although growing, the Canadian literature is thin in this area.

These findings enhance the case for governmental interventions to address barriers to participation in postsecondary education, many of which are not financial. For example, providing more information on the consequences of additional schooling is seen to be very important. Moreover, there is also support for the recent initiatives in some provinces to increase the age of compulsory schooling. Other recent studies, such as that by Carneiro and Heckman for the US (2002) and Marc Frenette for Canada (forthcoming) conclude that the most important factors explaining gaps in university attendance between children from low- and high-income families are parents' education and the academic ability of the child as measured by standardized test scores. The gaps in academic ability emerge early in life, suggesting that interventions are needed early as well. And as Riddell notes, while we can be more confident than in the past that education has large, positive impacts on a variety of individual and social outcomes, we need a better understanding of the pathways through which such effects occur. Riddell asks, "Does education alter the way that individuals access and process information?"

Some light is shed on this last question, among other issues, by Jacqueline Leighton. In "Increasing Adaptive Expertise: The Next Frontier in Human Capital Development," she outlines current knowledge in the psychology literature related to human capital development. Briefly, she finds that some of the major determinants of human capital development are: measured intelligence, neural efficiency, working memory, knowledge and the ability to use it within a particular context to solve problems, and the ability to "learn for meaning." She notes that variables such as neural efficiency and working memory predict measured intelligence, suggesting that more intelligent people use their brains and manage information processes more efficiently. While there is a strong inherited component to intelligence, Leighton points to research that indicates that education can make a difference. She refers to the work of Garlick, who concludes that "better organized brain systems are likely to arise when young children are exposed to learning environments that challenge their developing brains to create highly efficient connections in adaptation to difficult tasks." Garlick claims that theory-based reasoning should be introduced to students at a younger age than is currently the norm.

Leighton also points to findings that working memory can be enhanced *at any age* through intensive, deliberate practice and the "chunking" of information. Research in psychology also indicates that when children and adults are taught to engage in theory-based reasoning — thinking that seeks to uncover the underlying causal principles — they are better able to reuse their knowledge and transfer their skills to new areas and new problems. Leighton notes that human capital can be fostered by applying the results of systematic research on the development of adaptive expertise to teaching methods. Further research along these lines requires greater access by psychologists to children and student populations in classroom settings.

Issues regarding the education system are also the subject of the next paper in the collection, though from a different perspective. In "Human Capital Development and Education," Robert Crocker looks at research on the "education production function" — the relationship between resource allocation in our schools and learning outcomes — with a focus on the K to 12 system.

Crocker's main conclusion is that the research on the effects of changes in educational resource expenditures (e.g., reducing class size, alternative pedagogical approaches) is, at best, inconclusive. This situation makes it difficult to advise policymakers about funding priorities. There is some evidence that smaller class size (fewer students per teacher) in the primary grades yields higher achievement levels. However, the research indicates that it would take large reductions in class size, and therefore a large increase in funding, to obtain improvement in outcomes. In practice, when governments move to reduce class size, the reductions tend to be modest. The evidence suggests that the benefits of this are questionable. Crocker cites Hanushek's conclusion that what matters is not resources but how they are used. For example, there is some evidence from American studies that spending targeted on disadvantaged students does improve achievement.

Crocker also cites evidence that teachers with a few years of experience perform better (in terms of learning outcomes of their students) than neophytes, but notes that there isn't much evidence of gains from experience beyond that point. Specialization is an advantage, but there is no evident gain in student outcomes from teachers having higher degrees.

Regarding future research, Crocker points to the need to get inside the "black box" of educational processes through more collaboration between those looking at resources and outcomes and those studying education processes. The former group has tended to rely on secondary analysis of existing data sources; the latter on the micro world of the classroom, but with little examination of the resources needed for different teaching processes. Crocker argues that it is important to pay attention to resources, but that advances are more likely to come from micro-level research, such as field experiments focusing on particular education processes, than from the analysis of large-scale surveys.

Stephen Morgan and Mark McKerrow look at factors affecting educational attainment from a sociological perspective in their paper, "Human Capital Development and the Frontiers of Research in the Sociology of Education." They consider four broad explanations — family background, race, opportunities to learn and school effects — for motivation and commitment to schooling, learning and preparation for post-secondary education and resulting educational attainment.

Morgan and McKerrow rely mainly on American studies in their review of the literature, since the Canadian literature on the sociology of education is thin, in part because Canada lacks a national, school-based, longitudinal survey. The authors note that in the sociology of education, family background is universally considered to be the most important determinant of educational achievement and outcome. However, they also observe that although there has been substantial work on this issue in Canada, the literature lacks depth, particularly with regard to the causal effects of family background. The paper demonstrates the difficulty in generating unqualified support for one specific policy over another, given that there are relatively few consensus positions in the sociology of education, even based on US research. There are areas where strong research findings have allowed a consensus to develop, however, and the literature does point to policy recommendations. Three such examples are grade retention (requiring students who are not meeting standards to repeat the grade), ability streaming (placing high-school students in academic or non-academic tracks) and social capital development.

The theory behind grade retention is that the threat of retention stimulates student effort and the fact of retention enables poorly performing students to improve their understanding of the curriculum. However, the evidence examined by Morgan and McKerrow indicates that grade retention does more harm than good. Students who have been held back do not appear to learn more and they are far more likely to drop out of secondary school.

Evidence regarding the net effects of ability streaming is not as compelling, but still of policy relevance. While non-academic pathways can benefit some students, there are risks that streaming can be class-biased. Studies that control for academic achievement and ability find that students of higher socio-economic status are more likely to obtain higher-track placements. So, where streaming is in place, Morgan and McKerrow point to the need for steps to avoid this bias.

Morgan and McKerrow also note the potential gains associated with certain kinds of peer networks (social capital). Since the literature suggests that many disadvantaged students are uninterested in structured extracurricular activities, the question arises of whether schools should provide more mandatory activities, or expanded unstructured opportunities, for students to develop their peer networks. However, they also suggest that the opportunity for "the cultivation and re-inforcement of anti-schooling norms in some associational groups" must be recognized and challenged by school officials.

Morgan and McKerrow argue that our understanding of these issues could be improved by more comparative research, particularly Canada-US comparisons. As an example, they suggest an examination of factors affecting high-school completion and/or participation in postsecondary education in Canada and the United States.

The final paper in the collection is "Human Capital, Civic Engagement and Political Participation: Turning Skills and Knowledge into Engagement and Action," by Brenda O'Neill. O'Neill reports evidence that increased educational attainment is associated with higher levels of political participation, not only through imparting knowledge and developing citizenship skills, but also through enhancing the motivation to participate. The increase in motivation is particularly associated with higher education, partly through curriculum that conveys a sense of civic responsibility and duty.

However, O'Neill also points to a puzzle in the literature on political engagement. The empirical evidence indicates that today's generation of young Canadians is less likely to vote and less likely to pay attention to politics than was the case for previous generations of young people, despite growing levels of educational attainment over time. But the biggest decline in political participation is among less-educated youth, so the positive impact of education remains.

O'Neill also points to the role of social capital — the networks connecting people to each other — in fostering civic engagement. In particular, she notes evidence that mobilizing agencies, such as trade unions and religious organizations, help draw citizens into action, in part through building feelings of trust and reciprocity (social capital), and also through developing citizenship and political skills and through the direct opportunities they provide for volunteering.

Not only do the acquisition of human and social capital foster participation and engagement, but, to some extent, there is evidence that the converse is also true: participation in politics can help develop skills needed to work with others through collective action, and enhance people's capacity to appreciate other points of view. O'Neill cites several policy implications of this literature. Investment by governments in education, including higher education, is warranted, not only for considerations of productivity in an economic sense, but it also provides returns in terms of enhanced political participation and citizen engagement, and more effective articulation of values and interests in the political process. In particular, there is a need for a renewed commitment to a civics curriculum in our K to 12 system. Governments can foster civic engagement through support of voluntary associations. In their role as mobilizing agencies, such organizations provide an important avenue for developing citizenship skills, particularly among disadvantaged groups.

The papers in this collection focus on factors affecting, and outcomes associated with, the development of human capital from the perspective of multiple academic disciplines. However, some themes cut across more than one paper. For example, several authors point to the importance of early intervention in order to safeguard later potential. The paper by Mustard, Tompa and Etches, with its focus on avoidable child health conditions that can impair later learning and development, is the most explicit in this regard. Leighton points to the importance of teaching our children in ways that enhance their working memory and "neural efficiency." O'Neill calls attention to the value of including civics education in the K to 12 curriculum. Of course, the concept of human capital is inherently about investments that pay off over time, and these studies point to particular kinds of investment in our children that may call for a policy response.

Social capital is raised by several authors as a potentially important influence on the acquisition of skills and knowledge. For example, as we have just seen, O'Neill cites evidence that participation in voluntary associations is associated with increased levels of trust and co-operation within communities and that such social capital helps build citizenship skills. Morgan and McKerrow refer to research findings pointing out that community practices and norms that build trust among students, teachers and principals have contributed to the success of Catholic schools in the United States. They, as well as Riddell, refer to the effects of peer relationships on educational attainment. Although there is more work to be done to understand how these observations link to policy action, the density and quality of social networks appear to be key influences on both the acquisition and utilization of human capital.

Another cross-cutting theme is that the gains from the acquisition of human capital, particularly the gains from formal education, go well beyond improved employment prospects and earnings in the labour market. Other gains include: reduced crime, improved health, greater and more effective political participation and enhanced engagement by citizens in their communities. Similarly, the papers collectively point to the potential gains from integrating family, education and public health policies (as noted explicitly in the paper by Mustard, Tompa and Etches).

One policy recommendation that flows from this collection and is explicit in several papers is the benefit of keeping our young people in school. The gains from formal education seem clear and Riddell points to evidence that the incremental gains are particularly high for the less-educated. One province has very recently moved to extend the age of compulsory schooling. It will be important to monitor and evaluate the impact of this policy change.

All of the authors of papers in this volume point to areas where additional research would be particularly beneficial, such as the magnitude of the impact of childhood health problems on learning, the effects on human capital development of alternative pedagogies in formal schooling, and how the extent and nature of civics education of children affects civic and political engagement in adulthood. Several authors point to the value that longitudinal studies could provide in answering such questions.

Among promising areas for future work, we would add research questions that go beyond traditional disciplinary boundaries. The papers in this volume lead us to conclude that there is much that can be learned about determinants and effects of human capital acquisition by combining the research knowledge and approaches from different social science disciplines. Examples of topics that lend themselves to cross-cutting, integrative work include:

- the effects of early childhood experiences on subsequent learning;
- the impact of education/learning at different stages of the life course on health behaviours and health outcomes;
- the effects of different "vocational" programs in high school (e.g., co-op education, school-based vocational education, a mix of the two, apprenticeship or pre-apprenticeship programs) on subsequent learning and labour market activity;
- the distribution of returns to education/learning. For example, as participation in higher education increases, is there a form of polarization in the returns with some students reaping very large returns and others very little?

- the impact of access to, and the take-up of, health services on educational attainment and labour force participation;
- the impacts of education and training of various types on future human capital investment decisions;
- institutional barriers to lifelong learning;
- the effectiveness of alternative modes of delivery of skills upgrading programs for adult learners; and
- relationships between learning activity and life-satisfaction/well-being.

As the papers point out, reaching consensus regarding the answers to basic questions surrounding human capital development can be a long journey. But education is arguably the most important determinant of a host of positive outcomes, both at the individual and societal level, over which institutions and individuals have some control. This notion should place research regarding human capital development high on any priority list. Involving researchers from a number of disciplines would lead to a more integrated understanding of what factors contribute to the acquisition and utilization of skills and knowledge, and what outcomes — for individuals, for organizations and for society as a whole — are associated with the development of human capital. This volume is one step in that journey.

References

Carneiro, P. and J.J. Heckman. 2002. "The Evidence on Credit Constraints in Post-Secondary Schooling," *The Economic Journal* 112 (October):705-34.

Frenette, M. Forthcoming. *Why are Lower Income Students Less Likely to Attend University? Evidence from Standardized Tests Scores, Non-Cognitive Abilities, and Parental and Peer Influences*. Analytical Studies Research Paper. Ottawa: Statistics Canada.

2

The Effects of Deficits in Health Status in Childhood and Adolescence on Human Capital Development in Early Adulthood

Cameron Mustard, Emile Tompa and Jacob Etches

Important human capital is formed in childhood and adolescence, as a result of both formal education and the socialization experiences provided by families and peer groups. Health-status deficits in childhood and adolescence may influence human capital development primarily through effects on educational attainment. There is a need for additional research describing the pathways leading from childhood health status to early adult human capital attainment and to assess the economic consequences of public policies focused on mitigating the impact of social, economic and health disadvantage on child and adolescent developmental outcomes.

Introduction

Economists define human capital as the acquired skills and knowledge an individual can draw upon to generate outputs of value. Human capital may be applied to generate value in the labour market, or may be applied to produce other valued individual or societal outcomes such as improved personal health or active civic engagement.

An important portion of human capital is acquired in childhood and adolescence, as a result of both formal education and the socialization experiences provided by families and peer groups. It is plausible to expect that health status in childhood and adolescence will influence human capital development, primarily through effects on educational attainment. Children with poor physical or mental health may be impaired in gaining maximum benefits from primary and secondary schooling and may have lower expectations for postsecondary educational attainment. Children with robust physical and mental health may have more energy and personal resources to respond to the relatively high expectations of the current education curriculum. These differences in the opportunity to gain human capital, determined by health status, have the potential to shape, in part, the socio-economic mobility opportunities of individual birth cohorts.

In this paper, we assess the evidence for the influence of health-status deficits in childhood and adolescence on human capital attainment. As will be outlined in the following sections of this paper, we define health-status deficits broadly. Health-status deficits include physical, mental and/or cognitive deficits arising from injury or insult during gestation and birth. Deficits in physical and/or mental health can also arise from physical or toxicological injury during periods of heightened developmental vulnerability in early childhood. Injury to physical or cognitive function can occur during later periods of childhood and during adolescence. This paper also takes the perspective that deficits in behavioural development, represented by syndromes such as hyperactivity or conduct disorder, also represent deficits in health and function, broadly defined.

We apply this definition of health to review a sample of the epidemiologic literature in two primary areas: first, the potential for specific health-status deficits to influence developmental outcomes (with the potential for these deficits in developmental outcomes to influence human capital attainment), and second, the empirical evidence from longitudinal studies that have followed cohorts of children into adulthood to estimate the magnitude of effects on educational attainment and occupational attainment attributable to health-status deficits in childhood.

One perspective advanced in this paper is that the influence of child health status on human capital development is poorly understood and therefore given limited recognition in policy deliberations (Willms 2003). There are strong macroeconomic imperatives for ensuring optimal human capital development outcomes in Canadian society. The aging population profile will increase the productivity expectations of active labour-force participants. As the labour market demand for knowledge workers increases and the demand for manual labour declines, child and adolescent health-status deficits in the cognitive and behavioural domains may become increasingly consequential for understanding differences in young adult occupational attainment and labour-force success.

Epidemiologic studies of adult populations in the developed economies have consistently observed an inverse relationship between health status and socio-economic status. Persons in lower status occupations, with lower levels of educational attainment or residing in households earning lower incomes will typically have poorer health status than persons with more advantaged socio-economic circumstances. These socio-economic health inequalities in adult populations are frequently described as gradients. A gradient in population health status describes a monotonic pattern of increasing morbidity and risk of mortality with decreasing rank order in a socio-economic hierarchy. The Black Report, published in the United Kingdom in the early 1980s, was among the first studies to examine explanations that may account for these observed socio-economic health inequalities (Townsend, Whitehead and Davidson 1982; MacIntyre 1997). The Black Report considered two competing explanations for the causes of socio-economic health inequalities in populations: social causation (where the material and psychosocial conditions of socio-economic position influence subsequent health status) and health selection (where health status influences subsequent socio-economic status).

The authors of the Black Report concluded that social causation processes were dominant in producing socio-economic health inequalities. There is, for example, robust evidence, emerging from longitudinal observational studies of working-age adults, that exposures embedded in work experiences are important causes of the development of gradients in health status across occupational groups ranked by socio-economic position (Sorlie and Rogot 1990; MacKenbach 1997; Marmot *et al*. 1991). There are several prospective studies of young adults entering the labour market that have documented the health effects of adverse exposures in these early labour market experiences (Wadsworth, Montgomery and Bartley 1999; Morrell *et al*. 1997; Graetz 1993; Matthews *et al*. 1998; Power *et al*. 1997; Blane, Power and Bartley 1996). Figure 1 depicts the emergence of differences in health status over three to five years of follow-up among three large samples of labour-force participants in equivalent health at the beginning of the study period (Kingdon 1995). In each of the Danish, British and Canadian samples, workers in lower-ranked occupations were more likely to report a decline in their health status over the follow-up period relative to workers in the highest-ranked occupations.

The authors of the Black Report did acknowledge that health-related social mobility processes do explain a portion of socio-economic health

Figure 1. Odds Ratio for Decline in Health Status in the United Kingdom, Canada and Denmark

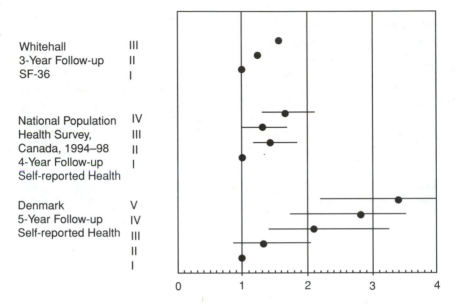

Note: In this figure, the horizontal axis scales odds ratios for health status declines, comparing the odds of health-status decline in the most advantaged occupational group (labelled I on the vertical axis) to the odds of health-status decline in less-advantaged occupational groups (labelled II to V on the vertical axis).
Source: Mustard, Lavis and Ostry (2005).

inequalities in populations. Health selection arises when current health status influences future socio-economic status. For example, healthy individuals may be more successful and unhealthy individuals may be less successful in ascending socio-economic hierarchies. As a further example, the onset of an illness resulting in work disability in an adult of working age can frequently result in a decline in socio-economic position. The evidence considered in the Black Report suggested that health-selection effects account for no more than 10 to 20 percent of the socio-economic health-status gradient observed in most developed country populations (Blane, Davey-Smith and Bartley 1993; MacIntyre 1997; Chandola *et al.* 2003; Cardona, Costa and Demaria 2004; Elstad and Krokstad 2003; Bartley and Plewis 1997; Marmot *et al.* 1997). The dominant process responsible for creating socio-economic health-status gradients in populations arises from the effects of socio-economic disadvantage on health status. Most of this research on health-related social mobility has examined cohorts of working-age adults and has therefore described the impact of health selection on socio-economic mobility within the adult period of the life course.

There has been less attention paid to health-related social mobility between childhood and adulthood, where childhood health status might influence adult socio-economic attainment. The growth of this area of inquiry has required the development of longitudinal research cohorts integrating measures of biology, behavioural development and health status and human capital attainment across the life course (Power and Hertzman 1997; Davey-Smith *et al.* 1998; Caspi *et al.* 2002; Lynch *et al.* 1994; Lawlor, Ebrahim and Davey-Smith 2002), novel conceptual frameworks (Hertzman 1999) and new approaches to the analysis of stability and change in health at different stages of life. Given the complexity of mounting prospective cohorts that have enrolled subjects in childhood and maintained follow-up into adulthood, there are relatively few sources of information on the influence of child and adolescent health on socio-economic mobility outcomes in adulthood (Hertzman and Wiens 1996; Barker 1992; Kuh and Ben-Shlomo 1997; Coe 1999).

What Does Existing Research Tell Us About the Influence of Childhood Health on Human Capital Development?

There are a limited number of cohort studies that have measured health status in a representative sample of children and followed these children into adulthood. The UK National Child Development Study (NCDS), a cohort of 17,414 children born during a single week in 1958, has reported extensively on health-related social mobility (Manor, Matthews and Power 2003; Power, Matthews and Manor 1996; Power *et al.* 2002). In Canada, the Ontario Child Health Study (OCHS) enrolled a sample of 3,200 children in 1983. These cohort members have recently been followed into adulthood, at ages 22–34 (Boyle *et al.* 1987; Boyle *et al.* 1993). Both the NCDS and the OCHS obtained measures of parental socio-economic status, emotional and behavioural function and physical health in childhood as well as social and economic characteristics and measures of health and function obtained in early adulthood. Results reported from both cohorts have found health selection effects (Mustard *et al.* 2005; Boyle *et al.* 2001; Power *et al.* 1990; Wadsworth

1986). At labour market entry, cohort members with poor health were more likely to be downwardly mobile and less likely to be upwardly mobile relative to their healthier peers over the follow-up period (intergenerational mobility).

In addition to this small but important body of literature based on long follow-up studies from childhood to adulthood, there is a larger body of literature that has estimated the impact of specific disorders and syndromes in childhood on pediatric and youth developmental outcomes. There is a range of disciplines contributing to this evidence. Epidemiologists are typically concerned with health outcomes, and thus, more attention has been spent examining the impact of child health on adult health rather than on human capital acquisition. Among social epidemiologists, there is a literature linking child health to the emergence of social inequalities in health in adulthood. Part of this literature describes the impact of child health on human capital acquisition. Pediatric epidemiology and the epidemiology of readiness to learn also contain findings relevant to human capital acquisition.

There are important definitional issues in examining the effect of child health on adult human capital acquisition. Aspects of childhood cognitive, emotional or behavioural health may be precursors of adult human capital as well as a component of adult human capital. So, for example, a childhood behavioural disorder like hyperactivity may lead to impaired academic performance in school, resulting in lower educational attainment in adulthood. This example is a model of pathway effects. Alternatively, hyperactive disorders in childhood may persist into adulthood as impulsive personalities with the potential that this adult trait impairs success in the labour market and in other socially desirable outcomes. In the remainder of this paper, the reader may generally assume that we are presenting evidence for pathway effects linking childhood health status to adult human capital.

In the following section, we review evidence of consequences to human capital acquisition for a selected range of child and youth health status and behavioural function measures. The review presented in this section is not comprehensive. The specific health conditions represented in the following discussion are not necessarily the most consequential for human capital attainment, nor are the conditions represented the only pediatric health impairments that may influence human capital attainment. The health conditions are selected to indicate the importance of examining health-status factors at specific stages of childhood in understanding the consequence for human capital development.

Fetal Alcohol Exposure

Fetal alcohol spectrum disorder (FASD) refers to the range of outcomes associated with all levels of fetal alcohol exposure. Sokol, Delaney-Black and Nordstrom (2003) have reviewed the evidence on its consequences and the disease burden in the United States. In addition to physical effects, FASD can include longer reaction times, inattention, hyperactivity and developmental delay at preschool ages; learning problems, attention and impulsivity problems, memory deficits, distractibility, restlessness, lack of persistence and mood disorders during school ages; and attention problems, executive functioning deficits leading to difficulty with problem-solving and functioning in everyday life, adult antisocial syndrome, and alcohol, drug and nicotine dependence in adulthood. Alcohol exposure is considered the most common cause of mental retardation and the leading preventable cause of birth defects in the US. While fetal alcohol exposure is difficult to measure, it is currently thought that social drinking levels during pregnancy can lead to reduced academic and social functioning in exposed children. FASD is associated with low socio-economic status, older mothers, and in the US strongly with African-American and especially with American Indian/Alaska Native status.

It has proven difficult to precisely estimate the incidence of FASD because exposure (alcohol consumption) is difficult to measure and the signs and symptoms of FASD are easily overlooked. One estimate suggests the incidence of FASD may be as high as 1 in 100 births in the US (ibid.). Fetal alcohol syndrome, or FAS, involves more severe symptoms, and is thought to have an incidence rate between 0.5 and 2 per 1,000 births in the US (Abel 1995; May and Gossage 2001). There is some evidence that the United States has unusually high incidence rates (Abel 1995), but there is no national estimate for Canada (Chudley *et al.* 2005). However, unless there is a large, unmeasured disease burden, the relatively low prevalence of both FAS and FASD means that these disorders will not be significant factors in human capital acquisition in the general population.

Childhood Lead Exposure

Compared to fetal alcohol exposure, childhood lead exposure is easier to measure, and therefore better understood. The mechanisms and consequences of lead toxicity have been reviewed by Lidsky and Schneider

(2003). Lead can substitute for calcium in many biochemical processes, and many of its diverse toxic effects can be traced to this property. Once absorbed, lead persists in the blood for weeks, in the brain for years and in bone for decades. Children can be exposed environmentally, by breastfeeding and during gestation. Since lead accumulates in bone, it can contaminate the fetal blood supply and breast milk years after maternal lead exposure ends. This maternally-derived lead can be the dominant source of fetal lead poisoning. Environmental lead exposure during childhood occurs by respiration and ingestion. Children are especially sensitive to lead toxicity. They absorb lead more efficiently by ingestion, and once absorbed, a greater amount reaches the brain as compared to adults, particularly before the age of five. The developing nervous system is also much more vulnerable to lead toxicity.

Although only high levels of exposure produce identifiable physical symptoms, lower levels of exposure remain neurotoxic. Among the consequences of lead toxicity are lowered IQ, impaired neuropsychological functioning and impaired academic achievement. Since parental socio-economic status is negatively associated with lead and positively associated with IQ, researchers have attempted to isolate the effect of lead. There is evidence, however, that lead has greater effects on children who are socio-economically disadvantaged, which would mean that previous studies may have underestimated its effects in these children.

One possible mechanism by which social disadvantage might exaggerate the toxicity of lead is that deficiencies in iron, calcium, zinc and protein increase lead absorption, and these deficiencies are more likely in disadvantaged children. Non-dietary mechanisms, however, are needed to explain the observation that lead-exposed rat pups show neurological damage and spatial learning deficits if they are raised in isolation with little stimulation, but if exposed to the same amount of lead and raised in groups with enriched environments, they were largely protected (Schneider *et al.* 2001).

It should also be noted that global tests such as IQ, which is the most common outcome in studies of childhood lead exposure, are insensitive to many forms of brain damage, and neuropsychological tests of more focused aspects of cognitive function typically reveal greater effects. Social and behavioural problems may be a result of lead poisoning, or might be a consequence of reduced cognitive function and academic difficulty. However, in a study of preschool children who could not yet have experienced academic difficulty, their social/emotional functioning scores on the Bayley Scales of Infant Development were negatively associated with lead exposure.

The impact of lead on human capital acquisition in the general population will have changed substantially over the last several decades, since efforts to reduce environmental lead have been successful and child blood-lead levels have decreased accordingly (Wang *et al.* 1997). However, recent research suggests that while IQ decreases with increasing lead exposure, the drop in IQ is steepest at the lowest levels of exposure, such that considerable toxicity occurs below levels officially considered safe in most jurisdictions (Lanphear 2005). It is now thought that there is no safe level of lead exposure.

Birth Weight

Birth weight is determined by gestational weight gain and by gestational age at birth, and one should try to distinguish between newborns who are light for gestational age and those who are premature. It is also important to distinguish between the consequences of unusually low birth weight and relationships that occur throughout the normal range of birth weights. One of the difficulties in research on the consequences of birth weight is discriminating between birth weight as a consequence of the fetal environment and birth weight as an indicator of subsequent growth patterns. This distinction is important for understanding mechanisms and proposing interventions.

Many aspects of physiology are determined during gestation in response to the uterine environment. For example, there is evidence that the number of muscle fibres is determined during gestation, and that although each fibre can grow larger through exercise, this does not fully compensate, so that grip strength in midlife is positively associated with birth weight, independently of postnatal, childhood and adult body size (Kuh *et al.* 2002).

In the British 1946 birth cohort, Richards *et al.* (2001) observed that birth weight was associated with increasing cognitive function at age eight, and that these differences in cognitive function persisted at ages 11, 15, 26 and 43. They also observed that birth weight was associated with increased educational achievement in a manner consistent with hypothesized mediation by childhood cognitive ability. Further analyses showed that this relationship was independent of subsequent body size (Richards *et al.* 2002).

In the 1958 British birth cohort, Jefferis, Power and Hertzman (2002) observed that birth weight was positively associated with both math scores and achieved education level. This association was independent of parental social class, parental education, parity, gestational age, maternal age and breastfeeding. They noted, however, that the effect of birth weight on achieved education level was smaller than that of social class, and that the effect of birth weight was constant over time, whereas that of social class increased during childhood. The effect of birth weight also did not depend on parental social class, nor did the effect appear to be the result of disability or preterm birth.

Unlike many measures of poor child health, which have showed declining temporal trends in incidence and prevalence, the incidence of low birth weight has generally remained unchanged in most jurisdictions. The current incidence of low birth weight in Canada is approximately 5 per 100 births. The incidence is approximately 1.5 to 2 times greater among lower socio-economic status women compared to higher socio-economic status women (Mustard and Ross 1994). Relative inequalities in low birth weight between social classes in England and Wales did not change over the period 1993–2000, a period of rising incidence of low birth weight (Moser, Li and Power 2003).

Breastfeeding

Breastfeeding is thought to promote cognitive development, and thereby educational achievement, by supplying specific long-chain fatty acids needed for brain and eye development during gestation and the first year of life which the infant cannot produce for itself after birth (Richards, Hardy and Wadsworth 2002). Childhood and adolescent cognitive ability is associated with length of breastfeeding independent of parental commitment to education (Anderson, Johnstone and Remley 1999). At age 53, word-reading ability remains associated with length of breastfeeding, but this appears to be mediated by adolescent cognitive function and educational achievement (Richard, Hardy and Wadsworth 2002).

Delayed Growth and Rates of Maturation

Delayed growth is likely to be due to poor nutrition, which is growth-limiting, and to disrupted sleep patterns, which reduce growth-hormone secretion. Since nutrition and sleep are needed for physical, cognitive and emotional development, as well as for academic success, it may be that delayed growth is indicative of an important role for childhood health in intergenerational social mobility (Montgomery *et al.* 1996). Dose-response relationships between air pollution and child growth have also been observed, but the mechanisms, if any, that would explain this association are unknown (Bobak, Richards and Wadsworth 2004). However, it may be that delayed growth is merely a marker of parental socio-economic status with greater precision than that of survey indicators such as parental occupational status and household crowding, such that the association between delayed growth and achieved socio-economic status is due to residual confounding by parental socio-economic status (ibid.). Because of the complexity of the putative mechanisms, and the difficulty of accurate and precise measurement of the relevant factors, causal inferences remain speculative.

Boys who grow slowly, as measured by their height at age seven, achieve lower levels of educational qualification and show a greater number of unemployment spells of three months or greater between the ages of 22 and 32. This association with unemployment does not appear to be due to social class at birth, household crowding, parental height, adult height (delayed growth is not always accompanied by decreased adult height), achieved education, behavioural problems at age 11 or chronic illness or disability in youth (ibid.).

Rapid childhood growth appears to increase and late adolescent weight gain to decrease cognitive function in early adulthood, and some plausible neuroendocrine pathways have been proposed to connect childhood skeletal growth and cognitive development (Richards *et al.* 2001).

Although delayed growth rates do not necessarily imply short adult stature, in the 1958 British birth cohort it appears that the positive association of height and occupational status at age 23 cannot be fully explained by the father's occupational class at birth or age 16 (Power, Fogelman and Fox 1986). This finding may reflect a mechanism by which both human capital acquisition and adult height are limited by childhood health factors (Li, Manor and Power 2004).

Childhood Behavioural Maladjustment

Like delayed growth, boys' behavioural maladjustment at age 11 also predicts unemployment at ages 22 to 32. Here the mechanisms may be more obvious, since behavioural maladjustment at age 11 likely precedes poor technical and social job performance (Montgomery *et al.* 1996). Using data from the Ontario Child Health Study, Mustard *et al.* (2005) observed that hyperactivity at ages 4 to 16 was associated with decreased upward occupational mobility in young adulthood for boys, with decreased upward educational mobility for boys and girls, and with increased downward educational mobility for boys. Hyperactive disorders affect 5 to 8 percent of children. Emotional problems at ages 4 to 16 were associated with increased downward occupational mobility in young adulthood in girls, decreased upward educational mobility in girls and boys, and with increased downward educational mobility in boys.

The strongest influences on behavioural development outcomes in children rest with aspects of parenting characteristics. For example, parenting styles consistent with "authoritative" standard-setting appear to be more beneficial than parenting styles consistent with "authoritarian" standards. Time committed by parents to involvement with children is also an important predictor of child behavioural outcomes. Suggestive evidence of the influence of parental commitment on child behavioural outcomes is provided by the history of abortion and crime in the US (Donohue and Levitt 2001; Levitt 2004). Abortion was legalized in the United States in 1973 (five states legalized abortion in 1970), and crime rates dropped dramatically in the 1990s when a sharp reduction in the number of unwanted boys aged 18 to 24 may have occurred. Birth rates fell by approximately 5 percent with the legalization of abortion, and the decrease was greater among teenage and minority women. By 1980, 1.6 million abortions were being performed annually. The number of infants put up for adoption also decreased dramatically. The decreases in crime appear to be timed according to the date of legalization across states, and the magnitude of the crime decrease appears to be proportional to the number of abortions. Canadian data have shown a similar effect (Sen 2003). Behavioural maladjustment, to which parental commitment can contribute, appears to be a predictor of poor labour market performance, of which criminality is an extreme example.

Illness that Interrupts Education

Serious illness in childhood has been shown to have negative consequences for later-life achievement. One of the first descriptions of the consequence of childhood serious illness on achievement was reported by Wadsworth, using longitudinal cohort data from the UK (1986). A more recent report from the UK, using data from the 1958 birth cohort, confirmed the original finding from Wadsworth. Self-rated health and extended sickness absence from school at age 16 was examined for its association with parental occupational status at age 16 and with the cohort's own occupational status at ages 23 and 33. Modest health-related effects on mobility during the two periods are observed for men, but not for women (Manor, Matthews and Power 2003). Two methodological concerns with this evidence are whether occupational status at ages 23 and 33 are equally valid as measures of socio-economic trajectory and whether there is residual confounding by parental socio-economic status. There are relatively few studies that have considered the impact of serious childhood illness on adult human capital attainment.

Functional Limitation

Functional limitations are defined as impairments in sensation, anatomy or physiology that result in limitations in normal function. Vision deficits, for example, can result in limitations in reading and mobility functions. Functional limitations were reported by 10.6 percent of subjects in the Ontario Child Health Study. These limitations were not associated with occupational mobility, but were linked to increased downward and decreased upward educational mobility in boys, and a similar, but weaker and not statistically significant pattern was seen for girls (Mustard *et al*. 2005). Using the same data, Boyle *et al*. (2001) estimate that a functional limitation in 1983 (at ages 4 to 16) is associated with about one year less educational achievement when adjusted for a wide variety of child, family and neighbourhood factors.

Discussion

In summary, this review has considered evidence for the long-term persistence of health-status deficits in childhood on human capital attainments in young adulthood. The review has considered only a selected range of dimensions of child health. Of the factors reviewed, none has a high prevalence. For example, fetal alcohol syndrome may affect two to five children per 1,000, the incidence of low birth weight is approximately 50 per 1,000 children and the prevalence of behavioural disorder is in the range of 50 to 80 per 1,000 children.

While the prevalence of any one condition may be low, the cumulative prevalence of all childhood disorders that may have consequences for human capital attainment will be in the range of 15 to 25 percent of the population of children. Of equal importance, there is significant evidence for long-term effects on human capital attainment for each of the child health-status factors considered in this review.

In the opening paragraphs of the second section, we note that the conditions reviewed in this paper do not necessarily represent a comprehensive inventory of all pediatric health-status deficits that may be consequential for human capital attainment. As examples of health conditions not considered in this paper which plausibly may influence human capital attainment, we would list traumatic injury, asthma and depression. All three conditions have relatively high prevalence in child and youth populations, and can result in substantial chronic disability. We expect that further work examining these conditions would extend the scope of the preliminary analysis presented in this paper.

Policy Implications

This paper will now turn to a focus on the primary policy approaches that have been applied in developed country settings to mitigate the effects of health-status deficits in childhood on human capital attainment.

There is good evidence that some of the negative impacts of these health-status deficits can be mediated by social, educational and clinical interventions. One important body of evidence comes from cross-national comparisons of human capital attainment. Some of the most interesting work in this field has been done by Douglas Willms, comparing literacy in youth at age 16 across socio-economic status groups for a sample of 12 OECD countries (Willms 2003). This work shows that some countries have reached relative equality in literacy achievements across socio-economic groups (Sweden and the Netherlands) while other countries have human capital outcomes that are very unequal across the socio-economic hierarchy (Figure 2). Willms's work has also shown that gradients in literacy converge at higher levels of socio-economic status in the developed economies. In other words, youth from relatively advantaged backgrounds tended to have high literacy scores in every country, or in every jurisdiction within a country, whereas, across countries, youth from less advantaged backgrounds tended to vary considerably in their literacy skills.

Socio-economic gradients in developmental outcomes such as literacy are a useful tool for informing policy, as they call attention not only to the level of learning but also to inequality in the distribution of literacy

Figure 2. Socio-Economic Gradients for Youth Literacy Scores for 12 Countries Participating in IALS by 1997

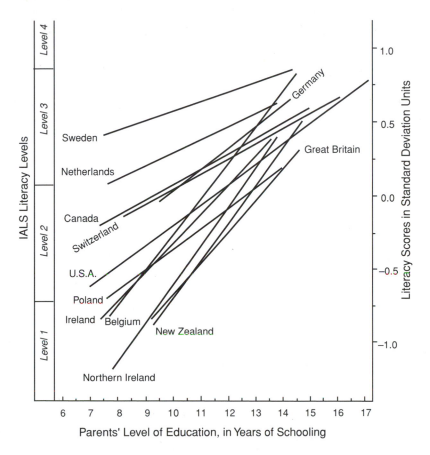

Source: Willms (2003).

skills. The analyses of socio-economic gradients in literacy skills provides good evidence that it is possible to achieve both high levels of proficiency and equality of proficiency among groups of differing socio-economic status.

What are the characteristics of an effective policy approach to mitigating the factors that impair societal achievement in literacy attainment in early adolescence? These factors include attributes of the household environment, the nature and quality of publicly provided resources and programs, and the health and function of children and adolescents. Willms has stated that "raising the literacy bar requires a comprehensive policy strategy aimed at safeguarding the health development of infants, strengthening early childhood education, improving the learning environments in schools and local communities, reducing segregation and the effects associated with poverty and creating a family-enabling society"(Willms 2003, 251).

This summary points to two key features of the policy response to inequalities in child and adolescent developmental outcomes relevant to optimal human capital formation. The first characteristic is the intersectoral policy requirement, integrating family policy, social welfare policy, education policy and public health policy and practice. The second characteristic points to the importance of targeting programs and resources to high-risk and vulnerable households and children.

On both dimensions, Canada has a record of accomplishment. The National Child Benefit is a strong example of intersectoral policy-making with a strong emphasis on targeted programs. The National Child Benefit (NCB) initiative is a partnership among the federal, provincial and territorial governments and First Nations that aims to help prevent and reduce the depth of child poverty, support parents as they move into the labour market and reduce overlap and duplication of government programs. The NCB combines two key elements: monthly payments to low-income families with children and benefits and services designed and delivered by the provinces and territories to meet the needs of families with children in each jurisdiction. Under the NCB, the Government of Canada has increased the benefits it pays through the NCB Supplement to low-income families with children, regardless of their source of income. Provinces and territories have the flexibility to adjust social assistance or child benefit payments by an amount equivalent to the NCB supplement. Expenditure reductions on social assistance benefits are expected to be allocated by provinces and territories to pay for new and enhanced benefits and services for low-income families with children. The extent to which these reallocations have been made is unevenly documented across provincial and territorial jurisdictions and there is little known of the impact of these reinvestments. The NCB seeks to reduce provincial expenditures on social assistance and income-security programs. The key feature of the federal-provincial agreement is that these provincial resources are to be reallocated to provide child development services to low-income households.

A good example of a public program targeting resources to high-risk and vulnerable households is the federal Canadian Prenatal Nutrition Program (CPNP). CPNP funds community groups to develop or enhance programs for vulnerable, pregnant women. Through a community development approach, the CPNP aims to reduce the incidence of unhealthy birth weights, improve the health of both infant and mother and encourage breastfeeding. CPNP enhances access to services and strengthens intersectoral collaboration to support the needs of pregnant women facing conditions of risk. As a comprehensive program, the services provided include food supplementation, nutrition counselling and support, education, referral, and counselling on health and lifestyle issues. CPNP targets those women most likely to have unhealthy babies due to poor health and nutrition. Over 95 percent of the projects are aimed at pregnant women living in poverty, teens, or women living in isolation or with poor access to services. Other client groups targeted include women who abuse alcohol or drugs, women who live with violence, women with gestational diabetes, Aboriginal women and immigrant and/or refugee women.

In 2001/02, over 44,650 women participated in CPNP projects. The annual budget for the non-reserve portion of CPNP was $30.8 million as of 2002/03. Prior to the establishment of the Public Health Agency of Canada, there were approximately 350 CPNP projects funded annually by the Population and Public Health Branch of Health Canada serving over 2,000 communities across Canada. In addition, over 550 CPNP projects are funded by the First Nations and Inuit Health Branch of Health Canada in Inuit and on-reserve First Nations communities.

Implications for Future Research Directions

There are four primary priorities for future research directions arising from the perspectives offered in this paper.

First, the paper has noted that the conditions reviewed in this paper do not necessarily represent a comprehensive inventory of all pediatric health-status deficits that may be consequential for human capital attainment. As examples of health conditions not considered in this paper, which plausibly may influence human capital attainment, we would list traumatic injury, asthma and depression. All three conditions have relatively high prevalence in child and youth populations, and can result in substantial chronic disability. We expect that further work examining these conditions would extend the scope of the preliminary analysis presented here. The paper has illustrated some of the challenges in conducting research on the human capital attainment consequences and, in the following paragraph, we emphasize the importance of longitudinal surveys in addressing some of these challenges.

Second, we also note that the assessment of the consequences of childhood health status on human capital attainment is an area of interdisciplinary research that would clearly benefit from more intensive activity. Only limited high quality information is available on the magnitude of effects on human capital attainment resulting from specific health-status deficits in children and youth.

Third, more emphasis should be given to the development of longitudinal population surveys that integrate health and function measures with labour market measures such as participation and human capital development measures. Canada has strong national longitudinal survey programs measuring health and function (the National Population Health Survey and the Longitudinal Survey of Children and Youth), and separately, strong survey programs in labour-force participation (the Survey of Labour and Income Dynamics). The current weakness of these national survey programs is that these two strengths are not integrated. In Canada, this could be accomplished by continuing the NLSCY, supplementing the SLID measurement of health and function among respondents aged 15 to 24 or further strengthening the NPHS labour market measures. A very important benefit of extending the NLSCY into the early adult life-course period will be the creation of a research database that will support understandings of the pathways leading from childhood health status to early adult human capital attainment.

Fourth, there is an ongoing need to assess the economic consequences of public policies focused on mitigating the impact of social, economic and health disadvantage on child and adolescent developmental outcomes. Large federal/provincial/territorial programs (such as the National Child Benefit) have a wide range of potential social, economic and developmental outcomes. Accurately measuring the costs and consequences of these programs and precisely attributing program effects is an important research mandate in support of strengthened policy development in this area.

Table 1. Childhood Health Factors by Stage of Life Course and Dimensions of Human Capital and their Sequelae in Young Adulthood

Fetal →	Perinatal →	Preschool →	School →	Young Adulthood
Alcohol	Birth weight	Breastfeeding	Cognitive function	Cognitive Function
Tobacco	Gestational age	Growth	Growth	Educational achievement
Illicit drugs	Ponderal index	Nutrition	Nutrition	Labour market attachment
Disease		Serious injury	Serious injury	Occupational status
Injury		Serious illness	Serious illness	Earned income
Growth		Hearing	Academic success	Workplace disability
Abortion		Sight	Sickness absence	Emotional health
Maternal age		Lead exposure	Sight	Behavioural health
Maternal nutrition		Exercise	Hearing	
Lead		Emotional health	Exercise	
		Behavioural health	Emotional health	
		Psychosocial stress	Behavioural health	
		Pregnancy	Psychosocial stress	

Note: Since health is an important part of human capital, factors such as cognitive function might be both predictors and outcomes, particularly at secondary school age.

References

Abel, E.L. 1995. "An Update on Incidence of FAS: FAS is Not an Equal Opportunity Birth Defect," *Neurotoxicol Teratol* 17(4):437-43.

Anderson, J.W., B.M. Johnstone and D.T. Remley. 1999. "Breast-Feeding and Cognitive Development: A Meta-Analysis," *American Journal of Clinical Nutrition* 70(4):525-35.

Barker, D.J.P., ed. 1992. *Fetal and Infant Origins of Adult Disease*. London: British Medical Journal Publications.

Bartley, M. and I. Plewis. 1997. "Does Health-Selective Mobility Account for Socio-Economic Differences in Health? Evidence from England and Wales 1971-1991," *Journal of Health and Social Behavior* 38:376-86.

Blane, D., G. Davey-Smith and M. Bartley. 1993. "Social Selection: What Does it Contribute to Social Class Differences in Health?" *Sociology of Health and Illness* 1:1-15.

Blane, D., C. Power and M. Bartley. 1996. "Illness Behaviour and the Measurement of Class Differentials in Morbidity," *Journal of the Royal Statistical Society. Series A. Statistics in Society?* 159:77-92.

Bobak, M., M. Richards and M. Wadsworth. 2004. "Relation Between Children's Height and Outdoor Air Pollution from Coal-Burning Sources in the British 1946 Birth Cohort," *International Archives of Occupational and Environmental Health* 77(6):383-86.

Boyle, M.H., K. Georgiades, Y.A. Racine and C.A. Mustard. 2001. "Neighbourhood and Family Influences on Educational Attainment: Results from the Ontario Child Health Follow-Up." IWH Working Paper No. 306. Toronto: Institute for Work and Health.

Boyle, M.H., D.R. Offord, H.G. Hofman, G.P. Catlin, J.A. Byles, D.T. Cadman *et al.* 1987. "Ontario Child Health Study: I: Methodology," *Archives of General Psychiatry* 44:826-31.

Boyle, M.H., D.R. Offord, Y.A. Racine, M. Sanford, P. Szatmari and J.E. Fleming. 1993. "Evaluation of the Original Ontario Child Health Study Scales," *Canadian Journal of Psychiatry* 38:397-405.

Cardona M., G. Costa and M. Demaria. 2004. "Social Mobility and Health in the Turin Longitudinal Study," *Social Science and Medicine* 58:1563-74.

Caspi, A.V., J. McClay, T.E. Moffitt, J. Mill, J. Martin, I.W. Craig *et al.* 2002. "Role of Genotype in the Cycle of Violence in Maltreated Children," *Science* 297:851-53.

Chandola, T., M. Bartley, A. Sacker, C. Jenkinson and M. Marmot. 2003. "Health Selection in the Whitehall II Study, UK," *Social Science and Medicine* 56:2059-72.

Chudley, A.E., J. Conry, J.L. Cook, C. Loock, T. Rosales, N. LeBlanc and Public Health Agency of Canada's National Advisory Committee on Fetal Alcohol

Spectrum Disorder. 2005. "Fetal Alcohol Spectrum Disorder: Canadian Guidelines for Diagnosis," *Canadian Medical Association Journal* 172(5 Suppl):S1-S21.

Coe, C.L. 1999. "Psychosocial Factors and Psychoneuroimmunology within the Lifespan Perspective," in *Developmental Health and the Wealth of Nations: Social, Biological and Educational Dynamics*, ed. D.P. Keating and C. Hertzman. New York: The Guilford Press.

Davey-Smith, G., C. Hart, D. Blane and D. Hole. 1998. "Adverse Socioeconomic Conditions in Childhood and Cause Specific Adult Mortality: Prospective Observational Study," *British Medical Journal* 316:1631-35.

Donohue, J.J. III and S.D. Levitt. 2001. "The Impact of Legalized Abortion on Crime," *Quarterly Journal of Economics* 116(2):379-420.

Elstad, J.I. and S. Krokstad. 2003. "Social Causation, Health-Selective Mobility and the Reproduction of Socio-Economic Health Inequalities over Time: Panel Study of Adult Men," *Social Science and Medicine* 57:1475-89.

Graetz, B. 1993. "Health Consequences of Employment and Unemployment: Longitudinal Evidence for Young Men and Women," *Social Science and Medicine* 36(6):715-24.

Hertzman, C. 1999. "Population Health and Human Development," in *Developmental Health and the Wealth of Nations: Social, Biological and Educational Dynamics*, ed. D.P. Keating and C. Hertzman. New York: The Guilford Press.

Hertzman, C. and M. Wiens. 1996. "Child Development and Long-Term Outcomes: A Population Health Perspective and Summary of Successful Interventions," *Social Science and Medicine* 43:1083-95.

Jefferis, B., C. Power and C. Hertzman. 2002. "Birth Weight, Childhood Socioeconomic Environment, and Cognitive Development in the 1958 British Birth Cohort Study," *British Medical Journal* 325(7359):305-11.

Kingdon, J.W. 1995. *Agendas, Alternatives and Public Policies*. New York: Longman.

Kuh, D. and Y. Ben-Shlomo, eds. 1997. *A Life Course Approach to Chronic Disease Epidemiology*. New York: Oxford University Press.

Kuh, D., J. Bassey, R. Hardy, A.A. Sayer, M. Wadsworth and C. Cooper. 2002. "Birth Weight, Childhood Size, and Muscle Strength in Adult Life: Evidence from a Birth Cohort Study," *American Journal of Epidemiology* 156(7):627-33.

Lanphear, B.P., R. Hornung, J. Khoury, K. Yolton, P. Baghurst, D.C. Bellinger, R.L. Canfield, K.N. Dietrich, R. Bornschein, T. Greene, S.J. Rothenberg, H.L. Needleman, L. Schnaas, G. Wasserman, J. Graziano and R. Roberts. 2005. "Low-Level Environmental Lead Exposure and Children's Intellectual Function: An International Pooled Analysis," *Environmental Health Perspectives* 113(7):894-99.

Lawlor, D.A., S. Ebrahim and G. Davey-Smith. 2002. "Socioeconomic Position in Childhood and Adulthood and Insulin Resistance: Cross-Sectional Survey Using Data from British Women's Heart and Health Study," *British Medical Journal* 325(7368):805.

Levitt, S.D. 2004. "Understanding Why Crime Fell in the 1990s: Four Factors that Explain the Decline and Six that Do Not," *Journal of Economic Perspectives* 18(1):163-90.

Li, L., O. Manor and C. Power. 2004. "Are Inequalities in Height Narrowing? Comparing Effects of Social Class on Height in Two Generations," *Archives of Disease in Childhood* 89(11):1018-23.

Lidsky, T.I. and J.S. Schneider. 2003. "Lead Neurotoxicity in Children: Basic Mechanisms and Clinical Correlates," *Brain* 126(Pt 1):5-19.

Lynch, J.W., G.A. Kaplan, R.D. Cohen, J. Kauhanen and T.W. Wilson. 1994. "Childhood and Adult Socioeconomic Status as Predictors of Mortality in Finland," *The Lancet* 343:524-27.

MacIntyre, S. 1997. "The Black Report and Beyond: What Are the Issues?" *Social Science and Medicine* 44:723-45.

Mackenbach, J.P. 1997. "Tackling Inequalities in Health: Great Need for Evidence-Based Interventions," *British Medical Journal* 310(May 6):1152-53.

Manor, O., S. Matthews and C. Power. 2003. "Health Selection: The Role of Inter- and Intra-Generational Mobility on Social Inequalities in Health," *Social Science and Medicine* 57:2217-27.

Marmot, M., C.D. Ryff, L.L. Bumpass, M. Shipley and N.F. Marks. 1997. "Social Inequalities in Health: Next Questions and Converging Evidence," *Social Science and Medicine* 44(6):901-10.

Marmot, M.G., G. Davey-Smith, S. Stansfeld, C. Patel, F. North, J. Head *et al.* 1991. "Health Inequalities among British Civil Servants: The Whitehall II Study," *The Lancet* 337 (June 8):1387-93.

Matthews, S., C. Hertzman, A. Ostry and C. Power. 1998. "Gender, Work Roles and Psychosocial Work Characteristics as Determinants of Health," *Social Science and Medicine* 46(11):1417-24.

May, P.A. and J.P. Gossage. 2001. "Estimating the Prevalence of Fetal Alcohol Syndrome: A Summary," *Alcohol Research and Health* 25(3):159-67.

Montgomery, S.M., M.J. Bartley, D.G. Cook and M.E. Wadsworth. 1996. "Health and Social Precursors of Unemployment in Young Men in Great Britain," *Journal of Epidemiology and Community Health* 50(4):415-22.

Morrell, S., R. Taylor, S. Quine, C. Kerr and J. Western. 1997. "A Cohort Study of Unemployment as a Cause of Psychological Disturbance in Australian Youth," *Social Science and Medicine* 38(11):1553-64.

Moser, K., L. Li and C. Power. 2003. "Social Inequalities in Low Birth Weight in England and Wales: Trends and Implications for Future Population Health," *Journal of Epidemiology and Community Health* 57(9):687-91.

Mustard C.A. and N.P. Roos. 1994. "The Relationship of Prenatal Care and Pregnancy Complication Birthweight Outcome: Results from Winnipeg, Canada," *American Journal of Public Health* 84:1450-57.

Mustard, C.A., C. Kalcevich, M. Boyle, Y.A. Racine and M. Dooley. 2005. "Childhood Health Status and Inter-Generational Socioeconomic Mobility in the Ontario Child Health Study." IWH Working Paper No. 270. Toronto: Institute for Work and Health.

Mustard, C.A., J. Lavis and A. Ostry. 2005. "New Evidence and Enhanced Understandings: Labour Market Experiences and Health," in *Creating Healthier Societies: From Analysis to Action,* ed. J. Heymann, C. Hertzman, M. Barer and R. Evans. New York: Oxford University Press.

Power, C. and C. Hertzman. 1997. "Social and Biological Pathways Linking Early Life and Adult Disease," *British Medical Bulletin* 53(1):210-21.

Power, C., K. Fogelman and A.J. Fox. 1986. "Health and Social Mobility during the Early Years of Life," *Quarterly Journal of Social Affairs* 2(4):397-413.

Power, C., S. Matthews and O. Manor. 1996. "Inequalities in Self-Rated Health in the 1958 British Birth Cohort: Life Time Social Circumstances or Social Mobility?" *British Medical Journal* 313:449-53.

Power, C., C. Hertzman, S. Matthews and O. Manor. 1997. "Social Differences in Health: Life-Cycle Effects Between Ages 23 and 33 in the 1958 British Birth Cohort," *American Journal of Public Health* 87(9):1499-1503.

Power, C., O. Manor, A.J. Fox and K. Fogelman. 1990. "Health in Childhood and Social Inequalities in Young Adults," *Journal of the Royal Statistical Society* (Series A)153:17-28.

Power, C., S.A. Stansfeld, S. Matthews, O. Manor and S. Hope. 2002. "Childhood and Adulthood Risk Factors for Socio-Economic Differentials in Psychological Distress: Evidence from the 1958 British Birth Cohort," *Social Science and Medicine* 55:1989-2004.

Richards, M., R. Hardy and M.E.J. Wadsworth. 2002. "Long-Term Effects of Breast-Feeding in a National Birth Cohort: Educational Attainment and Midlife Cognitive Function," *Public Health Nutrition* 5(5):631-35.

Richards, M., R. Hardy, D. Kuh and M.E. Wadsworth. 2001. "Birth Weight and Cognitive Function in the British 1946 Birth Cohort: Longitudinal Population Based Study," *British Medical Journal* 322(7280):199-203.

— 2002. "Birthweight, Postnatal Growth and Cognitive Function in a National UK Birth Cohort," *International Journal of Epidemiology* 31(2):342-48.

Schneider, J.S., M.H. Lee, D.W. Anderson, L. Zuck and T.I. Lidsky. 2001. "Enriched Environment during Development Is Protective against Lead-Induced Neurotoxicity," *Brain Research* 896(1-2):48-55.

Sen, A. 2003. "Does Increased Abortion Lead to Lower Crime? Evaluating the Relationship between Crime, Abortion, and Fertility." Working Paper. Waterloo, ON: University of Waterloo.

Sokol, R.J., V. Delaney-Black and B. Nordstrom. 2003. "Fetal Alcohol Spectrum Disorder," *Journal of the American Medical Association* 290(22):2996-99.

Sorlie, P.D. and E. Rogot. 1990. "Mortality by Employment Status in the National Longitudinal Mortality Study," *American Journal of Epidemiology* 132(5):983-92.

Townsend, P., M. Whitehead and N. Davidson. 1982. *Inequalities in Health: The Black Report and the Health Divide,* new edition. London: Penguin Books.

Wadsworth, M.E.J. 1986. "Serious Illness in Childhood and its Association with Later-Life Achievement," in *Class and Health: Research and Longitudinal Data,* ed. R.G. Wilkinson. London: Tavistock Publications.

Wadsworth, M.E.J., S.M. Montgomery and M.J. Bartley. 1999. "The Persisting Effect of Unemployment on Health and Social Well-Being in Men Early in Working Life," *Social Science and Medicine* 48:1491-99.

Wang, S.T., S. Pizzolato, H.P. Demshar and L.F. Smith. 1997. "Decline in Blood Lead in Ontario Children Correlated to Decreasing Consumption of Leaded Gasoline 1983–1992," *Clinical Chemistry* 43(7):1251-52.

Willms, J.D. 2003. "Literacy Proficiency of Youth: Evidence of Converging Socioeconomic Gradients," *International Journal of Educational Research* 39(3):247-52.

3

Socio-Economic Status and Human Capital: Recent Canadian Evidence

LORI J. CURTIS

Recent Canadian evidence supports international research linking socio-economic status (SES), parental income and education to health and educational outcomes. Individuals from high-SES households are much more likely to attend university, but slight gains are apparent for lower-SES households. Student loan programs may be responsible. Most decisions regarding human capital attainment are influenced very early in life — by parental SES, beliefs and attitudes — which suggests that policies to decrease the SES/human capital gradient should focus on early investments in human capital to create an equal playing field. Policymakers should not further disadvantage those already left behind.

Introduction

When economists refer to human capital they are most commonly referring to an individual's knowledge, skills and competencies; higher levels of human capital lead to better labour market (Riddell 2006), social (Schuller 2001) and other outcomes (Grossman 2005). An extra year of school, for example, has been shown to not only correlate with but cause an increase in wages by about 10 to 14 percent, on average, and an improvement in health, poverty and employment status for individuals in the US, UK and Canada (Oreopoulos 2003).

Grossman (2005), Currie (2006), and many others interested in population and public health suggest that, along with knowledge capital (attained through, for example, formal education or less formal on-the-job training), health should be included as an important aspect of human capital. They postulate that the two forms of capital interact in each other's production and in the optimal production of human capital. A plethora of international evidence examines the relationship between socio-economic status (SES) and health (see Deaton 2002; Marmot 2002; Case, Lubotky and Paxson 2002; Meara 2001) and education (see Oreopoulos, Page and Stevens 2004; Mahler and Winkelmann 2004; Jenkins and Schluter 2002). This paper focuses on recent Canadian evidence examining the relationship between SES and human capital (defined for our purposes as health and education).

Recent economic research concentrates on providing evidence on the causal pathways of the relationship between SES and human capital (Riddell 2006 discusses this at length). The focus here is the SES-human capital correlation, particularly recent literature on the intergenerational associations between SES and human capital (in the form of health and education), not the pathways through which SES affects levels of human capital (except for a brief review).

The SES-human capital relationship is relevant to policy on many fronts. Higher levels of human capital acquisition are related to better jobs, higher incomes, lower rates of social assistance participation, higher quality marriage partners, higher levels of social capital and better health for individuals and their children. Typically, decisions on whether or not a youth invests in postsecondary education are made jointly with parents and recent studies point out that values concerning life-long learning may be largely established very early in life, perhaps prior to entering the education system and certainly prior to making decisions regarding postsecondary education. Thus, families' economic and social states affect the child's future human capital acquisition and well-being and possibly that of future generations, and Currie (2001) provides justification for government intervention in what some may feel should be a private (family) decision, including market and informational failures, externalities and equity.

SES and Health

An abundance of research links the socio-economic status (SES) to health and well-being in adult populations (see Curtis and Phipps 2004; Deaton 2002; Marmot 2002), older populations (see Buckley *et al.* 2004; Decker and Reimler 2004) and child populations (see e.g., Curtis, Dooley and Phipps 2004; Currie and Stabile 2003; Case, Lubotky and Paxson 2002). The SES-health gradient is a robust finding with which few would argue. No such agreement exists, however, on the causal pathways for the relationship (Deaton 2002; Marmot 2002; Currie and Stabile 2003). Mustard, Tompa and Etches (2006) examine the consequences of some specific childhood/youth illnesses on human capital acquisition in early adulthood. Meara (2001) summarizes literature on pathways that operate in the opposite direction. Those with lower levels of SES may have poorer health because of lower ability to collect and process health information; unhealthy lifestyle choice; stress due to relative SES standing; and health-care access issues. This section of the paper will present literature that examines the relationship between SES and health (assuming the pathway is from SES to health, directly or indirectly). Perhaps in response to the recent policy focus on the plight of children, Canadian research has targeted the relationship between family SES and child health.

Prior to 1996, Canadian research on the link between SES and child health and well-being came mainly from the Ontario Child Health Study (OCHS), the only population-based longitudinal study of child health in Canada, (see, e.g., Curtis *et al.* 2001). The OCHS surveyed children in 1983 and again in 1987 and found significant associations between low-income and lone-mother family status and a variety of psychiatric, social and academic problems.

Dooley *et al.* (1998), among others, confirmed the OCHS results with findings from the release of the first wave of the National Longitudinal Survey of Children and Youth (NLSCY), a national sample of Canadian children completed in 1996 and then every other year. The survey produced evidence of a significant relationship between SES and child (and maternal) health. The availability of these data allowed researchers to focus on several measures of SES and child health, including, for example, the link between family income, maternal education, lone-parent status and neighbourhood characteristics and children's emotional problems, behavioural problems, cognitive problems and injuries (Curtis, Dooley and Phipps 2004; Kohen *et al.* 2002), and more recently, longer-term relationships between SES and child health using the longitudinal aspect of the data (Dooley and Stewart 2004; Currie and Stabile 2003).

The principle measures of lower SES utilized in the literature are low family (household) income or poverty, lone-mother family status and/ or low levels of maternal education; the presence of these characteristics is consistently related to worse outcomes for children, although the magnitude of the relationship often depends on the outcome measured and selection of control variables (many see this as evidence of indirect pathways for the SES to health relationship). For example, Curtis *et al.*

(2001) examine the relationships between current and longer-term low income, and current and longer-term lone-mother status, and child health, controlling for maternal education, and other demographic variables. They find that the association between current lone-mother status and the child's emotional status is more important (in magnitude and significance) than either current or long-term income measures. However, when measuring cognitive problems, longer-term low income is the strongest correlate. Curtis, Dooley and Phipps (2004) examine the relationship between several child-health outcomes and SES as measured by low family income, maternal education, lone-motherhood and neighbourhood status; low-income status was not significant when other SES variables were included. Low maternal education remained a strong correlate while lone-mother status and neighbourhood problems showed the strongest and most consistent relationships with child-health outcomes.

Dooley and Stewart (2004) investigate the relationship between family incomes and childhood cognitive outcomes following conventional regression methods, using fixed-effects models and including measures of consumption, a housing index, for example, (a pathway through which income may affect health). The standard income gradient is evident when using conventional methods; however, fixed effects models and the inclusion of other measures weaken the income-health relationship substantially. They conclude that the direct income-health relationship is apparent but may be weaker than previously thought.

In what is most likely the most convincing study to come out of the NLSCY to date, Currie and Stabile (2003) examine whether Case, Lubotky and Paxson's (2002) US finding — that the SES-child health gradient increases with child's age — holds in the Canadian context with a universal health-care system. Their results indicate that the US findings are similar to those for Canada and they infer that the SES health gap is therefore not driven by differences in access to health care across the two countries, a remarkable observation. Canadian children from low-income households respond to health shocks (episodes of ill-health) almost as well as children from higher-income households, but they experience more shocks and thus become increasingly less healthy in the long run. Their study also points out that, even when controlling for the child's prior health conditions, parental average income and maternal education are consistently related to a child's current health status (in both magnitude and significance). Interestingly, the average income effect is substantially (1.7 times) larger than the maternal education effect.

The importance of the link between family SES and childhood health is strengthened by recent results, using OCHS (1983, 1987 and newly released 2001 data), indicating that low-parental SES and poor child health affect individuals as they become adults. Dooley and Contoyannis (2005) find that low parental income is associated with educational and labour force outcomes (graduating from high school rather than postsecondary, hours of work, earnings and unemployment receipt) of the young adults after controlling for parental age and education, childhood health and family functioning problems. Maternal education is most consistently related to outcomes and childhood health problems are most commonly associated with poor outcomes of young adults; the relationship is stronger for lower-income individuals and females.

In sum, the consistent relationship between parental SES, particularly maternal education, and child health found in other jurisdictions also is demonstrated with Canadian data. As more years of longitudinal data become available in the NLSCY, studies similar to that of Dooley and Contoyannis will be possible at the national level (although they present a convincing argument that their results should be generalizable to Canada as a whole). Although SES is typically measured by low income, other measures such as lone-motherhood, maternal education, housing and neighbourhood status are also important. Low levels of maternal education seem to be particularly relevant when examining poor childhood health outcomes. Moreover, parental education levels are associated with marital outcomes, labour market outcomes and thus family income, and poor health behaviours such as smoking and inactivity, which in turn lead to poorer health for children now and into adulthood.

SES and Education

The previous section presents recent Canadian research on the existence of an SES gradient in one important aspect of human capital: health, child health in particular, and that poor child health leads to poor adult outcomes. SES also has been associated with lower levels of education (the most commonly used measure of human capital). The recent availability of some unique data has resulted in a surge of Canadian research suggesting that lower levels of parental SES are related to lower levels of educational attainment of their grown children (Drolet 2005 and Finnie, Lascelles and Sweetman 2004 offer excellent reviews of the recent economic literature) and lower academic scores and literacy for school-aged children (see Desjardins 2003; Willms 2003; Ma and Klinger 2000). The economic literature has tended to focus on the relationship between family SES (parental education and family income and to a lesser extent, lone-parent status) and participation in postsecondary education, particularly university. Recently released studies utilize varying data, time periods and methodologies to examine this relationship. The conclusions — regarding a strong relationship between family SES, particularly parental education and family status and young adults' educational attainments — are remarkably robust; there is a substantial SES gap in attainment of postsecondary education. The conclusions about the dynamics of the relationship, whether or not the strength of the relationship or the width of the gap has changed over time, are somewhat less robust.

Knighton and Mirza (2002) present a descriptive analysis of postsecondary participation rates of young individuals (18 to 21 years of age and no longer in school) in 1998, using the Survey of Labour and Income Dynamics (SLID) (1993–1998). On average, almost two-thirds of Canadian youth participate in postsecondary education (university, college, applied technical schools, trade school and CEGEP). However, a strong income (parental) gradient in participation is evident; over 75 percent of youths in the highest income quartile attend postsecondary school while only about half of the youths from the lowest income quartile do so. The income gradient is even more pronounced when examining university attendance: 39 percent of youths whose parents' incomes fall in the highest category attend university while only 17 percent of those living in the lowest-income circumstances do.

The findings are even starker when examining postsecondary attendance by the parents' education (parent with highest level): 52 percent of youths whose parents have high-school educations attend postsecondary education, 68 percent of those whose parents are college educated and 88 percent of those whose parents have a university degree attend postsecondary education. Again, the gradients are steeper for university attendance: 49, 29 and 17 percent of youths with university, college and high-school educated parents, respectively, attend university. The basic conclusions remain in multivariate analysis including parental income, education and region — parental income and education have strong (in magnitude and significance) associations with youths' participation in postsecondary education; youths with a university-educated parent are, by far, the most likely to attend.

As stated previously, many other studies, using alternate time periods, datasets and more sophisticated statistical analysis, have been completed over the past several years. Remarkably, the studies all present very similar findings to the simple descriptive statistics discussed here. For example, Christofides, Cirello and Hoy (2001) use data from the Survey of Consumer Finance (SCF), 1975 to 1993, to examine trends in participation rates in postsecondary education for youths by family income and education. Their prime interest is in exploring the regressivity of subsidies for postsecondary education. They find that postsecondary attendance rates are higher for children from higher-income families than from lower-income families; however, they note, a strong degree of convergence of participation rates over the period decreased the level of regressivity of student subsidies. In 1975, 18 percent of youth from the lowest-income quintile attended postsecondary school, while 53 percent of those in the highest-income quintile did (a 35 percentage-point spread). The percentages increased to 44 percent and 71 percent, respectively by 1993 (a 27 percentage-point spread). In general, they find that family income, parental education, proximity to a postsecondary institution and region are all independently associated with participation in postsecondary schooling; tuition fees were not a significant predictor.

Corak, Lipps and Zhao (2004) point out that the findings by Christofides, Cirello and Hoy pertained to the 1980s and early 1990s and may not hold in the higher tuition climate of the later 1990s and early 2000s. The later period saw gains to actual and perceived returns to education over the period, over 80 percent of families expected their children to participate in postsecondary education; however, tuition fee increases of 85 percent and more were also a reality. As well, the Christofides' study did not differentiate between universities and other types of postsecondary education. Knighton and Mirza (2002) found the largest SES gradients for university participation and none for college attendance or gender. Corak, Lipps and Zhao were concerned with the nature and strength of the relationship between postsecondary participation and family income as well as changes that may have occurred from 1980 to 2000.

Using instrumental variables estimation with complementary datasets of the Canadian population (SCF and the General Social Survey), a longer time frame and specific levels of postsecondary education, Corak,

Lipps and Zhao obtain results similar to previous studies. Slight increases in university participation of individuals from lower-income households are evident, but individuals from higher-income families are still much more likely to be engaged in university education. Increases in the participation of low-income individuals and declines in the rates of those from middle-income families lead to a slight narrowing of the long established gap in university attendance between the rich and the poor. No significant differences in college participation rates were seen across income classes (consistent with Knighton and Mirza 2002 findings). The correlation between parental income and university participation did become stronger up to the mid-1990s, just after substantial increases in tuitions, but the strength of the relationship subsequently weakened somewhat.

In support of previous work, Drolet (2005) examines the relationship between family income, parental education and family status and young adults' participation in postsecondary education using the SLID, 1993–2001 and her findings are very similar. Between 1993 and 2001, about 60 percent of young adults participate in postsecondary education; approximately 25 percent attend university. As other studies demonstrate, parental income and education are important factors in a young person's participation in postsecondary schooling. Young adults from lone-parent households are also less likely to attend university but equally as likely to attend college. In multivariate analysis, the relationships remain strong for university education; parental education exhibited the strongest relationship, in terms of magnitude and significance and those from higher-income families are significantly more likely to attend or have finished university than families with moderate incomes; however, young adults from very low-income families are not significantly less likely to attend when compared to those from families with low to moderate incomes. The lone-parent association remains significant even after controlling for parental income and education. Drolet claims that the parental SES gradient is apparent in young adults' postsecondary, particularly university, education and that the relationship does not change between 1993 and 2001. She also finds no evidence of an SES gradient in college attendance.

The School Leavers Survey (SLS) and the Youth in Transition Survey (YITS) were used by Finnie, Laporte and Lascelles (2004) to examine the relationship between family SES (measured by parental education and family structure; family income is not available) and participation rates in postsecondary education in 1991 and 2000. They find, as others

do, that postsecondary education participation rates rise over the period and that participation is strongly influenced by parental education. However, contrary to Christofides, Cirello and Hoy (2001); Corak,
Lipps and Zhao (2004) and Drolet (2005), they find that the association
strengthens over the 1990s and the gap widens, particularly when comparing youth with the most highly educated parents (whose participation rates increase over the period) to those whose parents have the
lowest education levels (whose participation rates increase more slowly
or decline, for males). Family type (lone-parent compared to coupled
families) is also strongly associated with postsecondary participation,
but the advantage of youths from two-parent families diminishes somewhat over the period.

Parental education, family type, ethnicity and location are also shown
to have strong direct and indirect relationships with postsecondary
participation by Finnie, Lascelles and Sweetman (2004) using the School
Leavers and Follow-up Survey. The authors point out that the strong
indirect effects, which operate through the youth's high-school outcomes
and related attitudes and behaviours, should lead researchers and
policymakers to focus on the period of life before postsecondary decisions are made.

Using the 2002 Post-Secondary Education Participation Survey (PEPS)
dataset, Finnie and Laporte (forthcoming) support findings that parental education is strongly related to any postsecondary and university
participation but not family income — Finnie, Laporte and Lascelles
(2004) suggest that this finding may be a result of problems with the
sample size). However, parental savings for education is a strong indicator. They surmise that parental savings may be associated with financial status earlier in youths' lives, and/or parental values toward
formal and informal learning. They also point out that lack of interest
in continuing education is reported substantially more often than monetary problems as a reason for not attending postsecondary training.
As in other studies, the results support the notion that the development of values toward education, set early in life, strongly influence
latter decisions.

Current evidence points toward a strong link between several
measures of SES, particularly parental education and youths' participation in postsecondary education. The relationship is driven mainly
by the SES gradient in university participation; in general, the gradient
does not appear for college attendance. However, de Broucker (2005)
points out that there is a SES gradient in college attendance if one

includes only individuals who did not attend university; college attendance rates do not make up for the SES differences at the university level and thus a SES gradient is seen when postsecondary education is taken as a whole. While there appears to be a debate over whether the strength of the SES-university relationship or the width of the gap has changed over the 1990s and early 2000s, a time of increasing tuition fees and higher admission standards (see, e.g., Finnie and Usher 2005), there is little doubt of the existence of a SES gradient in postsecondary or university participation rates. Recent evidence points strongly to the early development of attitudes and values as a "determinant" of the SES gradient in educational attainment.

SES Gradients in Human Capital: Conclusions and Policy Discussion

Current Canadian research supports a robust finding: despite the historical level of activity of the welfare state there is a substantial SES gradient in both the health and educational attainment aspects of human capital. The causal pathways are, however, not entirely clear, which makes policy proposals difficult. Low levels of human capital are related to relatively poor labour market outcomes, and thus income, social assistance (SA) participation and difficulty moving off SA into employment (Beaulieu *et al.* 2005; Johnson and Corcoran 2002; Thériault 2000) and a host of others. Low maternal education, child health problems and parental SA receipt are also associated with poorer labour market outcomes when the child becomes a young adult (Dooley and Contyannis 2005). Although no agreement exists on definitive causal pathways, it has been suggested that the relationship between SES and low levels of human capital may be a result of issues that are subject to policy such as income constraints, imperfect capital markets, imperfect knowledge, learned values and behaviours, or stress resulting from poor economic social circumstances relative to others.

Among others, Finnie and Laporte (forthcoming) and (Corak, Lipps and Zhao 2004) see student grant and loan programs that assist low-income individuals in solving educational problems associated with income constraints and imperfect capital markets as a practical policy. This set of policies is particularly important since tuition has increased in the last decade or so and, without adequate support, may hinder postsecondary access. But, to date, targeted funding for youth from less affluent households seems to be counteracting the increasing costs somewhat. Corak, Lipps and Zhao suggest that student loans helped narrow the low- to high-income gap in university attendance in the late 1990s. Nevertheless, postsecondary access issues associated with affordability clearly remain on the policy agenda and need watching.

However, Finnie, Lascelles and Sweetman (2004) point out convincingly that student funding can only ever be expected to ease a modest fraction of the relationship between SES and educational attainment (as do Carneiro and Heckman 2003 for the US). A substantial portion of the variance in postsecondary attendance across individuals in Canada is associated with decisions and events that occur well before postsecondary funding becomes an issue. Current research around the SES gradient in postsecondary education and human capital acquisition, in general, is moving the discussion back to the very early stages of children's lives. Studies indicate that SES gradients in readiness to learn and academic achievement patterns, like health, are seen early in life (see Desjardins 2003; Willms 2003; Ma and Klinger 2000; ISUMA 2000) and it is likely that values toward life-long learning are as well (Banting 2005; Dodge 2004; Carneiro and Heckman 2003; Heckman, 1999).

Canadian population and public health researchers, at least in the Canadian context, have been advocating policies that address the "broader (or non-medical) determinants of health" (see e.g., Evans and Stoddart 2003), particularly early childhood educational and developmental (ECE/ECD) for some time (see ISUMA 2000 for several articles on the topic). Investments in children in the way of health, nutrition, good parenting and education have been shown to have large impacts on outcomes throughout the life cycle. Researchers in the area of human capital and economic development are now backing the call for these types of programs (Banting 2005; Dodge 2004; Corak 2004; Cleveland and Colley 2003; Hô and Legault 2002).

In strong support of ECE/ECD programs, Heckman states that "the best evidence suggests that learning begets learning" (1999, 42). Although the evidence regarding these programs is not conclusive, many authors (particularly those in the US, where there have been extensive evaluations of ECE/ECD programs) believe that there is enough mounting empirical evidence to imply a significant positive association between ECE/ECD and human capital acquisition (particularly health and education) across the life cycle (Carneiro and Heckman 2003; Currie 2001; Heckman 1999) and that these programs are likely, when of high quality and properly targeted, to be cost effective. Currie (2001) suggests that income targets alone will likely not capture the children most in need. Children whose parents have low levels of education, who are at risk for neglect or abuse or have problems with the English language also should be included. She goes on to surmise that universal programs will not be as efficient as well-targeted programs but may make the program as a whole more palatable for tax payers. Lipman *et al.* (2002) support the suggestion for careful targeting in the Canadian context. They suggest that the policy implications of the strong association between low income, low maternal education and poor child outcomes should lead to policies that address these characteristics for all family types. While lone-parent families are at higher risk and have been a focus in Canada, other family types are also subject to adverse circumstances. Whether programs are universal or targeted, there is a clear need to start very early to support the highest potential outcomes. There is also a need to recognize, as can be deduced from the work by Currie and Stabile (2003), that some parts of the welfare state are working well (children recover from negative health events at roughly the same speed regardless of SES), while others are less successful (low-SES children experience a greater number of negative health events).

According to Banting (2005), Canada's new social policy paradigm shifts emphasis from income security or protection from market disruptions with policy levers such as employment insurance (EI) and SA to supporting the capacity to adapt to changing markets through human capital investment. Few would argue that human capital investment is a "bad" thing. Many, however, argue that the current EI and SA systems are "broken" (Banting 2005; Battle, Mendelson and Torjman 2005). Currently, far less than half of the unemployed meet eligibility requirements for EI; for those who do qualify, replacement rates are as low as 50 percent. In many cases, individuals who previously would have qualified for EI are turning to SA. Moreover, severe cuts to SA benefits over the 1990s and "make work pay" policies may move individuals off SA into low-paying marginalized work. While large subsidies offered in the Self-Sufficiency Project (SSP) provided strong incentive to find work, Card and Hyslop (2005) report that the majority of women who moved from SA to work earned within $0.05 to $1.00 of minimum wage, whereas SA benefits equaled 33 hrs/wk of minimum wage work. Dunifon, Kalil and Danziger (2002) conclude that leaving SA and increasing labour-force participation alone will not lead to better outcomes for families; they must escape poverty. However, Johnson and Corcoran (2003) find that SA recipients often have low levels of human capital and few job skills leading them into low-paying, part-time jobs that do not offer health-insurance coverage. Unsurprisingly, recidivism rates are high (Green and Warburton 2001; Barret and Cragg 1998).

Is human capital investment *the* answer? The evidence is not clear cut. While providing full support of very early investments in human capital via ECE/ECD programs, Heckman (1999), and Carneiro and Heckman (2003) produce a review of US literature that provides compelling arguments against public training programs for older, displaced workers. They go so far as to suggest that for this group, subsidizing jobs is likely a more efficient way of providing income security while not undermining work ethics, which pure income transfers might do. They recognize that programs for some younger, more trainable individuals, particularly those offered through employers or in conjunction with work (apprentice-type training), are more efficient, likely due to the fact that, in the private market, these opportunities will be offered to those with the highest likelihood of success. Moreover, private human capital investment in later life also shows an association with SES, with those in higher SES circumstances (higher income and more educated) likely to take up ongoing training.

Meyers and de Broucker (2006) argue that the evidence presented by Heckman and colleagues focuses heavily on government-sponsored skills upgrading. Although they claim the evidence on the efficiency of obtaining more formal job-related training later in life (early 30s or later) is sparse, they present recent Canadian and international studies that indicate, for some "older" individuals who "missed out" on graduating from high school or postsecondary school earlier in their lives, policies that promote job-related training or "second-chance" education may be efficient. However, the evidence does not seem to support large-scale publicly funded job-training programs that are not linked to work.

While governments, federal and provincial, have followed through on limiting income redistribution by reducing income supports, with large cuts to EI, SA benefits and workfare programs. They have been less effective at investing in human capital for the young and particularly for those who are (were) reliant on income security programs. Banting argues that the human investment agenda must begin with investments very early in the life cycle to decrease inequality in life chances and that even if done well, and Canada is not yet at that point, the investments are likely to take a generation or more to pay off. Society should not ignore that a socio-economic gradient in human capital attainment still exists and that many individuals who were not afforded interventions early in life are now stranded by the changing regime. Banting concludes that "investing in human capital cannot be divorced from issues of poverty and inequality" (2005, 427) and that for some time the human capital investment agenda must coexist with some type of income redistribution scheme, otherwise the new paradigm is a "recipe for lower levels of income security for low-skilled workers in this generation and perhaps several to come" (ibid.).

Notes

Curtis gratefully acknowledges the excellent research assistance provided by Caitlin Dooley, helpful comments received from Arthur Sweetman and an anonymous reviewer. As well, she acknowledges the financial support for her CRC from Social Sciences and Humanities Research Council (SSHRC), Canada Foundation for Innovation (CFI) and Ontario Ministry of Research and Innovation.

References

Banting, K.G. 2005. "Do We Know Where We Are Going? The New Social Policy in Canada," *Canadian Public Policy/Analyse de politiques* 31(4):421-29.

Barrett, G.F. and M.I. Cragg. 1998. "An Untold Story: The Characteristics of Welfare Use in British Columbia," *Canadian Journal of Economics* 31(1):165-88.

Battle, K., M. Mendelson and S. Torjman. 2005. "The Modernization Mantra: Toward a New Architecture for Canada's Adult Benefits," *Canadian Public Policy/Analyse de politiques* 31(4):431-37.

Beaulieu, N., J.-Y. Duclosz, B. Fortin and M. Rouleau. 2005. "Intergenerational Reliance on Social Assistance: Evidence from Canada," *Journal of Population Economics* 18(3):539-62.

Buckley, N.J., F.T. Denton, A.L. Robb and B.G. Spencer. 2004. "The Transition from Good to Poor Health: An Econometric Study of the Older Population," *Journal of Health Economics* 23:1013-34.

Card, D. and D.R. Hyslop. 2005. "Estimating the Effects of a Time Limited Earnings Subsidy for Welfare Leavers," *Econometrica* 73(6):1723-70.

Carneiro, P. and J.J. Heckman. 2003. "Human Capital Policy." NBER Working Paper No. 9495. Cambridge, MA: National Bureau of Economic Research.

Case, A., D. Lubotky and C. Paxson. 2002. "Economic Status and Health in Childhood: The Origins of the Gradient," *The American Economic Review* 92 (5):1308-34.

Christofides, L.N., J. Cirello and M. Hoy. 2001. "Family Income and Post-Secondary Education in Canada," *Canadian Journal of Higher Education* 31(1):177-208.

Cleveland, G. and S. Colley. 2003. "The Future Roles of Government in Supporting Early Childhood Education and Care in Ontario." Report to the Panel on the Role of Government in Ontario. Submitted 4 June.

Corak, M. 2004. "Do Poor Children Become Poor Adults? Lessons for Public Policy from a Cross-Country Comparison of Generational Earnings Mobility." Paper presented at the workshop, "The Welfare State in an Intertemporal Perspective."

Corak, M., G. Lipps and J. Zhao. 2004. "Family Income and Participation in Post-Secondary Education." IZA Discussion Paper No. 977. Bonn: Institute for the Study of Labor.

Currie, J. 2001. "Early Childhood Education Programs," *The Journal of Economic Perspectives* 15(2):213-38.

— 2006. "Child Health and Human Capital," *NBER Reporter: Research Summary* (Spring).

Currie, J. and M. Stabile. 2003. "Socioeconomic Status and Child Health: Why Is the Relationship Stronger for Older Children?" *The American Economic Review* 93(5):1813-23.

Curtis, L.J. and S. Phipps. 2004. "Social Transfers and the Health Status of Mothers in Norway and Canada," *Social Science and Medicine* 58(12):2499-507.

Curtis, L.J., M. Dooley and S. Phipps. 2004. "Child Well-Being and Neighbourhood Quality: Evidence from the Canadian National Longitudinal Survey of Children and Youth," *Social Science and Medicine* 58(10):1917-27.

Curtis, L.J., M. Dooley, E. Lipman and D. Feeny. 2001. "The Role of Permanent Income and Family Structure in the Determination of Child Health in the Ontario Child Health Study," *Health Economics* 10(4):287-302.

Deaton, A. 2002. "Policy Implications of the Gradient of Health and Wealth," *Health Affairs* (March/April):13 -30.

de Broucker, P. 2005. *Getting There and Staying There: Low-income Students and Post-secondary Education.* CPRN Research Report No. W I 27. Ottawa: Canadian Policy Research Network.

Decker, S.L. and D.K. Remler. 2004. "How Much Might Universal Health Insurance Reduce Socioeconomic Disparities in Health? A Comparison of US and Canada." NBER Working Paper No. 10715. Cambridge, MA: National Bureau of Economic Research.

Desjardins, R. 2003. "Determinants of Literacy Proficiency: A Lifelong-Lifewide Learning Perspective," *International Journal of Educational Research* 39(3):205-45.

Dodge, D. 2004. "Human Capital, Early Childhood Development and Economic Growth," in *Encyclopedia on Early Childhood Development*, ed. R.E. Tremblay, R.G. Barr and R. DeV. Peters. Montreal: Centre of Excellence for Early Childhood Development.

Dooley, M. and P. Contoyannis. 2005. "Intergenerational Economic Mobility in the Ontario Child Health Study." Working Paper. Hamilton: McMaster University.

Dooley, M. and J. Stewart. 2004. "Family Income and Child Outcomes in Canada," *Canadian Journal of Economics* 37(4):898-917.

Dooley, M.D., L.J. Curtis, E. Lipman and D. Feeny. 1998. "Child Psychiatric Disorders, Poor School Performance and Social Problems: The Roles of Family Structure and Low-Income," in *Labour Markets, Social Institutions, and the Future of Canada's Children*, ed. M. Corak. Ottawa: Statistics Canada.

Drolet, M. 2005. *Participation in Post-Secondary Education in Canada: Has the Role of Parental Income and Education Changed Over the 1990s?* Catalogue No. 11F0019MIE, 243. Analytical Studies Research Paper Series. Ottawa: Statistics Canada.

Dunifon, R., A. Kalil and S.K. Danziger. 2002. "Maternal Work Behavior under Welfare Reform: How Does the Transition from Welfare to Work Affect Child Development?" Ithaca, NY: Department of Policy Analysis and Management, Cornell University. Unpublished paper.

Evans R.G. and G.L. Stoddart. 2003. "Consuming Research, Producing Policy?" *American Journal of Public Health* 93(3):371-79.

Finnie, R. and C. Laporte. Forthcoming. *The Demand for Student Loans and Access to Post-Secondary Education*. Analytical Studies Research Paper Series. Ottawa: Statistics Canada.

Finnie, R. and A. Usher. 2005. "The Canadian Experiment in Cost-Sharing and its Effects on Access to Higher Education, 1990–2002." Working Paper No. 39. Kingston: School of Policy Studies, Queen's University.

Finnie, R., C. Laporte and E. Lascelles. 2004. *Family Background and Access to Post-Secondary Education: What Happened over the 1990s?* Catalogue No. 11F0019MIE, 226. Analytical Studies Research Paper Series. Ottawa: Statistics Canada.

Finnie, R., E. Lascelles and A. Sweetman. 2004. *Who Goes? The Direct and Indirect Effects of Family Background on Access to Post-secondary Education*. Catalogue No. 11F0019MIE, 237. Analytical Studies Research Paper Series. Ottawa: Statistics Canada.

Green, D.A. and W.P. Warburton. 2001. "Tightening a Welfare System: The Effects of Benefit Denial on Future Welfare Receipt." Discussion Paper No. 02-07. Vancouver: Department of Economics, University of British Columbia.

Grossman, M. 2005. "Education and Nonmarket Outcomes." NBER Working Paper No. 11582. Cambridge, MA: National Bureau of Economic Research.

Heckman, J.J. 1999. "Policies to Foster Human Capital." NBER Working Paper No. 7288. Cambridge, MA: National Bureau of Economic Research.

Hô, V.H.G. and G. Legault. 2002. "Les indices socio-économiques, outil de politique de l'éducation au Québec," in *Towards Evidence-Based Policy for Canadian Education/Vers des politiques canadiennes d'éducation fondées sur la recherche*, ed. P. de Broucker and A. Sweetman. Montreal and Kingston: The John Deutsch Institute at Queen's University in cooperation with McGill-Queen's University Press.

ISUMA. 2000. "Kids," *ISUMA* 1(2). Montreal: Les Presses de l'Université de Montréal.

Jenkins, S.P. and C. Schluter. 2002. "Does Low Income in Early Childhood Affect Adolescent School Attainment? Evidence from the German Socio-Economic Panel." Colchester, UK: University of Essex. Unpublished paper.

Johnson, R. and M. Corcoran. 2003. "The Road to Economic Self-Sufficiency: Job Quality and Job Transition Patterns after Welfare Reform," *Journal of Policy Analysis and Management* 22:615-40.

Knighton, T. and S. Mirza. 2002. "Postsecondary Participation: The Effects of Parents' Education and Household Income," *Education Quarterly Review* 8(3):25-32.

Kohen, D.E., J. Brooks-Gunn, T. Leventhal and C. Hertzman. 2002. "Neighborhood Income and Physical and Social Disorder in Canada: Associations with Young Children's Competencies," *Child Development* 73(6):1844-60.

Lipman, E., M. Boyle, M. Dooley and D. Offord. 2002. "Children Well-Being in Single-Mother Families," *Journal of the American Academy of Child and Adolescent Psychiatry* 41(1):75-82.

Ma, X. and D.A. Klinger. 2000. "Hierarchical Linear Modelling of Student and School Effects on Academic Achievement," *Canadian Journal of Education* 25(1):41-55.

Mahler, P. and R. Winkelmann. 2004. "Single Motherhood and (Un)Equal Educational Opportunities: Evidence for Germany." IZA Discussion Paper Series No. 1391. Bonn: Institute for the Study of Labor.

Marmot, M. 2002. "The Influence of Income on Health: Views of an Epidemiologist," *Health Affairs* (March/April):31- 46.

Meara, E. 2001. "Why is Health Related to Socioeconomic Status? The Case of Pregnancy and Low Birth Weight." NBER Working Paper No. 8231. Cambridge, MA: National Bureau of Economic Research.

Meyers, K. and P. de Broucker. 2006. *Too Many Left Behind: Canada's Adult Education and Training System*. CPRN Research Report No. W 134. Ottawa: Canadian Policy Research Network.

Mustard, C., E. Tompa and J. Etches. 2006. "The Effects of Deficits in Health Status in Childhood and Adolescence on Human Capital Development in Early Adulthood," in *Skills and Knowledge for Canada's Future: Seven Perspectives: Towards an Integrated Approach to Human Capital Development*. Ottawa: Canadian Policy Research Networks Inc.

Oreopoulos, P. 2003. "Do Dropouts Drop Out Too Soon? Evidence Using Changes in School Leaving Laws." NBER Working Paper No. 10155. Cambridge, MA: National Bureau of Economic Research.

Oreopoulos, P., M.E. Page and A.H. Stevens. 2004. "The Intergenerational Effects of Compulsory Schooling." Toronto: University of Toronto. Unpublished paper.

Riddell, W.C. 2006. "The Impact of Education on Economic and Social Outcomes: An Overview of Recent Advances in Economics," in *Skills and Knowledge for Canada's Future: Seven Perspectives: Towards an Integrated Approach to Human Capital Development*. Ottawa: Canadian Policy Research Networks Inc.

Schuller, T. 2001. "The Complementary Roles of Human and Social Capital," *ISUMA: Canadian Journal of Policy Research* 2(1):18-24.

Thériault, L. 2000. "Non-Financial Barriers to Employment Faced by Welfare Recipients: A Review of Recent American Literature." Social Policy Research Unit Working Paper No. 15. Regina, SK: University of Regina. At http://scratchpost.uregina.ca/spr/working_paper.html.

Willms, J.D. 2003. "Literacy Proficiency of Youth: Evidence of Converging Socioeconomic Gradients," *International Journal of Educational Research* 39:247-52.

4

The Impact of Education on Economic and Social Outcomes: An Overview of Recent Advances in Economics

W. CRAIG RIDDELL

Important advances have recently taken place in our understanding of a central issue: the causal relationship between education and labour market success. The causal effect of education on earnings is at least as large as, and possibly larger than, what was previously believed. The return to incremental investments in education, especially those that affected groups with relatively low levels of education, often exceed the average return for the labour force as a whole. The social benefits of education are also substantial. These results suggest that investments in human capital remain an important potential source of earnings growth.

Introduction

This paper surveys recent advances in our understanding of the consequences of human capital for individual and social outcomes. Particular attention is given to recent developments in the discipline of economics.

Over the past 10 to 15 years there has been a resurgence of interest among economists in education and human capital. Considerable progress has been made on several fronts. This paper focuses on what I regard as the most important advance in knowledge — that of obtaining credible estimates of the causal influence of education on individual and social outcomes. Distinguishing between correlation and causation has been a major challenge in this area for some time. As a consequence, the substantial recent progress in this area represents an important achievement. Nonetheless, it is worth noting that substantial research effort has also been devoted to several other issues relating to education and human capital. These include the consequences of changes in the intensity of resources devoted to schooling through such factors as class size and teacher training and remuneration, the implications of greater school choice and increased competition among schools, the role and implications of various forms of testing of students, and the significance of peer effects. Rather than providing a brief overview of recent research on all of these topics, I choose to focus on the central issue of the causal effect of education on individual and social outcomes.

The paper is organized as follows. The next section provides brief overviews of the leading theories that seek to explain the linkages between human capital formation and labour market and social outcomes. Although the treatment of these theories is necessarily brief and simplified, this section provides useful background for the main parts of the paper. The remaining sections deal with empirical evidence on the relationship between human capital and individual and social outcomes.

The third section discusses the challenges that arise in obtaining credible estimates of the causal impacts of education on private outcomes such as employment and labour market earnings. Although this task may seem to be straightforward, it has in fact represented a major challenge to empirical research for several decades. Important advances have recently been made in this area, and these are described in this section. The fourth section surveys recent advances in estimating the non-market and social benefits of education — impacts on outcomes such as greater civic participation, improved health and reduced criminal activity. As is the case for empirical research on the private impacts of schooling, important advances have recently occurred in obtaining estimates of a variety of social consequences. The statistical techniques used to advance our understanding of the private consequences of education have also been fruitfully employed to analyze non-market and social impacts.

Most research on the relationship between human capital formation and individual and social outcomes uses relatively crude measures of human capital such as educational attainment and years of work experience. However, education and experience are inputs into the production of human capital rather than outputs such as skills, competencies and knowledge. Only recently has data become available on direct measures of skills for the working-age population. Section five discusses recent studies that utilize such data to examine two issues. The first relates to the production of human capital — the nature of the relationship between inputs such as schooling and work experience and outcomes such as literacy and numeracy skills. The second issue relates to the way in which literacy and numeracy skills are rewarded in the labour market — the relationship between skills and outcomes such as employment and earnings. The final section concludes.

Models of Human and Skills Development

This section briefly outlines several key theories of human and skills development that are frequently used to explain observed relationships between human capital acquisition and labour market and social outcomes.[1] Three leading models are discussed: human capital, signalling or screening, and job-worker matching or information-based models. There are large theoretical and empirical literatures relating to each of these models. The objective here is not to survey these literatures, a task that would require a major effort, but to present the central ideas of these theories and their relevance to understanding the mechanisms through which human capital may influence labour market outcomes.

Human Capital Model

Human capital theory is widely used to explain labour market outcomes. The essence of the theory is that investments are made in human resources in order to improve productivity, and therefore employment prospects and earnings. Individuals acquire skills through formal schooling and/or work experience, and these skills increase the individual's value to employers and as a result, future earnings.

Several key elements of human capital theory are worth noting. First, it is a theory of investment decisions: individuals incur costs at the present time in return for benefits in the future. This investment dimension is particularly important because the benefits of human capital acquisition typically accrue over a long period, in the form of a higher earnings stream over many years. Second, because the benefits accrue in the future there will typically be uncertainty about the extent to which the investments will pay off. Human capital investments are generally risky investments. Third, a major component of the costs of acquiring human capital is typically the opportunity cost: the income foregone by not working.

Decisions about education — both the amount of time to devote to schooling and choice of educational programs — will be influenced by the "investment" and "consumption" components of human capital formation. The latter refers to the fact that learning may be a very enjoyable activity for some, but a less enjoyable or even unpleasant activity for others. Other factors being equal, individuals who enjoy learning are more likely to remain in school longer. Similarly, other things being equal, students are more likely to choose educational programs that they regard as interesting and stimulating.

An important distinction is that between private and social returns to human capital formation. Private returns are those based on the costs incurred by and benefits received by the individual acquiring the education. These benefits include both the consumption and investment consequences of schooling. Social returns are based on the costs incurred and benefits received by society as a whole. There may be differences between private costs and social costs, as well as between private and social benefits. This distinction is important because individuals can be expected to base their schooling decisions on the private costs and benefits, whereas it is in the interest of society as a whole to have educational decisions based on the social costs and benefits.

A final important concept is the distinction between general and firm-specific human capital. General human capital refers to skills and knowledge that are useful to many employers, while firm-specific human capital is useful to one employer but not to others. This distinction is useful in understanding the incentives for individual workers and employers to pay for education or training. In a competitive environment, firms will not be willing to pay for workers to acquire general skills because they will not be able to reap the benefits of this investment. Rather, workers will pay for general training because they are the ones who will receive the benefits in the form of higher earnings. On the other hand, workers do not have an incentive to invest in firm-specific skills because doing so does not raise their value to other employers. Firm-specific human capital investments will either be paid for by the employer or these investments will be shared, with both the employer and employee paying some of the costs and receiving some of the benefits.

In between the extreme cases of general and firm-specific human capital are situations in which the skills acquired are industry-specific or occupation-specific. I discuss these circumstances further below.

Lifetime earnings display two well-established patterns. First, the lifetime earnings profile of more educated workers lies above the equivalent earnings profile of less-educated workers. Second, earnings rise with work experience, albeit at a diminishing rate. The increase in earnings with experience is especially pronounced during the first five to ten years after entering the workforce. Human capital theory accounts for these well-established patterns through the mechanism of skill formation; education and work experience enhance the individual's skills, thereby raising the market value to employers. Human capital investments thus yield a private return in the form of greater employment opportunities and higher lifetime earnings. Because they increase worker productivity, human capital investments also yield social benefits: the increase in the total output of goods and services produced. They may also yield social benefits in excess of private benefits, as discussed more fully subsequently.

Signalling/Screening Model

Human capital theory emphasizes the role of education as enhancing the productive capacities of individuals. A contrasting view of education, where it has no effect on individual productivity, is the signalling/screening model. According to this theory, education may act as a signal of the productive capacity of individuals. Central to this theory is the importance of imperfect information. In their hiring decisions, employers are imperfectly informed about the capabilities of potential employees. They therefore may use education as a signal of a new hire's future productivity. If employers' beliefs are subsequently confirmed by actual experience (that is, if more educated workers turn out to be more productive), employers will continue to use education as a signal. Employers will thus offer higher wages to more educated workers. Facing a positive relationship between education (which is costly to acquire) and wages, individuals will have an incentive to invest in education. A central assumption of the signalling model is that education is less costly to acquire for individuals who are innately more skilled or able. If this assumption holds, higher-ability individuals will invest more in education than will lower-ability individuals. Both high- and low-ability individuals face the same potential benefits from investing in schooling, but low-ability workers face higher costs and therefore will acquire less education. In these circumstances, employers' beliefs about the relationship between education and worker productivity will be confirmed. Even though schooling has (by assumption) no effect on worker productivity, employers have an incentive to offer higher wages to more highly educated workers and higher-ability individuals have an incentive to invest in education. In this model, education serves as a "sorting device," separating the high-ability workers from the low-ability workers.

Like human capital theory, the signalling/screening model can explain the positive relationship that exists between schooling and labour market outcomes such as earnings. However, there are important differences between the two theories. In the human capital model, education is privately and socially productive. In contrast, in the signalling model education is privately productive (high-ability individuals benefit from investing in education), but not socially productive because education has no effect on the total goods and services produced by society. Another important difference is that in the human capital model, schooling exerts a causal influence on worker productivity and thus earnings. In the signalling theory, education has no effect on worker productivity so there is no causal influence of education on earnings. Rather, the positive relationship between schooling and earnings arises because both variables are related to a third factor: worker ability. In many circumstances, worker ability is unobserved so it is difficult to determine whether the positive relationship between education and earnings arises because schooling enhances workers' productive capacities (the human capital explanation) or because schooling sorts out high- and low-capacity individuals. However, as discussed subsequently, considerable recent progress has been made on identifying the causal effect of education on earnings. This evidence provides insights into the relative importance of skills development versus signalling in determining labour market outcomes.

Job-Matching or Information-Based Model

In the human capital model, individuals choose among alternative educational programs according to the costs of these programs and the associated lifetime earnings streams (and other benefits) that they generate. Information may play a role in helping to identify or forecast the benefits of alternative educational choices. An alternative view of the educational process is that it helps individuals to determine what types of careers they are most suited for. In this case, education plays the role of providing individuals with information about their comparative advantages — the types of occupations and jobs they are likely to do well in. This mechanism is characteristic of job-matching and information-based models. The perspective is similar to human capital theory in several ways, including the implication that education has both private and social benefits. However, the emphasis is different. Human capital theory emphasizes the acquisition of skills that are valued by the labour market, while job-matching models emphasize the acquisition of information about one's abilities and aptitudes. Human capital theory focuses on the direct increase in skills provided by schooling, whereas information-based models highlight the role of education in identifying the most productive applications of a given set of skills.

The job-matching approach also has important implications for the interpretation of returns to work experience. It views jobs as having an idiosyncratic, or firm-worker specific, value. The same job may be a better match for some workers than for others. In addition, the quality of the match usually cannot be observed in advance. It takes time for workers and firms to determine whether a particular relationship is a good fit.

One interpretation that follows from this view of the world is that some job instability — especially among young workers — is not a bad thing. Investment takes the form of workers learning about their comparative advantage by sampling and experiencing a variety of jobs in different industries and occupations. Additionally, there is a search for a good firm-worker match. Further, the model suggests that mobility should decrease with time in the labor market as workers learn about their own abilities and are more likely, as a result of moving from job to job, to find a good match.

This approach has led to a re-evaluation of the relative importance of general versus firm-specific human capital. Much empirical work observes that workers who have been with a firm a long time have higher wages than otherwise similar workers with less tenure. This was previously interpreted to mean that firm-specific human capital was very important and its accumulation was associated with increasing wages. However, the job search/shopping model suggests that causality may also go in the other direction. Good firm-worker matches have high wages because they benefit both parties, and are more likely to endure.

As with many perspectives on the labour market, empirical research has observed that both human capital and job-matching models explain some of what we observe. Related empirical research has altered the interpretation of "specific" human capital by showing that industry- and occupation-specific human capital are probably more important than firm-specific human capital. Industry- and occupation-specific human capital seems to be relatively easily transferred across firms. Further, the research shows the importance of general labour market experience to earnings growth, and the importance of job shopping to earnings growth among young workers.

Overall, the job-shopping model points out that early career job transitions are often productive, that training need not be firm-specific and that general labour market experience is especially valuable in the early stages of a career. It also reinforces the long-term value of formal education, not only because of its own labour-market productivity enhancing effects but also in its interaction in making general labour market experience more valuable. Finally, it emphasizes that educational programs may help people learn about their comparative advantages, in addition to directly enhancing skills and knowledge.

Evidence on the Consequences of Education and Skills Development

Many individuals invest in education in the belief that doing so will yield future benefits such as greater employment opportunities, higher earnings and more interesting and varied careers. Similarly, many public policies encourage individual citizens to increase their educational attainment and enhance their skills and knowledge. Increased educational attainment and skills are not necessarily valued for their own sake but often because they are believed to result in better labour market and social outcomes. But is there a solid empirical basis for this belief? How confident can we be that higher educational attainment and enhanced skills development deserve to be treated as objectives, if what we really care about are labour market and social outcomes?

This section addresses these questions. It reviews the empirical evidence on the relationship between education and earnings, including the extent to which schooling exerts a causal effect on employment and earnings versus acting as a sorting device. The studies discussed in this section typically examine the consequences of educational choices made by individuals many years, often several decades, ago. Although there is no assurance that the future will be like the past, this evidence nonetheless provides insights into the probable long-run consequences of individual decisions and policies designed to increase educational attainment.

Schooling may have numerous consequences for individuals and society. For many people, there is some consumption value from the educational process. Human beings are curious creatures and enjoy learning and acquiring new knowledge. Even focusing on the investment aspects, education may enable people to more fully enjoy life, appreciate literature and culture, and be more informed and socially-involved citizens. Although these and other potential consequences of schooling are important and should not be ignored, the consequences of education for employability, productivity and earnings are also of substantial importance.

As many studies have documented, schooling is one of the best predictors of "who gets ahead." Better-educated workers earn higher wages, have greater earnings growth over their lifetimes, experience less unemployment and work longer. Higher education is also associated with longer life expectancy, better health and reduced participation in crime. In this section we focus on evidence relating to the private returns to education, specifically those that result from higher lifetime earnings.[2]

Two principal approaches have been used to analyze the relationship between schooling and earnings. Both use standard multivariate methods such as ordinary least squares (OLS) estimation. As discussed below, both approaches suffer from the limitation that they may estimate the correlation between earnings and education, after controlling for other observed influences on earnings, rather than isolating the causal impact of education on earnings.

The first approach is illustrated by recent Canadian studies by Allen (2004), Rathje and Emery (2002) and Vaillancourt and Bourdeau-Primeau (2002). This method estimates life-cycle earnings profiles from data on groups of individuals with different levels of education. Combining these estimated earnings profiles with information on the costs of acquiring additional education — both the direct costs and the opportunity costs associated with the income foregone by not working — allows the implied rate of return on the investment in additional education to be estimated. For example, the rate of return to a university degree compared to a high-school diploma is estimated using the life-cycle earnings profiles for these two groups together with information on the direct and opportunity costs of attending university compared to entering the labour force after completing high school.

The second approach is based on estimation of an earnings function in which a measure of earnings is regressed on years of completed schooling (or highest level of educational attainment), years of labour market experience and additional variables that control for other influences on earnings. This earnings function approach is widely used because it readily provides estimates of the rate of return to education, as well as yielding insights into the relative magnitudes of other influences on earnings.

Canadian studies using these conventional OLS methods to analyze the relationship between education and earnings obtain estimates of the "return to schooling" that are similar to those obtained in many studies carried out in other developed countries: rates of return (in real terms, i.e., after adjusting for inflation) of approximately 8 to 10 percent for the labour force as a whole. Such estimates compare favourably with rates of return on investments in physical capital. In Canada, women tend to benefit more from education than men. For example, a recent study found real rates of return to investments in education of approximately 9 percent for females and 6 percent for males (Ferrer and Riddell 2002). Other Canadian research finds similar male-female differences.

The strong positive relationship between education and earnings is one of the most well-established relationships in social science. Many social scientists have, however, been reluctant to interpret this correlation as evidence that education exerts a causal effect on earnings. According to human capital theory, schooling raises earnings because it enhances workers' skills, thus making employees more productive and more valuable to employers. However, as discussed previously, the positive relationship between earnings and schooling could arise because both education and earnings are correlated with unobserved factors such as ability, perseverance and ambition (hereafter simply referred to as ability). If there are systematic differences between the less-educated and the well-educated that affect both schooling decisions and labour market success, then the correlation between education and earnings may reflect these other factors as well. According to signalling/screening theory, such differences could arise if employers use education as a signal of unobserved productivity-related factors such as ability or perseverance. In these circumstances, standard estimates of the return to schooling are likely to be biased upwards because they do not take into account unobserved "ability." More generally, those with greater ability or motivation may be more likely to be successful, even in the absence of additional education. That is, the correlation that exists between earnings and education, after controlling for other observed influences on earnings, may reflect the contribution of unobserved influences rather than a causal impact of education on earnings.

This "omitted ability bias" issue is of fundamental importance not only for the question of how we should interpret the positive relationship between earnings and schooling, but also for the emphasis that should be placed on education in public policies. To the extent that estimates of the return to schooling are biased upwards because of unobserved factors, estimated average rates of return to education may substantially over-predict the economic benefits that a less-educated person would receive if he/she acquired additional schooling. The estimated average rates of return in the population reflect both the causal effect of schooling on productivity and earnings and the average return to the unobserved ability of the well-educated. However, if those with low levels of education are also, on average, those with low ability or ambition, they can only expect to receive from any additional schooling the return associated with the causal effect of schooling on earnings. That is, average rates of return in the population reflect the causal effect of schooling on earnings and the return to unobserved factors. The marginal return — the impact of additional schooling for someone with low levels of education — may be substantially below the average return. In these circumstances, education may not be very effective in improving the employment or earnings prospects of relatively disadvantaged groups.

Unbiased estimates of the causal effect of education on earnings are thus important for individual decisions as well as for the design of public policies. How can such estimates be obtained? The most reliable method would be to conduct an experiment. Individuals randomly assigned to the treatment group would receive a larger "dose" of education than those assigned to the control group. By following the two groups through time we could observe their subsequent earnings and obtain an unbiased estimate of the impact of schooling on labour market success. Random assignment ensures that, on average, treatment and control groups would not be significantly different from each other in terms of their observed and unobserved characteristics. Thus, on average, the treatment and control groups would be equally represented by high-ability and low-ability individuals.

In the absence of such experimental evidence, economists have tried to find *natural experiments* or *quasi-experiments* that isolate the influence of education from the possible effects of unobserved ability. Many of these studies use instrumental variables (IV) methods to estimate the causal impact of education on earnings. These methods can be understood in the context of a simple two equation model of earnings and education. One equation is the earnings equation referred to above, in which the dependent variable is labour market earnings (often the logarithm of earnings) and the explanatory or right-hand side variables include education (usually measured as years of completed schooling or highest level of attainment), work experience and other observed influences on earnings. The dependent variable in the second equation is educational attainment and the explanatory variables include various influences on education such as family background. In this simple setting, unobserved factors such as ability or motivation enter the error terms in each equation because they may affect both educational choices and earnings outcomes. As a consequence, there is a correlation between the error term in the earnings equation and educational attainment, one of the right-hand side variables in the earnings equation. Such a correlation implies that OLS estimation of the earnings equation will yield estimates that are biased and inconsistent. Instrumental variables estimation is a method of obtaining consistent estimates in these circumstances.

An instrumental variable (or instrument) refers to a variable that is correlated with the right-hand side variable of interest — in this case educational attainment — but that is not correlated with the error term in the earnings equation. If a valid instrument can be found, IV estimation yields consistent estimates of the causal impact of schooling on earnings.

Many recent studies have obtained suitable instruments by finding natural experiments in which some policy change or other event causes changes in educational attainment among some individuals, and does so in a manner that is external to (or independent of) the decisions of the affected individuals. An example of such an external (or exogenous) event — one that has been extensively used in empirical studies — consists of changes in compulsory schooling and child labour laws. Such laws have existed in many countries throughout most of the past century. In Canada these laws operate at the provincial level, and they have been revised at different times in different provinces since the early 1900s. An increase in the minimum school leaving age — for example, from 15 years of age to 16 years of age — is expected to cause some individuals to remain in school longer than they would otherwise have. This policy change is also likely to be independent of the unobserved factors such as ability and motivation that influence the level of education that the individual would choose in the absence of such laws. In these circumstances, compulsory schooling laws represent a valid instrumental variable because they are correlated with educational attainment but are not correlated with factors that enter the error term in the earnings equation such as individual ability or motivation.

An alternative and useful way of thinking about instrumental variables is as follows. A valid IV influences the right-hand side variable which is correlated with the error term, in this case educational attainment, but does not directly influence the dependent variable, which in this case is labour market earnings. That is, a valid instrument for education in the earnings equation exerts its influence on earnings only indirectly through its effect on education: it does not influence earnings directly. The example of compulsory schooling laws illustrates these properties. Changes in such laws cause changes in educational attainment among some individuals, but it is unlikely that these legal changes would directly alter the earnings of the affected individuals, by which I mean the individuals who stay in school longer as a consequence of the changes in the laws. Thus if the affected individuals experience higher earnings, it is appropriate to infer that the increased earnings are the result of the additional schooling. We can be reasonably confident that the increased earnings are not due to unobserved factors such as individual ability since ability did not change for the individuals affected by the legal changes.

Of course, some — perhaps many — individuals are not affected by changes in compulsory schooling laws. According to human capital theory, those who would have remained in school beyond the new minimum school leaving age will make the same educational choices after the changes in the laws as before the legal changes because the costs and benefits of education have not changed for these individuals.[3] The fact that only a fraction of the population of interest is directly affected by changes in compulsory schooling laws does not affect the validity of IV estimation, but it does have two important consequences. One relates to the power of the IV estimates. If few people alter their educational choices in response to the legal changes then it is unlikely that precise estimates of the causal impact of education on earnings will be obtained. The second consequence relates to the interpretation of the IV estimates and is discussed below.

Another variable that has been used as an instrument for education is distance to a college or university at age 15 or 16. High-school graduates who live close to a college or university are more likely to attend a postsecondary educational institution than are those who live far away from a college or university, at least in part because the costs of postsecondary education is lower for such individuals. As a consequence, distance to a postsecondary institution is correlated with educational attainment but is arguably not correlated with unobserved ability. Living close to a university or college thus satisfies the conditions for a suitable IV.[4]

A large number of studies based on the natural experiment/instrumental variable methodology have recently been carried out, using data on sources of variation in education such as those arising from compulsory schooling laws or proximity to a college or university. Table 1 summarizes a number of these contributions, including several Canadian studies.[5] As is evident in Table 1, a consistent, and perhaps surprising, result is that conventional OLS estimates of the return to schooling tend to be similar in size or even smaller than their IV counterparts. According to these recent studies the true impact of education on earnings is at least as large as and perhaps larger than was suggested by earlier studies based on conventional OLS estimation.

The previous discussion of omitted ability bias suggested that OLS estimates are likely to be biased upward. Why then do IV estimates which correct for these omitted factors lie above the conventional OLS estimates? Research has provided two principal answers to this question.[6] One is that there is an additional source of bias that operates in the opposite direction. In particular, the presence of measurement error in educational attainment results in downward bias in the coefficient on education in the earnings equation.[7] The downward bias due to measurement error thus acts in the opposite direction to any upward bias associated with unobserved ability.

The second, and perhaps more fundamental, reason is that in some circumstances OLS and IV methods may measure different things. In particular, in the presence of heterogeneity in the net benefits of additional education across individuals, OLS and IV methods provide estimates of the return to education for different groups. In general, there are many reasons to expect that the returns to schooling are not the same for all individuals in the population. Rather, there is likely to be a distribution of such returns, with some individuals facing higher net benefits from acquiring additional schooling than others. In these circumstances the OLS and IV estimates have different interpretations, and considerable care is required when comparing these estimates.

For concreteness, consider the returns to acquiring an additional year of schooling. Doing so may raise the lifetime earnings of some

Table 1. OLS and IV Estimates of the Return to Education

Study	Country, Instruments	Returns to Schooling OLS	IV
Angrist and Krueger (1991)	US, compulsory schooling laws	0.070 0.063 0.052	0.101 0.060 0.078
Staiger and Stock (1997)	US, compulsory schooling laws	0.063 0.052	0.098 0.088
Harmon and Walker (1995)	UK, compulsory schooling laws	0.061	0.153
Kane and Rouse (1993)	US, tuition, distance to college	0.080 0.063	0.091 0.094
Card (1995)	US, distance to nearest college	0.073	0.132 0.097
Conneely and Uusitalo (1997)	Finland, living in university town	0.085 0.083	0.110 0.098
Lemieux and Card (2001)	Canada, WWII *Veterans Rehabilitation Act*	0.070 0.062	0.164 0.076
Meghir and Palme (2000)	Sweden, education reforms	0.028	0.036
Sweetman (1999)	Canada, Newfoundland education reform		
	females	0.146	0.170
	males	0. 108	0.221
Oreopoulos (2006)	Canada, compulsory schooling laws		
	without trends controls	0.115	0.070
	with trends controls	0.115	0.131

Source: Author's compilation.

individuals by (say) 6 percent but increase the lifetime earnings of others by 10 percent. One reason for such heterogeneity could be differential access to funds to finance human capital investments. A general principle of investment behaviour is that individuals should undertake investments as long as the expected rate of return exceeds the market rate of interest. If everyone faced the same market rate of interest and could borrow to finance educational investments, then everyone would invest in education up to the point where the expected rate of return equals the market rate of interest. In these circumstances, if everyone faces a common market interest rate, we would expect rates of return on educational investments to be similar across individuals. However, in contrast to the financing of physical capital investments, it is typically difficult for individuals to borrow to finance human capital acquisition. Some individuals may be able to access funds from family or other sources in order to acquire additional education, while others are unable to do so. As a consequence there may be some individuals who do not invest in additional education even though the expected return from doing so is high. In these circumstances there is likely to be heterogeneity in expected rates of return across individuals, with those who face above-average costs of schooling (perhaps due to credit constraints) also having above-average expected returns relative to market interest rates.

Inadequate information about the benefits of additional education may be another factor contributing to underinvestment in human capital. Individuals from relatively disadvantaged backgrounds appear to be less likely to be well informed about the benefits of acquiring more education and to be more adverse to the risks associated with such investments. Relative to those who are well informed about the consequences of additional education, such individuals behave as if the costs of education are high.

Consider the case of individuals who do not pursue higher education — perhaps because of low family income, limited ability to borrow in order to finance human capital formation, or a family background in which the importance of education is not emphasized. The low levels of completed schooling among these individuals may be principally due to above-average costs of additional education rather than below-average expected returns. For these individuals, whom I will refer to as the "high potential return" group, a policy intervention that results in increased educational attainment could have a substantial payoff. Indeed, the return to the investment may exceed the average return in the population. In these circumstances, the average return from existing investments in education may understate the payoff to incremental investments. That is, policy interventions that focus on increasing education among those with relatively low levels of schooling may be able to achieve rates of return that exceed those experienced by those who would invest in education even in the absence of any intervention.

When returns to education are heterogeneous, researchers must be careful in identifying what aspect of the distribution of returns they wish to estimate. One parameter that might be of interest is the average marginal rate of return to an additional year of schooling in the population. This measure provides a useful summary of the payoff to additional schooling for the population as a whole. It also provides an estimate of the expected rate of return that would be experienced by an individual chosen at random from the population. Using the language of program evaluation this concept is referred to as the average treatment effect (ATE).

However, the return to a specific group of individuals, rather than the population as a whole, might be of more interest for analyzing specific policy interventions. For example, one might wish to estimate the return for the group of individuals who are targeted by a policy. Consider a policy that would subsidize postsecondary education among students from less advantaged backgrounds. In order to determine whether this expenditure is worthwhile on cost-benefit grounds, analysts need to know the returns that would be experienced by the individuals affected by the policy rather than the rate of return for the population as a whole. This parameter is referred to as the average treatment effect on the treated (ATET) and measures the return for those individuals who actually receive treatment (in this case, for those less-advantaged individuals who were offered the subsidy to postsecondary education). However, empirical research relying on IV estimation techniques typically does not identify either the ATE or ATET parameters, except under special circumstances.[8]

What then does IV estimate? A key insight of recent research is that the causal effects that IV estimates are specific to the instrument used. In general, IV estimates the returns for those individuals who are induced to change their schooling decisions because of the instrument. For example, when the instruments are changes in compulsory schooling laws, IV estimates the average return for those individuals who acquire additional education as a consequence of the change to the laws. Such estimates are referred to as a local average treatment effect (LATE), and their interpretation is intimately tied to the instrument used. In general, different instruments estimate the returns for different groups and must be interpreted as such. Furthermore, unlike a true experiment where we know which individuals are assigned to the treatment and control groups, with IV methods applied to natural experiments it is generally not possible to identify the specific individuals whose behaviour was altered by the policy change.

This has consequences for analyzing specific policy interventions, since, while a particular IV estimate may be valid for the group studied, the results of this intervention may not readily generalize to other groups. Consider, for example, a policy to subsidize tuition for postsecondary education. We would expect IV estimation using college or university proximity as an instrument to be more informative than studies using compulsory schooling laws if we interpret distance to college or university as a cost of obtaining higher education (Kling 2000). In this case, we are concerned about the returns for those individuals for which cost might be a barrier to obtaining postsecondary education — a group that might be targeted by a tuition subsidy.

At this point, it might be useful to summarize the relationship between OLS, IV and the above concepts. When OLS is applied to a sample representative of the overall population, it yields an estimate of the ATE. In contrast, IV estimation provides an estimate of the LATE for the subset of the population that altered their behaviour due to the instrument used to obtain the IV estimates. This subset of the population is generally not a readily identifiable group, and care must be taken in interpreting the results since the estimates obtained may not provide valid inference for a specific policy intervention that affects a different group of individuals. In some circumstances, however, the IV estimates may be highly relevant since they provide estimates of the net benefits of additional education acquired by the group whose behaviour was influenced by a policy change or other intervention.

With these concepts in mind, let us now return to the summary of recent OLS and IV estimates in Table 1. These estimates indicate that the LATE of past educational interventions (accidental or otherwise) has generally been as large as or even greater than the average rate of return to education in the population as a whole. This suggests that policy and other interventions that caused some groups to acquire more education than they otherwise would have chosen to acquire have typically affected high potential return individuals. In the case of changes to compulsory schooling laws these are individuals who would have dropped out of secondary school prior to graduation.

Three recent Canadian studies provide good illustrations of this "natural experiment" approach. Lemieux and Card (2001) study the impact of the *Veterans Rehabilitation Act* (VRA) — the Canadian "G.I. Bill." In order to ease the return of World War Two veterans into the labour market, the federal government provided strong financial incentives for veterans to attend university or other sorts of educational programs. Because many more young men from Ontario than Quebec had served as soldiers, those from Ontario were significantly more likely to be eligible for these benefits. Lemieux and Card estimate that the VRA increased the education of the veteran cohort of Ontario men by 0.2 to 0.4 years. Further, their IV estimate of the rate of return to schooling is 14 to 16 percent, substantially higher than the OLS estimate with their data of 7 percent.

Sweetman (1999) investigates the impact on education and earnings of the education policy change in Newfoundland that raised the number of years of schooling required for high-school graduation from 11 to 12. He estimates that this intervention increased educational attainment of affected Newfoundland cohorts by 0.8 to 0.9 years. Estimated rates of return to the additional schooling are substantial: 17.0 percent for females (versus an OLS estimate of 14.6 percent) and 11.8 percent for males (compared to an OLS estimate of 10.8 percent).

Perhaps the most compelling Canadian evidence comes from the research of Oreopoulos (2006) on the effects of changes in compulsory schooling laws in Canadian provinces over the past century. He also concludes that the causal impact of the additional secondary level schooling brought about by the changes in these laws is large, with associated rates of return in the 12 to 15 percent range.

As with this growing body of international research, these Canadian studies conclude that for certain groups of individuals the returns to education are particularly high — even greater than conventional OLS estimates of the return to schooling that are believed to be biased upwards. Policy interventions that raised the educational attainment of certain groups many years ago evidently had large beneficial effects on the subsequent lifetime earnings of these individuals.

Two principal conclusions follow from this body of research. First, rates of return to investments in education made by certain groups are high, higher than has generally been believed on the basis of previous studies of the average impact of education on earnings for the population as a whole. Second, the payoff to incremental investments in education made by certain groups may exceed the average return in the population. In the past, interventions that raised educational attainment among groups with relatively low levels of schooling did not show evidence of diminishing returns to education because they required society to "reach lower into the ability barrel." This general finding is consistent with the view that these individuals stopped their schooling because they faced above-average costs of additional education rather than below-average expected returns. An important research and policy question is thus why, in the absence of the intervention, such individuals would have stopped their schooling "too early" and thus not benefited from the high-potential returns. A related important question is whether such high-potential return individuals can be identified. At the present time these questions are the subject of research and debate.[9]

Social Consequences of Education

This section reviews recent research on the social consequences of education and skills development. It is a lengthy section because there are numerous potential social benefits associated with education, because much of the relevant empirical literature is very recent and not well known, and because it is difficult to write a brief review without being superficial in nature. Readers who are not interested in the details can skip to the conclusions at the end of the section.

Social Returns to Education

Social returns to education refer to positive or negative outcomes that accrue to individuals other than the person or family making the decision about how much schooling to acquire. These returns are therefore benefits (potentially also costs) that are not taken into account by the decisionmaker. If such external benefits are quantitatively important they could result in significant underinvestment in education in the absence of government intervention. Many prominent social scientists, from Adam Smith to Milton Friedman to Kenneth Arrow, have suggested that education generates positive external benefits. A substantial amount of empirical evidence is now available on at least some of these outcomes. Most of the empirical evidence comes from the US. Much of the earlier literature focused on the correlation between educational attainment and various outcomes. Recent contributions have paid more attention to distinguishing between correlations and causal impacts.

It is also important to note that the social returns to education are not necessarily as high as the private returns. To the extent that education plays a signalling or screening role in the labour market, social returns can be less than private returns (Spence 1974). In the extreme case where schooling acts only as a signal and has no effect on individual productivity, the social returns to education are zero, but private returns continue to be positive.

The content of education clearly matters. In totalitarian societies schooling is often used as a form of indoctrination. The discussion here presumes that the nature of education is similar to that in Canada and other western democracies.

We first discuss social benefits that take the form of market outcomes such as productivity, earnings and output of goods and services. This is followed by an examination of non-market outcomes such as health, civic participation and criminal activity.

Innovation, Knowledge Creation and Economic Growth

The factors that determine long-term growth in living standards have received substantial attention in the past two decades. Much of this research has been dominated by "new growth theory" that emphasizes the contribution of knowledge creation and innovation in fostering advances in living standards over time.[10] The influence of these new perspectives has been reinforced by empirical evidence that supports the view that education plays an important role in economic growth (see, e.g., Barro 2001).

The importance of economic growth (growth in average living standards) deserves emphasis. Even apparently small differences in growth rates will, if they persist over extended periods of time, make huge differences to the living standards of the average citizen. For this reason many economists have noted that understanding the determinants of long-term growth is one of the most significant economic problems. As stated, for example, by Lipsey:

> All the other concerns of economic policy — full employment, efficiency in resource use, and income redistribution — pale into significance when set against growth ... All citizens, both rich and poor, are massively better off materially than were their ancestors of a hundred years ago who were

in the same relative position in the income scale. That improvement has come to pass not because unemployment or economic efficiency or income distribution is massively different from what it was a century ago but because economic growth has increased the average national incomes of the industrialized countries about tenfold over the period (1996, 4).

A central tenet of the new growth theories is that knowledge creation and innovation respond to economic incentives, and can thus be influenced by public policy. The education and skill-formation systems play an important role in fostering innovation and advancing knowledge. There are three main dimensions to this role. One is related to the research function of educational institutions, particularly universities. Such research can be an important source of new ideas and advances in knowledge. The other dimensions are related to the teaching function of universities and colleges. These educational institutions train many of the scientists and engineers who will make future discoveries. They also play a central role in the transfer of accumulated knowledge to new generations — not just in science and engineering but also across a wide range of fields of study. The human capital of the workforce is thus regarded as a crucial factor facilitating the adoption of new and more productive technologies.

The transfer of knowledge function should be reflected in the private returns to education. Those receiving education will become more productive and thus more valuable to employers. The "return" to this investment takes the form of higher earnings than would have been possible without additional education.

In contrast, there will generally be social benefits associated with encouraging innovation and scientific advances that arise from the "public-good" nature of knowledge. The potential market failure associated with the public-good nature of knowledge is recognized by adoption of patent laws and other institutional arrangements to encourage invention and innovation. In addition to these dynamic externalities that may contribute to greater growth in living standards over time, there may also be knowledge spillovers of a more static form if more educated individuals raise the productivity and earnings of those they work with or interact with in the community.

The magnitudes of these knowledge spillovers — both the dynamic and static types — has been the subject of substantial recent research. Davies (2002) provides a careful review of this literature. He concludes that there is substantial evidence of dynamic externalities associated with education, although he cautions that there remains considerable uncertainty about their magnitudes. These dynamic externalities appear to operate primarily via technology adoption and innovation. His estimate of the magnitudes of these growth-enhancing social returns in excess of private returns is one to two percentage points. This estimate is consistent with the results of a number of studies of the relationship between education and growth. For example, the ambitious study of both static and dynamic impacts of education on economic growth by McMahon (1999) covering 78 countries over the 1965–90 period obtains estimates of total returns to education for the US of 14 percent of which private returns constitute 11–13 percent. Comparable estimates for the UK are total returns of 15 percent and private returns of 11–13 percent.

Another noteworthy finding in this literature is that postsecondary education is relatively more important for explaining growth in OECD countries, while primary and secondary schooling is more important in developing countries (Gemmell 1995; Barro and Sala-i-Martin 1995). This result is consistent with the view that tertiary education has a special role to play in preparing workers for technological adoption and innovation in the more advanced countries.

Knowledge Spillovers

Static knowledge spillovers arise if more education raises not only the productivity of those receiving the education but also the productivity of those they work with and interact with. For example, in *The Economy of Cities*, Jane Jacobs (1969) argues that cities are an "engine of growth" because they facilitate the exchange of ideas, especially between entrepreneurs and managers. Such knowledge spillovers can take place through the exchange of ideas, imitation and learning-by-doing. Evidence of the role of knowledge spillovers in technological change has resulted in substantial attention being focused on the clustering of the agents of innovation: firms, end users, universities and government research facilities (Bekar and Lipsey 2002).

Rauch (1993) was the first study of human capital spillovers employing cross-sectional evidence on US cities. He found evidence that higher average education levels in cities is correlated with both higher wages of workers (even after controlling for the individual's own education) and higher housing prices. Similarly, Glaeser, Scheinkman and Shleifer (1995) found that income per capita grew faster in US cities with high initial human capital in the postwar period. In one of several studies of

specific industries, Zucker, Darby and Brewer (1998) note an impact of
the concentration of outstanding scientists in particular cities on the
location decisions of new biotech firms. These studies provide some
indirect evidence of human capital externalities. However, they are not
conclusive because cities with higher average schooling levels could
also have higher wages for a variety of reasons other than knowledge
spillovers. In addition, the direction of causation could be the reverse —
higher incomes could lead to more schooling. Recent contributions have
used "natural experiments" and instrumental variables methods to assess whether there is evidence of knowledge spillovers that is causal in
nature.

Acemoglu and Angrist (2001) use variation in educational attainment
associated with compulsory schooling laws and child labour laws in
the US to examine whether there is evidence of external returns to higher
average schooling at the state level.[11] They find small (about 1 percent)
social returns in excess of private returns, but these are imprecisely estimated and not significantly different from zero. Because compulsory
schooling laws principally influence the amount of secondary schooling received, these results suggest that there are not significant knowledge spillovers associated with additional high-school education. In
subsequent research using an alternative approach Ciccone and Peri
(2006) examine the impact of changes in the average level of schooling
in a city or state, and also find no evidence of significant externalities.
Similarly, Topel (1999) and Lange and Topel (forthcoming), using data
on aggregate output per worker, find little evidence of external effects
of education on productivity and earnings at the level of US states or at
the country level using a large sample of countries. However, subsequent studies by Moretti (1998, 2003a, 2004) and Iranzo and Peri (2006)
find stronger evidence of externalities associated with postsecondary
education (graduates of four-year colleges in US). These studies use a
variety of data sources and focus on spillovers at the city level. Moretti
(2003b) provides a useful survey of evidence on these city-level
spillovers.

Although this literature is still in its infancy, the most recent research
indicates little or no human capital spillovers associated with secondary schooling or changes in the average level of schooling in a city or
region. However, there is evidence of moderately large social returns
due to knowledge spillovers from postsecondary (college in US or university in Canada) education. A cautious assessment of this recent

literature would be that there are social returns of 0 to 1 percent associated with static knowledge spillovers from postsecondary education in advanced economies. Together with the growth-enhancing dynamic effects, this evidence suggests that social benefits associated with technological adoption, innovation, and productivity enhancement from knowledge spillovers may yield social returns in the range of 1 to 3 percent.

Non-Market Effects of Education

Berhman and Stacey (1997), McMahon (1997), Wolfe and Zuvekis (1997) and Wolfe and Haveman (2001) provide recent surveys of the literature that attempt to quantify the social and non-market effects of education. The non-market benefits of education considered are consequences other than those received in the form of higher wages or non-wage benefits from working. Some of these non-market effects — such as improved own health or child development — may be considered private in nature, or at least private to the family, and thus may be taken into account by individuals in choosing the amount of education to acquire. If so, they should not be treated as social benefits. Nonetheless, they are benefits that accrue to the individual or family, and thus should be added to the private benefits associated with higher lifetime earnings. In addition, even effects such as improved health outcomes may be of some public value if they reduce reliance on publicly funded programs.

The empirical studies that these authors survey generally find considerable impacts of education on a wide variety of non-market and social benefits, even after controlling for such factors as income, age, race, etc. The research analyzed data from both developed and developing countries. Here is a list of the benefits (other than those discussed previously) that are considered:

- effect of wife's schooling on husband's earnings;
- effect of parents' education on child outcomes (intergenerational effects): education, cognitive ability, health and fertility choices;
- effect of education on own health and spouse's health;
- effect of education on consumer choice efficiency, labour market search efficiency, adaptability to new jobs, marital choice, savings and attainment of desired family size;

- effect of education on charitable giving and volunteer activity;
- effect of schooling on social cohesion: voting behaviour, reduced alienation and smaller social inequalities;
- effect of education on reducing reliance on welfare and other social programs; and
- effect of schooling on reduced criminal activity.

Many of the studies surveyed also found relationships between the average education levels in the community and positive non-market benefits. For example, higher average education levels in the community (particularly young adults) lowered school dropout rates of children. Note, however, that not all of this research was able to control appropriately for unobserved factors that may impact both education and these non-market outcomes. Thus considerable care needs to be exercised in treating correlations between education and various outcomes as being causal in nature.

Brief summaries of the state of knowledge relating to these non-market social benefits of education are provided below. Special attention is devoted to recent research, which has generally devoted considerable attention to trying to estimate the causal impacts of education on various outcomes.

Intergenerational Effects

Parents' education has strong effects on children, resulting in large intergenerational effects. As a consequence, the benefits of higher education accrue over extended periods. Surveys by Greenwood (1997) and Maynard and McGrath (1997) summarize the earlier literature on these effects. The research shows an impact of parental education on a number of child outcomes, including:

- Higher parental education is associated with lower fertility, via increased efficiency of contraception, as well as via raising the age of both marriage and first pregnancy. The resulting lower population growth is positive for economic growth in developing countries.
- The incidence of teenage childbearing is much higher for children of less educated parents. Teenage parents have elevated probabilities of dropping out of high school, demonstrate lower parenting skills and experience higher rates of poverty. This has subsequent

negative impacts on the children of teenage parents, as outcomes for these children are generally worse than for other children.

- Child abuse and neglect are also associated with parental education levels.
- Higher parental education is associated with more substantial family investments in children, and these investments have an effect far greater than the societal educational investments made when the child enters school. Children of more educated parents generally perform better in school and in the labour market, and have better health. These impacts are significant even after controlling for parental income. The higher family investments typically take the form of parental time and expenditures on children.
- Children of less educated parents generally cost more to educate, needing special compensatory programs, as well as being more likely to require expensive programs like foster care and juvenile diversion.
- Higher parental education is associated with lower criminal propensities in children. It is also associated with lower probabilities of parental abuse and neglect, which also may reduce criminal behaviour and the need for the removal of children from the home.
- Higher parental education is associated with improved child health.

Although many of these consequences are internal to the family, and thus should be treated as private benefits, a number of these intergenerational effects of education also have benefits for society. These include: lower education costs, less use of foster care and juvenile diversion, lower crime, lower health costs and lower dependence on welfare transfers.

Health and Longevity

Grossman and Kaestner (1997) and Wolfe and Haveman (2001) survey a huge amount of empirical research on the relationship between education and health. The overriding conclusion of these authors is that there is a strong association between education and health outcomes in the US and other developed countries, as well as in developing countries. However, there are several reasons why both education and health may be related to other variables such as innate ability. Thus, as discussed elsewhere in this survey, the evidence of a strong correlation should not be taken to imply causation. Furthermore, the direction of

influence could be the reverse — better health may lead to higher education. A number of studies, including Berger and Leigh (1989), Adams
(2001), Arendt (2005) and Lleras-Muney (2005), address this issue and
do uncover evidence of causal impacts of education on health outcomes.
In addition, as noted previously, there is also considerable evidence
that child health is positively related to parental education (Wolfe and
Haveman 2001).

A good example of this line of research is the study by Lleras-Muney
(2005) which concludes that there is a strong causal effect of education
on mortality in the US. She finds that an extra year of schooling results
in a decline in mortality of at least 3.6 percent over a ten-year period, an
impact that is larger than prior estimates of the effect of education on
mortality. To deal with unobserved characteristics that impact both
education and health she uses variation in educational attainment due
to compulsory schooling laws as employed by Acemoglu and Angrist
(2001) and others. This methodology results in estimates that focus on
the impact of additional high school on mortality, rather than on higher
levels of postsecondary education.

The possibility that both educational attainment and health outcomes
are related to cognitive ability is highlighted by Auld and Sidhu (2005)
who find that the correlation between education and health drops substantially when one controls for ability using the Armed Forces Qualification Test (AFQT) scores as a measure of ability. They conclude that
studies that do not control for cognitive ability are likely to overstate
the impact of education on health. Nonetheless, even after controlling
for ability their IV estimates do imply that education exerts a causal
impact on health, albeit one that is smaller than that reported in some
earlier studies. They also conclude that education only exerts a strong
influence on health at low levels of schooling; thus their results suggest
that increasing the fraction of the population with postsecondary education may not have much impact on the health of the population. This
conclusion is consistent with evidence from studies that use compulsory schooling laws as IVs, since those studies identify the local average treatment effect (LATE) associated with the subset of the population
that altered their level of schooling as a consequence of such laws, a
group with relatively low levels of education.

There is less evidence on the actual pathways by which education
impacts health. Education may impact how individuals assess information on how to improve health, and it may increase the efficiency by
which individuals use that information in lifestyle choices. It may also

impact the rate of time preference of individuals, with more educated individuals discounting the future less, and thus undertaking actions that improve health (e.g., smoking less). In a widely cited study, Kenkel (1991) found that education is not only associated with better health outcomes but also superior health behaviours such as reduced smoking, more exercise and lower incidence of heavy drinking. Interestingly, however, the influence of schooling does not mainly operate through its impact on health knowledge — the estimated impact of additional education did not decline substantially when controls were included for health knowledge. This suggests that the effect of education on health occurs mainly through the utilization of health knowledge rather than the acquisition of such knowledge.[12]

Lleras-Muney and Lichtenberg (2002) examine one of the mechanisms by which education may impact health outcomes. They investigate whether education is correlated with adoption of newer prescription drugs. If more educated people are more likely to adopt newer drugs, due to more information or better ability to learn, and those newer drugs improve health, then this may be one mechanism by which education leads to better health. They find that education is correlated with the purchase of drugs that are more recently approved, after controlling for the medical condition, individual income and health insurance status. The impact of education is generally felt only for chronic conditions, where prescriptions are bought regularly for the same condition. This suggests that the more educated are better able to learn from experience.

Although better health is principally a private return, it may also be a social benefit if it means less reliance by people on publicly provided health care or welfare payments. In this respect, there is an important difference between morbidity and mortality. From the perspective of the public finances, reduced morbidity has a positive effect whereas increased longevity is more likely to negatively affect publicly funded programs such as pensions and medical care.

Criminal Activity

Until recently the evidence from empirical studies of the impact of education on crime was mixed. For example, in their reviews of the literature, Witte (1997) and McMahon (1999) concluded that the available evidence does not find that education impacts crime once other factors are controlled for.[13] However, recent work by Grogger (1998),

Lochner (1999) and Lochner and Moretti (2004) focuses specifically on the role of education and does find an impact of schooling on crime. Higher education levels may lower crime by raising wage rates, which increase the opportunity cost of crime. Education may also raise an individual's rate of time preference (the extent to which future consequences are discounted), thus increasing the cost of any future punishment as a result of crime. Lochner (1999) estimates the social value of high-school graduation through reductions in crime, taking into account the costs of incarceration and costs to victims. The extra social benefits amount to almost 20 percent of the private returns to increases in high-school completion. This may even be a conservative estimate as a number of crimes are not included in the analysis, nor are the potential benefits to citizens associated with feeling safe. In addition, some of the costs (such as criminal justice and law-enforcement costs) are also not taken into account.

In subsequent research, Lochner and Moretti (2004) utilize a variety of datasets to examine whether increasing education levels causes reductions in crime among adult males in the US. They employ three sources of information: incarceration, arrests and self-reports of criminal activity. The authors find that higher education levels, particularly graduating from high school, consistently lower the probabilities of incarceration, of criminal arrests and of self-reports of undertaking criminal activity. In US census data the probability of incarceration is negatively correlated with education levels, and is much higher for blacks than whites. This correlation may not be causal, however, if there are unobserved individual characteristics which both raise education and lower criminal activity. Following the methods used by Acemoglu and Angrist (2001) discussed previously, the authors employ compulsory school attendance laws as an independent source of variation in educational attainment. Their casual estimates of the impact of education on incarceration indicate that high-school graduation lowers incarceration probabilities by 0.8 percentage points for white males and 3.4 percentage points for black males. Differences in educational attainment can explain as much as 23 percent of the black-white gap in male incarceration rates.

Data from the FBI's crime reports allow the impact of education on different types of crime to be estimated. Education was most effective in lowering violent crime rates like murder and assault, as well as motor vehicle theft. The third dataset employed was a longitudinal survey that asked respondents about crimes they have committed. This source of information usefully supplements the data on arrests and incarceration because it is possible that more educated people commit as much crime as less educated people, but are better at avoiding arrest or obtaining lighter sentences. The evidence, however, is that education has very similar impacts on self-reported criminal activity to that which it had on arrests and incarceration.

On the basis of this evidence, Lochner and Moretti (2004) calculate that raising the high-school graduation rate by 1 percent will reduce the costs of crime by approximately $1.4 billion per year in the US.

Civic Participation

The impact of education on civic participation has been analyzed by political scientists for a long time.[14] The correlation between education and voting is strong. Higher education is also associated with greater charitable giving and more volunteerism. Helliwell and Putnam (1999) also find that education is correlated with typical measures of social capital: trust and social participation (club memberships, community work, hosting dinner parties). However, only recently have studies attempted to determine whether education exerts a causal influence on civic participation, or whether the correlation arises because both education and civic participation are jointly influenced by unobserved factors. Two recent papers that attempt to do so are Milligan, Moretti and Oreopoulos (2004) and Dee (2004).

Milligan, Moretti and Oreopoulos (2004) analyze the question of whether education improves citizenship. The authors focus on the US and the UK, but provide some results for Canada also. The main question is whether people who have more education are more likely to vote in elections. Analysis is also conducted on whether education raises the "quality" of people's involvement in society. Here, quality is measured by such things as whether people: (i) follow the news and political campaigns, (ii) attend political meetings, (iii) work on community issues, (iv) try to persuade others to share their views, (v) discuss political matters with friends, (vi) consider themselves politically active, (vii) consider themselves close to a political party, and/or (viii) trust the federal government.

As in previously discussed studies by Acemoglu and Angrist (2001) and others, Milligan, Moretti and Oreopoulos (2004) use variation in educational attainment generated by compulsory school attendance laws and child labour laws. The estimates thus relate to the impact of additional secondary schooling on civic participation.

Generally the authors find that having a higher level of education does raise the probability of voting in the US, but not in the UK. They suggest that this may be due to different voter registration methods in the two countries. In the US, registration is the responsibility of the individual, and thus many people are not registered. In the UK, registration is undertaken by local authorities, and registration is required. Thus the vast majority of citizens are registered. If estimates of the impact of education on voting are made conditional on registration, the effect of education becomes much less in the US. There is little change in the UK, as we would expect given the high level of registration. Canada has registration laws more closely resembling the UK, and the impact of education on voting behaviour is much more muted than in the US. Having graduated high school raises the probability of voting by close to 30 percent in the US (not conditional on registration), while the estimated impact is around 9 percent in Canada. The authors also find strong impacts of education on the measures of the quality of citizenship listed above.

Dee (2004) analyzes the impact of education on voting and civic behaviour in the US, using comparable methods to Milligan, Moretti and Oreopoulos (2004) but with different data sources. He also finds a strong causal impact of education on voting behaviour, the probability of reading newspapers and support for free speech by various groups. Some of his results also provide evidence on the impact of postsecondary education on voting behaviour. For example, he finds that college entrance raises the probability of voter participation by approximately 20 to 30 percentage points. He also concludes that an additional year of high school increases the probability of voting in presidential elections by around seven percentage points. Education also increases certain measures of civic engagement and knowledge: the frequency of newspaper readership and support for free speech by anti-religionists, communists and homosexuals. He also finds that additional education does not increase support for free speech by militarists (someone who advocates outlawing elections and letting the military run the country) or racists.

In addition to these studies based on individual data, cross-country studies find that higher education has a positive effect on democratization and political stability. For example, McMahon (1999, 2001) finds significant effects of secondary schooling on measures of democratization, human rights and political stability, after controlling for income per capita and military spending as a proportion of total public expenditure. McMahon finds strong feedback effects on economic growth that operate through democratization and political stability.

Tax and Transfer Effects

Several studies discussed by Wolfe and Haveman (2001) find that those with more education are less likely to rely on public transfers, even when eligible for benefits. Indeed, evidence indicates that the mother's education even lowers take-up of welfare by eligible children. Although these consequences of education should not be ignored, the quantitatively most important effect is the impact of higher lifetime earnings on government tax receipts (Davies 2002). For example, in Canada the modal marginal tax rate on university graduates — taking into account sales, excise and income taxes — is in excess of 50 percent. Thus each additional $1,000 in labour market earnings generates an additional $500 in tax revenue. Collins and Davies (2003) recently estimated the gap between before-tax and after-tax rates of return to a university bachelor's degree in Canada and the US. In Canada, for men and women together, the median reduction in the rate of return due to taxes was 1.9 percentage points. In the US the corresponding reduction was 1.1 percentage points. On the basis of these calculations, Davies (2002) notes that the tax revenue associated with higher earnings adds approximately two percentage points to the social benefits of higher education.

Because of the progressive nature of income tax, the reductions in the rate of return due to taxation are larger at higher income levels. For example, Collins and Davies (ibid.) estimate reductions of 2.8 percentage points for Canadian men at the ninetieth percentile of the earnings distribution and 1.9 percentage points for corresponding US men. This calculation highlights an important point made by Allen (2004). The combination of higher earnings associated with additional education and a progressive income tax system implies that those who earn more as a consequence of additional education also pay more over their lifetimes in tax revenue.

Education, Skills and Labour Market Outcomes

Education and labour market experience are "inputs" into the production of human capital, not direct measures of the "outcomes": a set of skills, competencies and knowledge. Although the relationships between inputs such as education and experience and outcomes such as employment and earnings have been extensively investigated, relatively little is known about the relationship between direct measures of skills and labour market outcomes.

Green and Riddell (2003) use the Canadian component of the International Adult Literacy Survey (IALS) to investigate the relationship between education, skills and labour market earnings. The IALS data contain standard questions on demographics and labour force behaviour, but also measures literacy in three domains: prose, document and quantitative literacy. Ferrer, Green and Riddell (2006) carry out a similar analysis for immigrants to the province of Ontario using the Ontario Immigrant Literacy Survey (OILS).

Conventional estimates of the return to schooling and to labour market experience confound two effects. The first is the impact of education and experience on skill production — the relationship between human capital inputs such as education and experience and outputs such as literacy skills or problem-solving skills. The second is the value placed on various skills in the labour market — the relationship between literacy or problem-solving skills and market earnings.

When skills are not directly observed, the best researchers can do is to analyze the relationship between human capital inputs and labour market outcomes. However, the availability of directly observed skills in datasets that also contain information on labour force behaviour allows researchers to "unpack" these two effects to some extent — to obtain estimates of both the skill production effect and the market valuation effect.

Green and Riddell (2003) find that formal education exerts a substantial effect on the production of literacy skills in Canada. However, they conclude that labour market experience has essentially no net effect on literacy production. These results suggest that policies aimed at improving cognitive skills such as literacy should focus on formal schooling. Policies designed to increase work experience can lead to earnings growth but they appear unlikely to enhance the cognitive skills of the workforce. Ferrer, Green and Riddell (2006) find a similar strong relationship between formal education and literacy skills among immigrants. However, in the case of immigrants they conclude that work experience in Canada also has some effect on literacy skills. Given that these surveys assess literacy skills in English or French, this finding may reflect the acquisition of language skills with work experience in the new country.

Another important result is that the Canadian labour market places a high value on literacy skills. A 20-point increase in the literacy score — equivalent to one-third of a standard deviation of the literacy score distribution — produces an increase in earnings equal to that associated with an extra year of formal schooling. Furthermore, Ferrer, Green and Riddell (2006) find that immigrants receive returns to literacy and numeracy skills that are as large as those received by native-born Canadians.

Together these results imply that a significant amount of the return to education as conventionally measured represents the combined effects of the contribution of schooling to producing literacy skills and the value placed on literacy in the labour market. Indeed, Green and Riddell (2003) estimate that about one-quarter to one-third of the return to education is associated with these effects. The remainder reflects the impact of education on the production of other (unobserved) skills that are valued in the labour market.

Summary and Conclusions

Many researchers have produced estimates of the economic return to schooling using conventional multivariate methods in which a relationship is estimated between earnings (or some other measure of labour market success) and education, after controlling for other observed factors that influence earnings. Canadian studies using such conventional methods to analyze the relationship between education and earnings obtain estimates of the return to schooling that are similar to those obtained in many studies carried out in other developed countries: approximately 8 to 10 percent rate of return when the analysis is based on annual earnings and 6 to 9 percent when the analysis is based on weekly earnings. Such estimates compare favourably with rates of return on physical capital investments. However, many social scientists have been skeptical about these estimates because they do not control for unobserved factors such as ability, motivation and perseverance that may influence both educational attainment and labour market success. Such unobserved factors are likely to imply that conventional estimates of the return to schooling are biased upwards. Furthermore, according to signalling/screening theory one may observe a positive correlation between education and earnings even when education has no causal effect on individual productivity and earnings. These concerns raise important questions about the nature and magnitude of public investments in education.

Important advances have recently taken place in our understanding of the relationship between education and labour market success. These advances have occurred from the use of natural experiments and instrumental variables methods that employ variations in educational attainment brought about by policy changes or unique events, variations that are arguably unrelated to the unobserved factors that influence both schooling and labour market outcomes. Such variations allow one to identify the causal impact of education on earnings and other measures of labour market success. A large number of such studies have now been carried out in numerous countries. A distinct pattern is evident from this research. A common finding is that estimates of the return to the additional schooling brought about by these policy changes are generally higher than conventional OLS estimates of the return to schooling for the population as a whole, despite the fact that such conventional estimates are widely believed to be biased upwards. The return to past incremental investments in education, which typically affected groups with relatively low levels of education, often exceeded the average return for the population as a whole. Although there is no guarantee that the future will be like the past in this respect, these results suggest that investments in human capital are likely to remain an important potential source of growth in earnings.

Important advances have also taken place in our knowledge regarding the non-market and social consequences of education. A central, if not the primary, reason for public funding, and in many cases also provision, of education has been the belief that there are major social benefits from additional schooling, in addition to the private benefits. Policy interventions designed to raise educational attainment among youth have also sometimes been justified on this basis. Evidence on the magnitudes of these external benefits has, however, been lacking until recently. Beginning in the 1960s and 1970s, with the availability of large micro-data files on individuals, social scientists have confirmed that educational attainment is correlated with numerous individual and social outcomes such as lifetime earnings, health and civic participation. However, it remained unclear to what extent the positive correlation between schooling and outcomes such as earnings and health reflected a causal impact of education or was due to both schooling and individual outcomes being related to some unobserved factors. Resolution of this issue is crucial as the case for public subsidization or intervention is much stronger if education leads to social benefits in addition to private benefits. Recent research using natural experiments and instrumental variables estimation methods has strengthened the case for believing that the social benefits of education are substantial.

Summarizing the evidence surveyed in the paper yields the following approximate estimates of the social returns to schooling:

• Dynamic externalities associated with economic growth	1–2 percentage points
• Static knowledge spillovers	0–1 percentage points
• Non-market external benefits	3–4 percentage points
• Social benefits associated with taxation	2 percentage points
Total	6–9 percentage points

The quantitative estimate for non-market benefits is based on calculations by Wolfe and Haveman (2001) after removing benefits associated with intergenerational effects and health, both of which are arguably principally private to the individual or family. The other estimates were discussed previously.

These estimates suggest that the social benefits of education may be similar in magnitude to the private benefits associated with higher life-time earnings, which are also in the above range. If so, the social returns to education are substantial and justify significant public subsidization of this activity.

The estimated (real) social return of 6 to 9 percent is arguably a conservative estimate. After a detailed survey of the available evidence, Wolfe and Haveman (2001) conclude that the social return from non-market effects of schooling are of the same order of magnitude as the private returns to education from higher earnings. They do not, however, include the social benefits from higher tax revenue or the growth-enhancing effects of knowledge creation and innovation. On the other hand, they do include in their calculations the intergenerational effects and the impacts of education on health, both of which are excluded from the above estimates on the basis that they are principally private in nature. Similarly, Davies (2002) also concludes that the social returns are similar in size to the private returns. His estimates are similar to those above except that he estimates a value of zero for static knowledge spillovers, whereas we assign a range of values from 0 to 1 percent.

Several additional observations are warranted. First, there remains considerable uncertainty about the magnitudes of the social benefits of schooling. In contrast to the substantial amount of research that has been carried out on the relationship between schooling and earnings, much less is known about the causal impact of education on other outcomes. This is particularly the case with respect to Canadian evidence. As indicated in this literature survey, most of the evidence on causal impacts comes from US studies. Some of the impacts of schooling may be universal in nature, but others are likely to depend on the social and institutional setting. This situation was evident in the case of civic participation, where education appears to have a much larger effect on voting behaviour in the US than it does in Canada and the UK, for reasons that seem to be related to systems of voter registration in the respective countries. It is quite possible that the magnitudes of the impacts of education on Canadian criminal activity and health outcomes are different from those in the US, even if the direction of the influence is the same in the two countries.

Second, there is substantial uncertainty about the size of the social benefits associated with postsecondary education. Much of the US evidence on causal impacts of schooling uses as a source of independent variation in educational attainment the changes in compulsory school attendance laws and child labour laws. As discussed, these studies provide evidence on the causal impact of additional schooling at the secondary level. The clearest evidence of positive social benefits from postsecondary education is that associated with growth-enhancing effects from technological change and innovation and knowledge spillovers from more educated workers. There is also some evidence that postsecondary education enhances civic participation. Many of the studies of intergenerational effects also report evidence of significant impacts associated with postsecondary education.

A third observation is that we have not included in the above calculation of social benefits the evidence of intergenerational effects such as those on child development, health and education associated with the educational attainment of the parents. Nor have the effects on the individual's health behaviours and health outcomes (as well as those on the spouse) been included. Whether these are appropriately viewed as private or social benefits depends to an important extent on whether individuals take these consequences into account at the time they choose how much education to acquire. The case for regarding these consequences of additional schooling as private benefits is based on the argument that a rational individual should take these effects into account in making their educational choices (even if they do not yet have a spouse or children). Although many individuals appear to be motivated in part by career prospects in making their educational decisions, it is less clear that they take into account these other benefits. If they generally do not do so, there is a case for including these consequences as social benefits, as scholars such as Wolfe and Haveman (2001) do. In these circumstances, the above estimates understate the social benefits from education. On the other hand, if we treat the intergenerational effects and health and longevity consequences as being strictly private benefits, then the total private benefits are much larger than is commonly believed. This conclusion would enhance the case for government involvement in the financing of postsecondary education, in order to help ensure that individuals from disadvantaged backgrounds can take advantage of investments with potentially high returns. In addition, there may also be a case for governments providing more information than is currently available on the non-market consequences of additional schooling, rather than focusing principally on the consequences for future employment and earnings.

In summary, although more research on these issues is needed (especially more Canadian research), the social benefits of education appear to be substantial, perhaps as large as the private market returns to education from higher lifetime earnings. Thus the benefits of education are considerable, and any decisions regarding public support for education and the design of educational policies should take social and non-market benefits into account.

Advances in the collection of data on the skills of the workforce have also resulted in progress in our understanding of the acquisition of human capital and its labour market consequences. Conventional estimates of the return to schooling and to work experience confound two effects: the impact of education and experience on skill production and the value placed on skills in the labour market. The availability of data on directly observed skills allows researchers to unpack these two effects. Recent evidence indicates that formal education exerts a substantial effect on the production of literacy skills in Canada. However, work experience has no net effect on literacy production. In addition, Canada's labour market places a high value on literacy skills. A 20-point increase in the literacy score — equivalent to one-third of a standard deviation of the literacy score distribution — produces an increase in earnings equal to that associated with an extra year of formal schooling. These results imply that a substantial fraction, one-quarter to one-third, of the return to education as conventionally measured represents the combined effects of the contribution of schooling to producing literacy skills and the value placed on literacy in the labour market.

At the present time we can be more confident than in the past that education has large and wide-ranging impacts on a variety of individual and social outcomes. Much less is known, however, about the pathways through such effects that occur. Does education alter the way in which individuals access and process information? Does it improve the quality of the decisions that are made on the basis of a given amount of information? Does education result in more "forward-looking" behaviour, so that individuals are more likely to make investments that will yield dividends in the future? Does increased education enable people to adapt more readily to changing circumstances? Addressing these questions about causal pathways is an important subject for future research.

Notes

An earlier version of this paper was written for the workshop: "An Integrated Approach to Human Capital Development," sponsored by Canadian Policy Research Networks (CPRN), the School of Policy Studies at Queen's University and Statistics Canada, and appeared as CPRN Working Paper June 2006. I am grateful to Ben Sand for very helpful comments. Important advances have recently taken place in our understanding of a central issue: the causal relationship between education and labour market success. The causal effect of education on earnings is at least as large as, and possibly larger than, what was previously believed. The return to incremental investments in education — especially those that affected groups with relatively low levels of education — often exceed the average return for the labour force as a whole. The social benefits of education are also substantial. These results suggest that investments in human capital remain an important potential source of earnings growth.

1. This section draws on Riddell and Sweetman (2004).
2. Earnings is the most commonly used measure of labour market success because it captures both the wage rate or "price" of labour services and employment (hours, weeks and years of work).
3. Lang and Kropp (1986) point out that, in a model of educational signalling, changes in compulsory schooling laws may alter the schooling choices of those not directly affected by them.

4. Distance to a postsecondary institution would not satisfy the conditions for being a suitable IV if parents of high-ability children were more likely to locate near a university or college than parents of low-ability children.
5. See Card (1999, 2001) for a detailed review of empirical studies and of recent advances in this area.
6. Other potential explanations are discussed in Card (2001).
7. Measurement error in an explanatory variable causes the estimated coefficient to be biased toward zero.
8. See Imbens and Angrist (1994) and Heckman (1997) for a discussion of the assumptions required for IV to identify the above parameters.
9. See for example Kling (2001), Carneiro and Heckman (2002) and Carneiro, Heckman and Vytlacil (2003).
10. Previous theories of economic growth placed greater emphasis on inputs into production — i.e., on the accumulation of physical and human capital.
11. As discussed in the previous section, such laws result in variation in educational attainment (in this case, additional secondary schooling) that is independent of individuals' educational choices.
12. An important exception is the case of smoking, where Kenkel (1991) found evidence of an important interaction between health knowledge and education. Those with more schooling reduced their smoking more for a given increase in knowledge of the consequences of smoking. He also points out that prior to the report of the US Surgeon General in the 1960s (which had a major impact on knowledge about the health consequences of smoking) higher education was not related to lower incidence of smoking.
13. There is, however, strong evidence of a link between time spent productively occupied, either employed or in school, and crime.
14. The issues discussed in this section are examined more fully by O'Neill (2007).

References

Acemoglu, D. and J. Angrist. 2001. "How Large are Human Capital Externalities? Evidence from Compulsory Schooling Laws," *NBER Macroeconomics Annual 2000*, pp. 9-59.

Adams, J. 2001. "Educational Attainment and Health: Evidence from a Sample of Older Adults," *Education Economics* 10(1):97-109.

Allen, R.C. 2004. "Education and Technological Revolutions: The Role of the Social Sciences and the Humanities in the Knowledge-based Economy," in

Educational outcomes for the Canadian workplace, ed. J. Gaskell and K. Rubenson. Toronto: University of Toronto Press.

Angrist, J.D. and A.B. Krueger. 1991. "Does Compulsory School Attendance Affect Schooling and Earnings?" *Quarterly Journal of Economics* 106:979-1014.

Arendt, J. 2005. "Does Education Cause Better Health? A Panel Data Analysis Using School Reforms for Identification," *Economics of Education Review* 24(2):149-60.

Auld, C. and N. Sidhu. 2005. "Schooling, Cognitive Ability and Health," *Health Economics* 14:1019-34.

Barro, R.J. 2001. "Human Capital and Growth," *American Economic Review* 91(2):12-17.

Barro, R.J. and X. Sala-i-Martin. 1995. *Economic Growth*. New York: McGraw-Hill.

Behrman, J.R. and N. Stacey. 1997. *The Social Benefits of Education*. Ann Arbor, MI: The University of Michigan Press.

Bekar, C. and R.G. Lipsey. 2002. "Clusters and Economic Policy," *ISUMA: Canadian Journal of Policy Research* 3(1):62-70.

Berger, M. and J. Leigh. 1989. "Schooling, Self-Selection and Health," *Journal of Human Resources* 24(3):433-55.

Card, D. 1995. "Using Geographic Variation in College Proximity to Estimate the Return to Schooling," in *Aspects of Labour Market Behaviour: Essays in Honour of John Vanderkamp*, ed. L.N. Christofides, E.K. Grant and R. Swidinsky. Toronto: University of Toronto Press.

— 1999. "The Causal Effect of Education on Earnings," in *Handbook of Labor Economics*, Volume 3A, ed. O. Ashenfelter and D. Card. Amsterdam: North Holland.

— 2001. "Estimating the Return to Schooling: Progress on Some Persistent Econometric Problems," *Econometrica* 69(September):1127-60.

Carneiro, P. and J.J. Heckman. 2002. "The Evidence on Credit Constraints in Post-Secondary Schooling," *Economic Journal* 112(October):705-34.

Carneiro, P., J.J. Heckman and E. Vytlacil. 2003. "Understanding What Instrumental Variables Estimate: Estimating Marginal and Average Returns to Education." Working Paper. Chicago: University of Chicago.

Ciccone, A. and G. Peri. 2006. "Identifying Human Capital Externalities: Theory with Applications," *Review of Economic Studies* 73(2):381-412.

Collins, K. and J.B. Davies. 2003. "Tax Treatment of Human Capital in Canada and the United States: An Overview and an Examination of the Case of University Graduates," in *North American Linkages: Opportunities and Challenges for Canada*, ed. R.G. Harris. Calgary: University of Calgary Press.

Conneely, K. and R. Uusitalo. 1997. "Estimating Heterogeneous Treatment Effects in the Becker Schooling Model." Working Paper. Princeton, NJ: Industrial Relations Section, Princeton University.

Davies, J. 2002. "Empirical Evidence on Human Capital Externalities." Paper prepared for Tax Policy Branch, Department of Finance, Government of Canada. London: Department of Economics, University of Western Ontario. Unpublished paper.

Dee, T.S. 2004. "Are there Civic Returns to Education?" *Journal of Public Economics* 88(August):1696-712.

Ferrer, A. and W.C. Riddell. 2002. "The Role of Credentials in the Canadian Labour Market," *Canadian Journal of Economics* 35(November):879-905.

Ferrer, A., D.A. Green and W.C. Riddell. 2006. "The Effect of Literacy on Immigrant Earnings," *Journal of Human Resources* 41(2):380-410.

Gemmell, N. 1995. "Endogenous Growth, the Solow Model and Human Capital," *Economics of Planning* 28(2/3):169-83.

Glaeser, E.L., J.A. Scheinkman and A. Shleifer. 1995. "Economic Growth in a Cross-section of Cities," *Journal of Monetary Economics* 36(August):117-43.

Green, D.A. and W.C. Riddell. 2003. "Literacy and Earnings: An Investigation of the Interaction of Cognitive and Unobserved Skills in Earnings Generation," *Labour Economics* 10(April):165-85.

Greenwood, D.T. 1997. "New Developments in the Intergenerational Impacts of Education," *International Journal of Education Research* 27(6):503-12.

Grogger, J. 1998. "Market Wages and Youth Crime," *Journal of Labor Economics* 16(October):756-91.

Grossman, M. and R. Kaestner. 1997. "Effects of Education on Health," in *The Social Benefits of Education*, ed. J. Behrman and N. Stacey. Ann Arbor, MI: University of Michigan Press.

Harmon, C. and I. Walker. 1995. "Estimates of the Economic Return to Schooling for the United Kingdom," *American Economic Review* 85:1278-86.

Haveman, R. and B. Wolfe. 1984. "Schooling and Economic Well-Being: The Role of Non-Market Effects," *Journal of Human Resources* 19(Summer):377-407.

Heckman, J.J. 1997. "Instrumental Variables: A Study of Implicit Behavioral Assumptions Used in Making Program Evaluations," *Journal of Human Resources* 32 (Summer):441-62.

Helliwell, J.F. and R.D. Putnam. 1999. "Education and Social Capital." NBER Working Paper No. 7121. Cambridge, MA: National Bureau of Economic Research.

Imbens, G. and J. Angrist. 1994. "Identification and Estimation of Local Average Treatment Effects," *Econometrica* 62(March):467-75.

Iranzo, S. and G. Peri. 2006. "Schooling Externalities, Technology and Productivity: Theory and Evidence from U.S. States." NBER Working Paper No. 12440. Cambridge, MA: National Bureau of Economic Research.

Jacobs, J. 1969. *The Economy of Cities*. New York, Random House.

Kane, T.J. and C.E. Rouse. 1995. "Labor Market Returns to Two- and Four-Year College: Is a Credit a Credit and Do Degrees Matter? *American Economic Review* 85:600-14.

Kenkel, D.S. 1991. "Health Behavior, Health Knowledge, and Schooling," *Journal of Political Economy* 99(April):287-305.

Kling, J.R. 2001. "Interpreting Instrumental Variables Estimates of the Returns to Schooling," *Journal of Business and Economic Statistics* 19(3):358-64.

Lang, K. and D. Kropp. 1986. "Human Capital vs Sorting: The Effects of Compulsory Attendance Laws," *Quarterly Journal of Economics* 101(August):609-24.

Lange, F. and R. Topel. Forthcoming. "The Social Value of Education and Human Capital," in *Handbook of the Economics of Education*, ed. E. Hanushek and F. Welch. Amsterdam: Elsevier Science.

Lemieux, T. and D. Card. 2001. "Education, Earnings, and the 'Canadian G.I. Bill,'" *Canadian Journal of Economics* 34(2):313-44.

Lipsey, R.G. 1996. *Economic Growth, Technological Change, and Canadian Economic Policy*. C.D. Howe Benefactors Lecture. Toronto: C.D. Howe Institute.

Lleras-Muney, A. 2005. "The Relationship Between Education and Adult Mortality in the United States," *Review of Economic Studies* 72(1):189.

Lleras-Muney, A. and F.R. Lichtenberg. 2002. "The Effect of Education on Medical Technology Adoption: Are the More Educated More Likely to Use New Drugs?" NBER Working Paper No. 9185. Cambridge, MA: National Bureau of Economic Research.

Lochner, L. 2004. "Education, Work and Crime: Theory and Evidence," *International Economic Review* 45(3):811-44.

Lochner, L. and E. Moretti. 2004. "The Effect of Education on Crime: Evidence from Prison Inmates, Arrests and Self-Reports," *American Economic Review* 94(March):155-89.

Maynard, R.A. and D.J. McGrath. 1997. "Family Structure, Fertility and Child Welfare," in *The Social Benefits of Education*, ed. J. Behrman and N. Stacey. Ann Arbor, MI: University of Michigan Press.

McMahon, W.W., guest ed. 1997. "Recent Advances in Measuring the Social and Individual Benefits of Education," *International Journal of Education Research* Special Issue 27(6):447-532.

McMahon, W.W. 1999. *Education and Development: Measuring the Social Benefits*. Oxford: Oxford University Press.

— 2001. "The Impact of Human Capital on Non-Market Outcomes and Feedbacks on Economic Development," in *The Contribution of Human and Social Capital to Sustained Economic Growth and Well-being*, ed. J. Helliwell. Vancouver: University of British Columbia Press.

Meghir, C. and M. Palme. 2005. "Educational Reform, Ability and Family Background," *American Economic Review* 95(March):414-24.

Milligan, K., E. Moretti and P. Oreopoulos. 2004. "Does Education Improve Citizenship? Evidence from the U.S. and the U.K.," *Journal of Public Economics* 88(August):1667-95.

Moretti, E. 1998. "Social Returns to Education and Human Capital Externalities: Evidence from Cities." Working Paper No. 9. Berkeley: Center for Labor Economics, University of California.

— 2003a. "Workers' Education, Spillovers and Productivity: Evidence from Plant-Level Production Functions." Working Paper. Los Angeles: University of California.

— 2003b. "Human Capital Externalities in Cities." *Handbook of Regional and Urban Economics*. Amsterdam: North Holland-Elsevier.

— 2004. "Estimating the Social Return to Higher Education: Evidence from Longitudinal and Repeated Cross-Sectional Data," *Journal of Econometrics* 121(1/2):175-212..

O'Neill, B. 2007. "Human Capital, Civic Engagement and Political Participation: Turning Skills and Knowledge into Engagement and Action," in this volume.

Oreopoulos, P. 2006. "The Compelling Effects of Compulsory Schooling: Evidence from Canada," *Canadian Journal of Economics* 39(February):22-52.

Rathje, K.A. and J.C.H. Emery. 2002. "Returns to University Education in Canada Using New estimates of Program Costs," in *Renovating the Ivory Tower*, ed. D. Laidler. Toronto: C.D. Howe Institute.

Rauch, J.E. 1993. "Productivity Gains from Geographic Concentration of Human Capital: Evidence from the Cities," *Journal of Urban Economics* 34(3):380-400.

Riddell, W.C and A. Sweetman. 2004. "Evaluation of Youth Employment Programs." Background paper prepared for the Youth Employment Strategy Evaluation Workshop. Ottawa.

Spence, A.M. 1974. *Market Signaling: Informational Transfer in Hiring and Related Screening Processes*. Cambridge, MA: Harvard University Press.

Staiger, D. and J.H. Stock. 1997. "Instrumental Variables Regression with Weak Instruments," *Econometrica* 65:557-86.

Sweetman, A. 1999. "What If High School Were a Year Longer? Evidence from Newfoundland." WRNET Working Paper No. 00-01. Vancouver: Faculty of Education, University of British Columbia.

Topel, R. 1999. "Labor Markets and Economic Growth," in *Handbook of Labor Economics,* ed. O. Ashenfelter and D. Card. Amsterdam, New York: North Holland.

Vaillancourt, F. and S. Bourdeau-Primeau. 2002. "The Returns to University Education in Canada, 1990 and 1995," in *Renovating the Ivory Tower,* ed. D. Laidler. Toronto: C.D. Howe Institute.

Witte, A.D. 1997. "Crime," in *The Social Benefits of Education,* ed. J. Behrman and N. Stacey. Ann Arbor, MI: University of Michigan Press.

Wolfe, B. and R. Haveman. 2001. "Accounting for the Social and Non-Market Benefits of Education," in *The Contribution of Human and Social Capital to Sustained Economic Growth and Well-being,* ed. J. Helliwell. Vancouver: University of British Columbia Press.

Wolfe, B. and S. Zuvekis. 1997. "Nonmarket Outcomes of Schooling," *International Journal of Educational Research* 27(6):491-502.

Zucker, L.G., M.R. Darby and M.B. Brewer. 1998. "Intellectual Human Capital and the Birth of U.S. Biotechnology Enterprises," *American Economic Review* 88(1):290-306.

5

Increasing Adaptive Expertise: The Next Frontier in Human Capital Development

JACQUELINE P. LEIGHTON

This chapter examines the variables that explain the efficiency and success with which highly skilled, expert performers manage knowledge and why knowledge management is a goal in the development of human capital. Valued forms of thinking should be introduced to students at a younger age than is currently the case in educational settings. Individual differences in measured intelligence have been found to predict school grades, occupational outcomes and job success, especially for knowledge-intensive occupations including professional, scientific and upper management jobs. Unleashing the potential inherent in human capital, therefore, will require a shift in standards and the expectations made of students.

Introduction

At least two books represent the fascination with experts on the one hand and the need for knowledge management on the other. In the recent *New York Times* bestseller *Blink* by Malcolm Gladwell (2005), we learn that expertise or very good decision-making involves frugality of thought. This frugality means that experts use a few good variables to generate conclusions, without being overloaded by irrelevant and excessive information. This might seem paradoxical at first. If experts have more knowledge than novices, should they not consult this accumulated knowledge every time they make a decision? Actually, not really. If there is one thing that psychologists have learned over 40 years of research it is that experts within content domains such as chess, physics, medicine, mathematics and logic are extraordinarily efficient in their thinking (de Groot 1965; Ericsson and Smith 1991; Gigerenzer, Todd and the ABC Research Group 1999; Haverty *et al.* 2000; Leighton 2006; Priest and Lindsay 1992).

In another book, *Thinking for a Living*, by Thomas H. Davenport (2005), we learn that knowledge workers are important because they are "closely aligned with the organization's growth prospects ... without [them] there would be no new products and services, and no growth" (ibid., 7). Davenport goes on to describe the single most important capability for knowledge workers: *the management of personal information and the knowledge environment.* Those few, highly skilled individuals who have mastered the management of personal information and the knowledge environment have "much more sophisticated strategies, including minimizing the number of devices they use, learning one piece of organizational software very well, and devoting considerable time to organizing and managing their information flows" (ibid., 139). My objective in this paper is to examine the variables that explain the efficiency and success with which highly skilled, expert performers manage their knowledge and why knowledge management is a goal in the development of human capital.

Human Capital and Expertise

Human capital is an economic term used here to describe the skills and knowledge that individuals draw upon to generate outputs of value. In other words, human capital refers to the generation of ideas, processes and products that lead to success in job performance and economic growth. An assumption in human capital development is that all individuals possess rich cognitive resources (knowledge and skills), which, if developed and managed appropriately, can be used to maximize their participation in and contribution to the creation of new and better ways of doing things.

Skilled performers in all domains possess human capital in the form of acquired knowledge and skills in the service of outstanding thinking, judgement and decision-making (Ericsson and Smith 1991). Experts draw on their human capital to quickly understand the nature of problems and to solve problems efficiently. A psychological perspective for developing human capital must focus on what makes experts who they are and how other individuals can be trained to acquire the intellectual prowess experts have developed. Many questions can be asked from a number of different perspectives about how to unleash human capital. One objective of this paper is to consider questions from a broad, policy-focused perspective, such as:

1. What does existing research in psychology tell us about the factors that influence human capital development?
2. Which causal connections are well established, and which are more speculative? Which influences have the greatest impact?
3. What key questions are not being answered or asked? What new ways of framing the issues might be worth exploring?
4. How can we look beyond conventional disciplinary boundaries? Where could those boundaries be breached in the most interesting, creative, and useful manner, in terms of subject matter, methodology or in any other respect?

Questions 1 and 2 will guide the discussion in the present paper, and I will address questions 3 and 4 in the discussion and conclusion to the paper. As I address these four questions, I will also address another set of four questions because they help set the theoretical and empirical stage for understanding human capital from a psychological perspective. These questions are:

5. How is human capital conceptualized within the psychological domain?
6. Assuming indicators of human capital can be identified, do individuals differ in their human capital?
7. If individuals do differ in human capital, which variables account for most of the differences?
8. How is human capital enhanced?

In the first section of the paper, I define human capital from a psychological perspective and discuss the two branches of psychology that focus on human capital development. In the second section, I review the differential psychology branch and its focus on the neural basis of general intelligence.[1] In the third section, I discuss the information-processing mechanism (working memory) that translates intelligence into effective knowledge management, including learning and productivity. In the fourth section, I discuss the cognitive psychological perspective and its focus on the person-based and contextual variables associated with knowledge management and skilled performance. In the fifth section, I discuss adaptive expertise and ways to promote the reuse of knowledge and transfer of skill. After each section, I discuss policy-relevant conclusions and implications. I summarize the paper by highlighting key questions for examining how adaptive expertise can be trained and how this research, which will most likely involve educational interventions, will rely on new partnerships between research organizations and school systems.

Human Capital as a Psychological Construct

If human capital refers to the skills and knowledge that individuals draw upon to generate outputs of value, then there are two main branches of psychology that focus on the study of human capital. These two branches include differential psychology and cognitive psychology. Differential psychologists study intelligence, broadly defined as the ability to learn from experience and adapt to the surrounding environment (Sternberg and Ben-Zeev 2001, 368) and narrowly defined as what intelligence tests measure[2] (Hunt 2005; see Sternberg and Grigorenko 2002 for a review of the debate). Tests of general intelligence in particular have been found to aid in the prediction of school grades, occupational outcomes (especially academic, professional and management) and performance on the job (Ceci 2000; Schmidt and Hunter 2004). It is for this reason that it is important to consider intelligence in any discussion of human capital; simply put, intelligence tests predict performance in knowledge-intensive domains.

Cognitive psychologists study complex cognition, broadly defined as the causal mechanisms or processes that people use to manage knowledge (Sternberg and Ben-Zeev 2001, 360). For example, adults and children who provide explanations for events within the physical, biological, mathematical and psychological domains have been shown to learn and perform better in knowledge-intensive or academic domains than individuals who do not provide such explanations (Wellman and Lagattuta 2004). This occurs because in the process of providing an explanation, individuals teach themselves about the underlying principles of the domain. Studies in cognitive psychology aim to identify why some variables are correlated; for example, why performance on intelligence tests predicts performance in knowledge-intensive domains. Both of these disciplines are therefore equally important to understanding how to develop human capital.

Differential psychology. Psychologists who study intelligence operationalize intelligence as the kind of behaviour that can be measured by intelligence tests, such as the Wechsler Adult Intelligence Scale (WAIS) or the Raven's Advanced Progressive Matrices. Intelligence tests are thought to be measures of knowledge or past academic achievement (Barnett and Ceci 2005). Investigations of intelligence have led to the identification of two dimensions of intelligent behaviour — crystallized and fluid (Carroll 1993; Cattell 1971; Horn and Noll 1994; Hunt 2005). Crystallized intelligence consists of context-dependent knowledge, defined as the ability to apply previously learned methods to solve current problems. Fluid intelligence is a context-independent skill, and is defined as the ability to develop solutions to relatively novel problems. Individuals who score high on measures of crystallized intelligence also tend to score high on measures of fluid intelligence (Jensen 2005). In other words, the two forms of intelligence are positively correlated. One possible explanation for this relationship is that persons use their fluid intelligence to acquire crystallized intelligence. For example, a person who reasons rapidly in novel domains is able to use this skill to learn concepts quickly (Cattell 1971). The other possible explanation is that persons use their crystallized intelligence to gain fluid intelligence. For example, persons who know a lot of things are able to reason effectively in new domains because their vast background knowledge matches aspects of the novel tasks they are solving.

Cognitive psychology. Cognitive psychologists study the information processes implicated in the management of knowledge. Knowledge management is necessary for all types of reasoning and problem-solving tasks that require the person to read, interpret, plan, compute, estimate, decide, infer, evaluate and execute. Cognitive psychologists have made unique contributions to what is known about the mental representations individuals create, and the processes individuals use as they apply strategies to reason about and solve tasks, together with the factors that facilitate or hinder problem-solving. In comparison to differential psychologists, who focus on the performance differences among individuals, cognitive psychologists tend to focus more on the process similarities among individuals. In particular, they seek to uncover what is common to the processes people use to interpret information and execute solutions. This focus on what is common has led to the creation of theories about how individuals make sense of their environments, and how tasks may be better created, presented and articulated for maximum comprehensibility (Girotto 2004). The limitation of the cognitive psychological approach is that group differences, such as gender differences, are generally downplayed in favour of what is common to all. An exception is the study of experts (Charness and Schultetus 1999), in which the focus of study is entirely on what is different about the information-processing of individuals who are considered highly knowledgeable and skilled in a domain from those individuals who are not. In the next section, I discuss the neural basis of intelligent performance.

Neural Efficiency and Plasticity

One avenue to understanding how individuals use their human capital to generate outputs of value begins by considering the neural basis of intelligent performance. Why do some people score better on tests of intelligence than others?

In terms of an actual location of the brain associated with intellectual performance, there is general consensus among cognitive neuroscientists that the frontal lobes are the areas underlying this form of behaviour (Duncan *et al.* 2000; Prabhakaran *et al.* 1997).[3] Using a range of methods from positron emission tomography (PET) to functional magnetic resonant imaging (fMRI), studies of individuals with frontal lobe lesions show impairments in higher-level cognitive processes such as planning, decision-making and goal-evaluation (Duncan, Burgess and Emslie 1995; Fiez 2001; Kessels *et al.* 2000).

Intelligence and Neural Efficiency

Outside of identifying the frontal lobes as the specific location of the brain associated with higher-level cognitive processes, researchers have focused on identifying the specific neural processes associated with measured intelligence. This bottom-up approach to understanding intelligence has largely involved examining "neural efficiency" (Neubauer and Fink 2005; Vernon 1987). I mentioned at the beginning of this paper that very good decision-making comprises frugality of thought. Neural efficiency is similar to this idea. Neural efficiency is quite simply the hypothesis that highly able people use their brains more proficiently than less able people (Neubauer and Fink 2005). However, the question of what specific brain processes actually serve as evidence for the neural-efficiency hypothesis has been challenging to answer. The challenge has arisen because some anticipated measures of neural efficiency such as evoked potentials (EP) latency (Deary and Caryl 1993; Neubauer 1997) and peripheral nerve conduction velocity (PNVC) have failed to show a reliable relationship to intelligent performance (Barrett, Daum and Eysenck 1990; Reed and Jensen 1991, 1992). Nevertheless, more reliable measures have been found such as positron emission tomography (PET), which can be used to assess glucose metabolism rate (GMR).

Glucose metabolism rate (GMR). Like other organs in the body, the human brain consumes energy in the face of environmental demands. More specifically, in cognitively difficult situations, the brain compensates for the loss of energy by metabolizing glucose (Haier *et al.* 1988; Neubauer and Fink 2005). To measure the GMR of the brain, neuroscientists inject a metabolic tracer into participating research subjects. During the uptake phase, the brain absorbs the tracer and the effects of cognitive activity on the GMR of different brain regions can be examined. The cognitive activity usually requires participants to solve the kinds of tasks found in traditional intelligence tests such as the Raven's Advanced Progressive Matrices. Figure 1 is an example of a matrix completion problem in which the participant must select from a set of options the one that will best complete the perceptual pattern.

After the uptake phase and cognitive activity are completed, individuals are moved to the PET scanner where their GMR is measured. Negative relationships have been found between GMR and cognitive

Figure 1. An Example of a Matrix Completion Problem

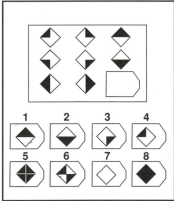

activity (Haier *et al.* 1988; Haier, Siegel, MacLachlan *et al.* 1992; Haier, Siegel, Tang *et al.* 1992; Parks *et al.* 1988). For example, Haier *et al.* (1988) found that individuals with higher IQs (intelligence quotient) exhibited lower GMRs during performance on the Raven's Advanced Progressive Matrices than individuals with lower IQs (correlations between –0.44 to –0.84 for different brain regions).

Event-related desynchronization (ERD). Another promising measure for establishing the relationship between neural efficiency and intelligence is the ERD or event-related desynchronization (Pfurtscheller and Aranibar 1977; Pfurtscheller and Lopes da Silva 1999) in the human electroencephalogram (EEG). Using this method, EEG background activity is assessed in two trials; one control trial involves no cognitive activity and the other activation trial involves cognitive activity where participants are asked to process task information. The task information presented to participants is again similar to tasks found in traditional intelligence tests. The ERD is measured by calculating the percentage of decrease in power from the control trial to the activation trial. With this approach, neuroscientists (Neubauer, Freudenthaler and Pfurtscheller 1995; Neubauer, Sange and Pfurtscheller 1999) have found that individuals with lower IQs were more likely to display stronger and relatively unspecific cortical activation (positive increase in ERDs) compared to individuals with higher IQs. Higher-IQ participants generally showed weaker, but specific, cortical activation on cognitive tasks such as the well-known sentence-verification task (Carpenter and Just 1975). Although the ERD seems to share a negative relationship with measured intelligence (weak but specific activation is associated with higher intelligence), it seems particularly related to individual differences in fluid rather than crystallized intelligence (Neubauer and Fink 2003) and in male cognitive activity rather than female cognitive activity (Neubauer and Fink 2003; Neubauer, Fink and Schrausser 2002). Studies have found that although higher-ability males tend to show the weak but specific cortical activation associated with efficient neural processing, higher-ability females do not. Moreover, the strong but unspecific cortical activation associated with lower-ability individuals is observed with lower-ability males but not with lower-ability females. In other words, cortical activation has been found to be unrelated to ability in female participants. Other studies have also shown that males and females display distinct patterns of cortical activation on verbal, numerical and figural-spatial tasks (see Neubauer, Fink and Schrausser 2002).

In addition to the findings that higher measured intelligence is associated with greater neural efficiency, there is also evidence that higher measured intelligence is associated with stronger myelination of axons. Stronger myelination translates into higher speed of nerve conduction, less leakage and anatomically larger brains (Miller 1994). Other sources of evidence suggest that redundant synaptic connections (also referred to as deficiencies in neural pruning) are associated with lower measured intelligence (Haier 1993). Finally, there is some evidence that in adaptation to environmental demands, more efficient brains grow dendritic trees and axon branches compared to less efficient brains and these changes are again associated with differences in measured intelligence (see Garlick 2002).

Intelligence and Neural Plasticity

There is strong evidence for individual differences in neural efficiency and, in some cases, these differences predict performance on tests of intelligence. At a basic level, then, it might seem that what influences human capital is neural anatomy. However, the statistical relationship between neural efficiency and measured intelligence has some limitations. Although better problem-solvers appear to have more efficient neural systems, this could be the case for at least two different reasons (Hunt 2005). It could be the case that when faced with a problem to solve, better problem-solvers simply have more efficient (faster) neural processing and thus take advantage of this asset. Alternatively, better problem-solvers may simply have better-organized brain systems due to unique learning patterns and opportunities, such that less neural processing is required to achieve a solution to a task.

In an impressive review of the literature, Garlick (2002) explains this second alternative in depth. He claims that better-organized brain systems are likely to arise when young children are exposed to learning environments that challenge their developing brains to create highly efficient connections in adaptation to difficult tasks. Garlick proposes that "neural plasticity" is the most likely process responsible for individual differences in neural efficiency and measured intelligence. Neural plasticity includes "the processes that involve major connectional changes of the nervous system in response to experience and that are observed to cease to operate at maturity" (Garlick 2002, 120). He explains that neural efficiency naturally arises in (young) brains that have been exposed to a wide array of stimuli and have therefore been given the opportunity to create the optimal connections necessary to deal with an equally wide range of complex task situations. Integrating neuro-science and computer simulation studies, Garlick concludes that these connections are largely generated during a critical period for intellec-tual development, starting at birth until age 15. In support of this neural-plasticity hypothesis, many cognitive skills such as learning a second language, playing a musical instrument and thinking in knowledge-intensive disciplines such as science and math have been found to be encountered and practiced early in life by those considered to be highly gifted in their performance (Albert 1978; Tomlinson-Keasey and Little 1990).

Policy Implications

What does this research imply for educational policy? For starters, outside the obvious importance of prenatal precautions and care for brain development, Garlick indicates that valued forms of thinking, whether in science and math or music and art, should be introduced to students at a younger age than is currently the case in educational set-tings. More succinctly, Garlick states that "the educational system ... presents these phenomena to people in college when they are past the critical period. It [educational system] is then surprised when these young adults cannot acquire these abilities" (2002, 127). The main im-plication of this research, then, is that if we want to enhance outputs of value in knowledge-intensive domains, the efforts must begin early by exposing young minds to the variety of the knowledge and skills we deem valuable as a society. Waiting until adulthood to create educa-tional interventions to develop human capital may be too late (see Hansen, Heckman and Mullen 2004 for an econometrics approach to this argument).

The research on the neural basis of intelligence is important to re-view when considering human capital development. Consider that in-dividual differences in measured intelligence have been found to predict school grades, occupational outcomes (Barrett and Depinet 1991; Ceci 2000) and job success, especially for knowledge-intensive occupations, including professional, scientific and upper management jobs (Schmidt and Hunter 2004). Although Sternberg (1999) claims that intelligence tests simply measure one form of expertise — performing well on (sim-ple) inductive problems that resemble academic tasks — it is also the case that performance on these seemingly simple problems predicts a highly valued output for human capital development; that is, the management of knowledge. Leaving aside for a moment the neural processes implicated in measured intelligence, I now turn to a discussion of the most likely information-processing mechanism that translates measured intelligence into outputs of value. In the next section, I review the information-processing link between intelligence and skilled performance — working memory.

Working Memory

Working memory is an integral component of the human information processing system. It is a temporary holding station for information required for a range of cognitive activities involving knowledge management, including language learning, reasoning and problem-solving (Baddeley 2000, 2003). Working memory is used to rehearse, interpret and transform information so that it can be transferred into long-term memory (where it resides as permanent knowledge for later retrieval). Outside of being a location where information is managed and manipulated, working memory also maintains existing information as active while new information arrives via sensory channels or long-term memory (Baddeley 2000).

Working memory is such a central component of human information-processing that some differential psychologists claim working memory and general intelligence are indistinguishable (Kyllonen 1996; Kyllonen and Christal 1990). In support of this claim, laboratory measures of working memory and intelligence have been found to be strongly correlated (0.90 at the latent variable level between working memory and fluid intelligence, Kyllonen and Christal 1990; see also Engle *et al.* 1999; Hambrick, Kane and Engle 2005).

Working memory is a limited-capacity system, where capacity refers to the quantity of information an individual can simultaneously and consciously attend to without becoming overloaded (Baddeley 2000; Nairne 2003; see also Ericsson and Simon 1993 for how working memory influences cognitive performance). Working memory is especially susceptible to overload when faced with new tasks or situations. Consider the first time you drove a car or visited a new city. The newness of the task or situation makes every detail relevant and it is impossible not to consciously attend to and evaluate every piece of information. When working memory is overloaded, there is a rapid decay in the information held, causing a breakdown in knowledge management. Thus, the information and any chance of successful performance are lost. Only when a task has been performed many times and is well learned to the point of being performed automatically (for example, driving after five years of experience), is working memory essentially bypassed and it no longer functions as a bottleneck. Working memory can be bypassed when conscious or controlled attention to task details is no longer required for successful performance.

Increasing the capacity of working memory would be expected to improve performance on measures of intelligence and, in turn, performance on all the tasks that measures of intelligence seem to predict (e.g., school grades, occupational outcome). But how could working memory be increased? Much like an express cashier at a local grocery store — moving foods through as quickly as or even more quickly than the rate at which they are coming in — working memory can be increased by sheer practice. In the next section, I describe expertise and how deliberate practice increases working memory capacity.

Working Memory and Expert Problem-Solving

Expertise is defined by Charness and Schultetus as "consistently superior performance on a set of representative tasks for the domain that can be administered to any subject" (1999, 58). Studies of expertise suggest that expert performance is a reliable phenomenon that can be measured using standard tasks or conditions for competition in laboratory settings (for a review, see Ericsson 1996). Identified experts within a domain seem to share a cluster of features about their training and performance. First, peak performance results after many years of intense preparation and practice within the domain — 10,000 hours, for example, are normally required to reach top-level performance within a domain (Charness and Schultetus 1999). Second, experts do not simply spend more "leisure" time in their respective domain in comparison to others, but rather spend more hours engaging in *deliberate* practice (Ericsson and Charness 1994). Deliberate practice normally involves solitary study with the purpose of improving knowledge management and performance.

Experts have been found to have an amplified working-memory capacity in the domain of their expertise. This amplified capacity is the result of efficient organization and automation — experts organize their vast knowledge into chunks of facts and strategies in long-term memory and they practice accessing this knowledge repeatedly to the point of making information retrieval automatic (Chase and Simon 1973; de Groot 1965; Gobet 1997; for a review, see Johnson 2003 and Leighton and Sternberg 2003). For example, their vast knowledge buys them the enviable skill of recognizing patterns (or chunks) of relevant and important features within a problem quickly (Allard and Starkes 1991; Chase and Simon 1973; de Groot 1965; Gobet 1997; Gobet and Simon 1996). These task features are interpreted, transformed and matched to previously learned and catalogued templates (schemas) in the expert's long-term memory.

This ability to match task features to previously catalogued templates allows experts to demonstrate extraordinary recall and management of information. For example, Gobet and Simon (1996) found that in contrast to less accomplished players, champion chess players could recall more than nine chess positions that had been presented to the players briefly and without breaks between presentations. Likewise, Allard and Starkes (1991) found that élite athletes were able to abstract and recall more information about game situations after a brief exposure than non-élite athletes. In other words, retrieval of accurate information is exceedingly efficient for experts because recall does not take place piecemeal. All the associated and relevant pieces of information come along with it in a chunk. Distilling these chunks of information allows experts to form highly complex representations of the problem situation, allowing them to integrate task information with background knowledge to select and evaluate courses of action (Charness and Schultetus 1999; Ericsson 1996; Ericsson and Charness 1994; Ericsson and Kintsch 1995; Ericsson and Smith 1991; Johnson 2003; Sternberg 1999).

Organizing knowledge into chunks effectively increases the capacity of working memory. Unlike novices within a domain, experts function as thriving businessmen and women, producing their outputs through economies of scale. When a maker of widgets first begins to make widgets, he or she will take time to ensure that the widgets are well crafted and even consider the different strategies to market and distribute them. After considerable time refining the production and distribution of widgets, however, and with sufficient market demand, the producer now has enough practice to automate the process. The widgets can be produced in large scale. One can see how this might extend to experts' thinking and performance. The vast knowledge and experience experts have allow them to automate much of their thinking within a domain, such that their performances become performances of scale —

working memory is freed up to manage new, additional information because basic information-processing has been refined and no longer takes time. Experts' organized knowledge therefore functions to increase working-memory capacity because it (a) permits working memory to operate on chunks of information instead of on single pieces of information, and (b) often bypasses working memory entirely for basic information-processing, freeing the single-channel system to operate on other newer and relevant information.

Surprisingly, experts learn to manage or chunk their knowledge by sheer practice within their domains. In fact, in contrast to the popular opinion that skilled performance within a contextual domain originates solely from superior intelligence, research on expertise suggests the opposite. The main message from this line of research is that skilled and even exceptional performance develops largely, although not exclusively, from basic hard work, effort and intense preparation (Ericsson and Charness 1994; see also Johnson 2003). Studies of expertise are intriguing because they suggest that human cognitive abilities are flexible and can adapt to meet increasingly higher demands and expectations. Although studies of expertise have been carried out largely with a limited range of problem-solving tasks within laboratory settings (e.g., Chase and Simon 1973; Chi, Glaser and Farr 1988; de Groot 1965; Gobet 1997; Holding 1992), this line of research offers concrete avenues for developing human capital (see Ceci and Liker 1986a, b; Ceci and Ruiz 1992, 1993). Increasing working-memory capacity presents another opportunity for policy initiatives in human capital development.

Policy Implications

After reviewing numerous studies of expertise, Gobet has eight recommendations for educators to develop working memory and skilled performance in their students:

1. Devote time to task for the purpose of improving performance (essential to gaining knowledge).
2. Direct learners' attention to key features of the material to be learned (segment curriculum).
3. Provide feedback and highlight important features of a problem so as to focus the acquisition of correct knowledge.
4. Supplement the teaching of specific knowledge with the teaching of *metaheuristics* (or metacognitive) — strategies about how to learn, how

to direct one's attention in novel domains and how to regulate memory.

5.   Pay attention to the ordering of presented material to be learned by presenting simple material first, followed by more complex material (that builds on previously presented material), noting discriminative features or cues in the material that signal avenues for problem-solving.

6.   Focus on the conditions for applying newly learned procedures.

7.   Maintain variety in presentation by using many examples to show the parameters or underlying principles of the concept: "without variation, schemata [general principles] cannot be created" (Gobet 2005, 197).

8.   Avoid new technologies (e.g., hypertexts) that "present distractions that interfere with what should ideally be learnt" (ibid., 198).

These eight recommendations are designed to promote working memory and expert performance for individuals regardless of pre-existing differences in intelligence. In fact, Gobet (see also Bloom 1984) claims that pre-existing individual differences should be taken into account only to tailor teaching for expertise. He states that "first, while individual differences tend to be diluted by large amounts of practice, they play a large role in the early stages of studying a domain, which characterizes much of classroom instruction ... taking into account individual differences may lead to better instruction, because instruction can be optimized for each student, including feedback on progress, organization of material, and choice of learning strategies to be taught" (Gobet 2005, 199).

Training to become an expert in a knowledge-intensive domain should not only increase working-memory capacity but should also boost measured intelligence to the extent that the tasks used in the training domain overlap with the kinds of tasks found on intelligence tests; namely, academic tasks (Ceci 2000; Sternberg 1999). In contrast, training to become an expert in a non-academic domain may improve working memory within that domain but will not likely boost performance on tests of intelligence because the tasks in the two domains would not share enough similarity (Beckmann and Guthke 1995; Ceci and Liker 1986*a*, *b*; Ericsson, Krampe and Tesch-Romer 1993; Funke 1995; Sternberg *et al.* 2001; see also Wenke, Frensch and Funke 2005). For example, Ceci and Liker (1986*a*, *b*) compared a group of experts and novices in their abilities to handicap horse races. The two groups were matched on many variables, such as their years of track experience, education and psychometric intelligence. The only variable on which the experts differed from novices was their ability to correctly predict the post-time odds (on the basis of *a priori* factual information) for the top three horses in ten real races. When experts and novices were asked to handicap 50 experimentally contrived races, there were significant differences between the two groups. In particular, experts used a sophisticated combination of variables (e.g., lifetime speed of the horse, claiming price, track surface condition) in their handicapping compared to novices, suggesting increased working-memory capacity to better manage their comprehension of task features and their relatedness. When numerical weights were assigned to the variables selected and combined by the experts, the weights correlated highly with handicapping performance but not with their measured IQ.

Research on expertise indicates that working memory can be reasonably enhanced at any age, thereby permitting experts to flourish within domains throughout the lifespan. In the next section, I describe the effects of knowledge and context and how these can be used to promote expert performance.

Developing Reuse and Transfer

So far in this discussion, I have identified two avenues for enhancing human capital: neural plasticity and working memory. Both these avenues could lead to improvements in the outputs of value within a domain, albeit at different stages of development. On the one hand, improvements in neural plasticity function to develop human capital at very early stages of the individual lifespan (birth to age 15). On the other hand, increases in working memory function to develop human capital at any age. Both in academic and non-academic domains, working memory allows individuals to think efficiently and successfully within their domains by attending to specific perceptual cues and foregoing redundant information. Gobet calls this the expert's professional eye, and it seems to select successful courses of action instinctively by "allowing [experts such as nurses and firefighters] to be highly selective in their search and to solve routine problems without exploring many alternatives" (2005, 184).

However, we do not want to simply enhance neural plasticity and working memory to predict school grades and occupational outcomes. This is not the end goal. Part of the goal is also to enhance the performance of those already in knowledge-intensive occupations. So the question we must now ask is: What allows some experts to become adaptive experts; that is, individuals who reuse their knowledge and transfer their skills to new domains? We have seen that measured intelligence (via working memory) predicts acquired knowledge within academic domains and deliberate practice (via working memory) predicts acquired knowledge within all domains. But what predicts the reuse of knowledge and the transfer of skills? Gobet recognizes, as do others (for example, Sternberg 1999), that "transfer seems to be minimal from one domain of expertise to another" (2005, 184). Certainly this is an important question to ask for developing human capital. We must consider what information processes permit the expert firefighter to become the expert fire chief or the expert assembly worker to become the expert salesman. Especially in knowledge-intensive professions, experts who want to reuse their knowledge and transfer their skills must now push the envelope to broaden the flexibility of their knowledge management. In the next section, I explore the variables that must be considered if reuse and transfer are to occur.

The Effect of Knowledge and Context

Knowledge mobilizes reasoning and problem-solving skills (Barnett and Ceci 2005; Cosmides 1989; Leighton and Sternberg 2003, 2004; Nickerson 2004). Unless a person thinks they have adequate knowledge and skills to solve a task, he or she will not be able to solve it successfully. Alternatively, constantly developing new knowledge and skills to tackle new problems that resemble old problems is inefficient. Davenport adds that "in many cases the goal is to reuse knowledge more effectively. We can greatly improve performance by having a lawyer reuse knowledge created in another case, or having a programmer employ a subroutine that someone else created" (2005, 71). The issue then is how to make tasks more accessible for the reuse of knowledge (Cheng and Holyoak 1985, 1989; Cosmides 1989) and how to help individuals see the similarities between new and old tasks so that their background knowledge mobilizes the transfer of skills.

Investigations of abstract and logical reasoning have underscored the importance of task presentation and the presence of relevant knowledge to "kick start" the use of appropriate reasoning and problem-solving skills (for a review see Leighton and Sternberg 2003). Studies of college students who are asked to solve the so-called Wason selection task (see Figure 2), a reasoning task named after the famous British psychologist Peter Wason (Wason 1966), demonstrated how miserably they could perform when the task was framed in an unfamiliar context (see Leighton and Sternberg 2003, 2004 for reviews).

Figure 2. Adaptation of the Wason Selection Task

Consider the rule: If there is a vowel on one side of the card, then there is an even number on the other side. Now examine the four cards below, each of which has either a

letter or number on one of the sides. Choose the fewest numbers of cards that can test the truth or falsity of the rule.

Note: See Leighton and Sternberg (2003).

Only 10 percent of college students normally select the appropriate cards, which happen to be the E and the 7. Students' poor performance in these studies was not due to their inherent deficiencies in information-processing. The participants in most of these studies were college students. In fact, the most likely reason for students' poor performance was that most of them had never taken a course in symbolic logic (Girotto 2004; Stenning and Yule 1997) and thus had no idea how to interpret the conditional rule formally, let alone the instructions for "testing the truth or falsity" of a rule.

The Wason task might seem at first glance to be no more than a toy problem. However, consider that student performance on more familiar versions of the Wason task predict performance on the SAT, a measure of college readiness (a correlation of 0.47), statistical reasoning (0.26) and the ability to evaluate arguments (0.31). In other words, when the Wason task is presented in a format that permits individuals to reuse their knowledge, the task can be used to discriminate abstract thinkers from not-so-good abstract thinkers (Stanovich, Sá and West 2004;

Stanovich and West 1998). Consider a more familiar version of the Wason task (adapted from Cosmides 1989):

Figure 3. An Adaptation of the Thematic Version of the Wason Selection Task for Social Contract Theory

---

Your job is to enforce the following law: If you take the benefit, then you must pay the cost.

The cards below have information about four people. Each card represents one person. One side of the card tells whether a person accepted the benefit, and the other side of the card tells whether the person paid the cost. Indicate only those card(s) that definitely need to be turned over to see if any of these people are breaking the law.

| Benefit Accept | Benefit Not Accept | Cost Paid | Cost Not Paid |

Note: See Cosmides (1989); reviewed by Leighton and Sternberg (2003).

When college students were asked to solve the familiar task shown in Figure 3, approximately 75 percent of them selected the correct cards, the Benefit Accepted and Cost Not Paid cards. Although the framework of this new, more thematic task is similar to the traditional Wason task, more able students solved it correctly because the familiar context facilitated their reuse of existing knowledge (e.g., Cosmides 1989). Most people learn extensively about rule enforcement from an early age, and therefore have the necessary background knowledge about potential rule violators. Participants who have this background knowledge recognize quickly which cards must be chosen to ensure that potential cheaters are identified and punished.

The context of a task can be manipulated in many ways to promote the reuse of previously learned knowledge (Girotto 2004; Leighton 2004; Newell and Simon 1972; Sperber, Cara and Girotto 1995). For example, some studies have found that depending on the perspective individuals are asked to adopt on a reasoning task (such as whether they stand to gain or lose), their performance can be manipulated in predictable ways (see cheating detection theory, Gigerenzer and Hug 1992;

Manktelow and Over 1991; Manktelow *et al.* 2000). The instructions participants receive prior to a task have also been found to influence their performance. For instance, instructing participants about the importance of searching for alternative solutions to a problem has been shown to improve their reasoning on categorical syllogisms (Cheng and Holyoak 1985; Cosmides 1989; Cosmides and Tooby 1996; Liberman and Klar 1996; Newstead and Evans 1993; Pollard and Evans 1987).

In general, persons' perceived relevance of a task, which determines whether they will entertain the prospect of solving it, is based on their background knowledge. After examining the experimental literature on the Wason task and conducting several studies where perceived relevance was manipulated, Sperber, Cara and Girotto (1995) concluded that people gauge the benefits and costs (effort) of solving a task. A task is perceived as increasingly relevant the more its benefits outweigh its costs. Moreover, Sperber, Cara and Girotto explain that perception of task relevance is related to background knowledge. Individuals who believed they were knowledgeable about the task perceived it as less effortful and more relevant than those individuals who believed they were not knowledgeable enough to solve the task.

When we consider how knowledge and skills relate to outputs of value, it is useful to consider how best to invoke that knowledge and those skills on a given task, so as to fairly judge what people can maximally or optimally produce. Otherwise we risk underestimating what people are capable of producing and contributing to the creation of valued goods. Our understanding of the specific variables that promote knowledge management in the service of skilled reasoning and problem-solving is still in its infancy, prompting Barnett and Ceci (2002, 2005) to suggest that we need a theory of context in order to understand the interaction of person-based and environmental variables that affect successful performance in a variety of contexts. In the effort to contribute to a theory of context, there are person-based variables or dispositions that correlate with successful performance in a variety of domains.

Effect of Person-Based Variables

Nickerson (2004, 415) has identified the following abilities, qualities and propensities that good reasoners tend to possess: intelligence, domain-specific knowledge, general knowledge about human cognition, knowledge of common limitations, foibles and pitfalls, self-

knowledge, knowledge of tools of thought, ability to analyze and evaluate arguments, good judgement, ability to estimate, sensitivity to missing information, ability to deal effectively with uncertainty, ability to
take alternate perspectives, ability to reason counterfactually, ability to
manage own reasoning, reflectiveness, curiosity and inquisitiveness,
strong desire to hold true beliefs and willingness to work at reasoning.
Nickerson argued that these abilities and qualities "are supportive of
good reasoning independently of who does it or the subject on which it
is focused. They do not guarantee that one will reason well, but they
increase the likelihood" (ibid., 414). Other investigators have also identified similar abilities and qualities (Kuhn 2001; Norris, Leighton and
Phillips 2004; Perkins 1995; Stanovich and West 2000; Sternberg and
Ben-Zeev 2001).

In answer to the question of how best to promote the individual abilities and qualities associated with successful knowledge management
and performance, we turn not to a theory of context but rather to a
theory of mind (Wellman and Lagattuta 2004). The term theory of mind
refers "to our everyday understanding of persons in terms of their in-
ner psychological states" (ibid., 479). An important aspect of theory of
mind for our purposes is its relationship with metacognition (or
metaheuristics) — how a child views the use of the mind to memorize
facts, learn knowledge, and use strategies effectively in learning contexts (Adams, Treiman and Pressley 1998). Increasingly, research studies
show (see Dunn *et al.* 1991; Meins *et al.* 2003) that children who are
adept at providing psychological explanations for a person's actions or
experiences as the cause or consequences of their mental states tend to
also make more references to underlying causal mechanisms.

After reviewing experimental studies where children are asked to
provide explanations for characters' actions and situations, Wellman
and Lagattuta (2004) concluded that children who are asked to provide
causal explanations also improve their perspective-taking and
knowledge of the tasks presented to them. In their words, explanations
are critical to learning because "attempting to better explain such anoma-
lous behaviour (including seeking and receiving explanations from others), causes children to develop further, deeper conceptualizations.
Regardless of differing theoretical emphases, empirically the data are
clear: explanations have a special role in theory of mind development"
(ibid., 491). The ability to generate causal explanations for events within
domains promotes the successful transfer of skills across domains (Chi,
Feltovich and Glaser 1981). The types of underlying principles used to

generate causal explanations are precisely those that are used to map meaningful relations across seemingly disparate domains (Dunbar 1995; Loewenstein, Thompson and Gentner 1999; Rattermann and Gentner 1998).

Policy Implications

Although there is need to conduct more research to identify the best methods to cultivate abilities and qualities that will promote knowledge management, practices that facilitate knowledge acquisition such as directing learners' attention to key features of the material to be learned, and providing feedback and highlighting important features of a problem so as to focus the acquisition of correct knowledge (see Gobet 2005) should increase the perceived relevance of a task and the likelihood that background knowledge will be reused in solving it. Moreover, encouraging children to provide explanations for physical and social phenomena and to comment on others' explanations is an important teaching tool for stimulating meaningful learning (see Chi *et al.* 1994; Pine and Siegler 2003; Siegler 2002). In fact, the payoffs of teaching children about the use of explanations may be a key to promoting adaptive expertise and, ultimately, both the reuse of knowledge and the transfer of skills. The reason for this is that experts who can adapt their skills most readily to new situations are those who understand the underlying principles for using rules in particular situations. Davenport comments on this capacity by sharing the remarks of one high-performing project manager: "I learned management not from a class, but through reflecting on my past experiences of being managed, through simple trial and error, and through conscious observation and reflection on the acts of other managers" (2005, 149). An individual's theory of mind can be used to promote the learning of underlying principles and causal mechanisms of a domain, which, in turn, can promote the flexible, theory-based reasoning shown by adaptive experts in response to new situations.

Adaptive versus Routine Expertise

Ensuring that the knowledge and skills people learn in one domain are applicable to other domains is an essential part of developing human capital and outputs of value. Investigators of problem-solving agree that managing knowledge and having the skills to solve tasks across conceptually similar domains is the hallmark of adaptive thinking, broadly conceived (Anderson 1983; Barnett and Ceci 2005; Bransford and Stein 1984; Ericsson 1996; Holyoak 1991; Johnson-Laird 1999; Leighton and Sternberg 2003, 2004; Newell and Simon 1972; Roberts and Newton 2005). But transfer of knowledge does not occur spontaneously (Adey and Shayer 1994; Nickerson 2004; Salomon and Perkins 1989; Sternberg and Ben-Zeev 2001). For example, the knowledge that people gain in a mathematics class is often not used to solve problems in a symbolic logic class, even though the underlying structure of problems in the two contexts may have similarities. This lack of reuse and transfer underscores the domain-specific nature of most of human learning. However, deficiencies in the reuse of knowledge and transfer of skills can be minimized so as to avoid having individuals continually relearning concepts and skills previously acquired. For example, Davenport (2005) claims that continually relearning how to make sense of and solve organizational tasks limits the optimization of output. Output is limited because the individual is constantly bogged down with basic information and cannot focus on new, advanced information about the domain.

Theory-Based Reasoning

One area of research that stands to inform the reuse of knowledge and transfer of skills distinguishes the learning patterns of two kinds of experts: adaptive and routine (Hatano 1982, 1988; Hatano and Inagaki 1984, 1986; Holyoak 1991; see also Barnett and Koslowski 2002). The difference between adaptive and routine expertise involves, fundamentally, the ability to reuse knowledge and transfer skills to novel tasks within conceptually similar domains. Holyoak summarizes the distinction succinctly: "Whereas routine experts are able to solve familiar types of problems quickly and accurately, they have only modest capabilities in dealing with novel types of problems. Adaptive experts, on the other hand, may be able to invent new procedures derived from their expert knowledge" (1991, 310). Holyoak claims that routine experts are proficient skill-learners but are essentially algorithmic in their understanding of a domain. These are the individuals who know a lot about what they do and can solve many problems as long as they have learned a rule for it (Barnett and Koslowski 2002). In contrast, adaptive experts do not only know how to apply the rules of their field effectively but they also have the depth of knowledge in the form of underlying principles to understand what makes the domain "tick." They often invent their own successful rules for solving problems if previously learned rules are ineffective. Davenport claims these high performers to be "intentional, flexible, and proactive learners over time" (2005, 145). Adaptive experts are believed to hold the key to knowledge reuse and transfer of skills because they are practiced at using what they already know to solve novel, yet conceptually similar tasks successfully.

In a study examining important group differences in knowledge re-use and transfer of skill, Barnett and Koslowski (2002) had two expert groups and one novice group read a story about a hypothetical restaurant. The groups included general business consultants, restaurant managers and a group of novices (non-business graduates). The groups of business consultants and restaurant managers were matched in age (approximately 35 years) and number of years of formal education (approximately 16.5 years). However, the groups differed on other variables. The business consultants had all earned business degrees, whereas only 42 percent of the restaurant managers had done the same. In addition, the business consultants had an average of six years of consulting experience but no restaurant experience, whereas the restaurant managers had no experience consulting but had an average of eight years of restaurant experience. The novice group was generally younger, at 20 years of age, and had 14 years of education and no business education, consulting experience or restaurant experience. Using individual interviews, Barnett and Koslowski posed four open-ended questions to the participants within each group, asking them to identify possible solutions to challenges facing the hypothetical restaurant.

After conducting individual interviews, the interviews were transcribed and then given to "super-expert" referees. These super-experts were university professors whose research focused on restaurant management in a faculty department specializing in the hotel and restaurant business. These super-experts had previously managed restaurants and also had broader consulting experience. In essence, these super-experts represented the combination of skills possessed by both business consultants and restaurant managers in the study. The super-experts coded the interviews, without knowing from which group they originated, for whether participants mentioned the optimal solution to the hypothetical restaurant challenge, and for whether participants expressed extraneous solutions that would not address the challenge. In the analysis of responses, business consultants were found to provide more optimal solutions (average score of 41 percent) than restaurant managers (average score of 24 percent) or novices (average score of 20 percent). Even though the scores of the business consultants were generally below 50 percent, they were still better than the other two groups (see Leighton 2006 for a discussion of expertise in novel domains and its impact on performance).

After reviewing the interviews for optimal solutions, a second analysis was conducted to examine the knowledge management and problem-solving skills of business consultants. Using a combination of qualitative and quantitative analytical methods, Barnett and Koslowski found that even though business consultants had no restaurant experience, they engaged in deep, theory-based reasoning in response to the challenge faced by the hypothetical restaurant. In particular, the consultants made use of theory-based reasoning, including the reuse of previously learned theoretical concepts, and the transfer of causal reasoning skills, causally-supported solutions and complementary alternatives in their thinking compared to restaurant managers and the novice students. Theory-based reasoning is believed to facilitate knowledge reuse and transfer to novel tasks because it provides an organizing framework with which to make sense of novel information in a conceptually similar domain (see also Dunbar 1995; Gentner 1999; Newell and Simon 1972). The organizing framework highlights what might be relevant in the problem and the main goals for task solution (see Carpenter, Just and Shell 1990; Kuhn 2001). Knowing and understanding the theory-based reasons for organizing problem-solving skills, including the fundamental principles at work within a domain, helps to distinguish experts who perform well within *narrow* domains based on algorithmic knowledge from those who can perform well within *broadly* defined domains based on adaptive thinking (see Kuhn 2001).

Consider the reasoning of one business consultant in response to the problem of having one of the roads leading to the hypothetical restaurant becoming a one-way street, without parking:

> depending on which way the one way is, it would be busy in one rush hour and not busy in another rush hour, so the road heading to town from suburbia would be busy in the morning and the other at night ... so if it turned out that it didn't matter and this was a destination decision I wouldn't worry about it, if there was significant impulse traffic I would be concerned and then I'd look into options such as a sign on the other road, billboard on the road "make a right turn for Luigi's" (Barnett and Koslowski 2002, 245).

According to Barnett and Koslowski, the business consultant who provided this answer considered the alternative of having different kinds of customers stop by the restaurant, such as customers who planned in advance to eat at the restaurant and other (impulse) customers who might stop in by chance. The consequences of the one-way road were considered for both kinds of customers. In contrast, restaurant managers often leapt to a conclusion and then used the available evidence to rationalize it: "put in their ads a reasonable place to park that is not too far away, advertise the fact that it is still very accessible for people, and that it is still very much worth coming to." Recommendations were sometimes justified, and typically these justifications came after the recommendation: "it would definitely affect the restaurant because people don't want to go too much out of their way unless it's a special occasion or they really, really like it there."

In a final set of analyses, Barnett and Koslowski examined possible answers to the question of why some experts, such as the group of business consultants, make use of theoretical reasoning more often than others, and what types of experiences encourage the formation of these theoretical perspectives. In search of answers, they looked at participants' backgrounds, comparing their age, years of education, the presence or absence of business education, and number of years of experience in restaurant management and business consulting. The analyses revealed that the only characteristic predicting both the amount of theory-based reasoning and overall performance was consulting experience. None of the other background characteristics (for example, age, years of formal education) predicted use of theory-based reasoning or performance on the task. Although consulting experience was found to be the most influential predictor of performance, the investigators acknowledged that they were unable to examine pre-existing differences in ability or intelligence among the participants. This is a limitation with most studies of expertise (Gobet 2005). Although Barnett and Koslowski examined whether the grade point average (GPA) of students in the novice group was associated with better problem-solving, they found no effect of GPA. This finding suggests that successful knowledge management across domains does not simply result from proximal academic success (GPA), seniority (age) or even years of formal education, but rather, is also a result of a method of thinking that involves in large part managing the reuse of theoretical concepts learned previously and the transfer of causal reasoning skills (see Wellman and Lagattuta 2004).

Policy Implications

Barnett and Koslowski's study is one of the few expert studies (however, see also Alexander *et al.* 2004; Barnett and Ceci 2005; Leighton 2006 for examples) to examine the differences between algorithmic and adaptive expertise and the form of thinking that characterizes the latter. Until recently, most research in skilled performance has not addressed this difference, focusing instead on simple comparisons between experts and novices (see e.g., Chi, Feltovich and Glaser 1981; Johnson *et al.* 1982) without distinguishing among different kinds of experts and their respective methods to manage knowledge.

From a policy perspective, then, what prompts knowledge reuse and the transfer of skill in the form of theoretical-based reasoning? Again, there is research suggesting that the breadth of an individual's prior experience may be the key to the development of deep, theory-based reasoning in the service of knowledge reuse and transfer of skill (Brown 1989; Catrambone and Holyoak 1989; Cummins 1992; Dunbar 1995; Gick and Holyoak 1983; Hatano 1982; Holyoak 1991; Leighton and Bisanz 2003). In addition to the research and recommendations already discussed by Garlick (2002), Gobet (2005), and Wellman and Lagattuta (2004), Brown (1989) found that four-year-old children who were trained with a broad range of distinct examples to illustrate mimicry-like defence mechanisms in animals (such as playing dead or changing shape) were more likely to reuse their knowledge to a new situation than children who were presented with a single type of example (ways to look dangerous). This is also supportive of Garlick's (2002) contention that variety or breadth (see earlier section) in the tasks presented during a child's intellectual critical period is a key to maximizing neural plasticity and the connections for complex problem-solving. In a similar vein, Dunbar (1995) discovered in his work with real scientists in microbiology laboratories that the collective span of relevant experience possessed by the scientists in the lab was a major determinant of their rate of effective problem-solving leading to new discoveries.

Overall, the substantive variety in an expert's background experience appears to be associated with forms of flexible thinking that focus on underlying principles which can be used to make sense of new problems in conceptually similar domains. Again this is reminiscent of Gobet's (2005) recommendations for educators. Activities that promote learning for meaning should be encouraged because they influence the ability to acquire flexible forms of thinking that make adaptive expertise possible. In short, there is strong evidence that exposing children to a variety of educational stimuli during their intellectual critical period, presenting them with stimulating problems and fostering them to seek deep, theory-based explanations for the occurrences they see in their environments, leads children to learn for meaning because they can abstract general principles about phenomena and understand (through explanations) why these principles exist. These general principles then facilitate the reuse of knowledge and transfer of skill by making visible the relational similarities in conceptually new domains (Dunbar 1995; Gentner 1999; Loewenstein, Thompson and Gentner 1999; Rattermann and Gentner 1998).

Summary and Discussion

To conclude, I provide summary answers to the questions posed at the beginning of this paper:

1. *What does existing research in psychology tell us about the factors that influence human capital development?* The factors that influence human capital development are (a) *measured intelligence* because it predicts school grades and occupational outcomes in knowledge-intensive do-mains, (b) *neural efficiency* and *neural plasticity* because they predict measured intelligence, (c) *working memory* because it predicts knowl-edge management within academic and non-academic domains, (d) *knowledge (expertise)* and *context* because individuals who can use what they know in familiar contexts can solve problems more successfully and view problem-solving tasks as more relevant, and (e) *learning for meaning* through variety, explanations and discriminating features so that emerging experts can reuse their knowledge and transfer their skills to conceptually new domains.

2. *Which causal connections are well established and which are more specula-tive? Which influences have the greatest impact?* Although causal connec-tions are not fully established at the present time, there are predictive relationships that are well established: (a) measured intelligence pre-dicts school grades and occupational outcomes in knowledge-intensive domains; this means that anything we can do to meaningfully boost measured intelligence in children will have payoffs for human capital development. Garlick (2002) suggests that we can do this by introducing

valued forms of thinking (for example, theory-based reasoning in order to learn for meaning) to students at a younger age than is currently the case in educational settings. (b) Deliberate training within a domain to become an expert is associated with increases in working memory capacity and skilled performance; this means that anything we can do to meaningfully boost deliberate training for children and adults with have payoffs for human capital development. As mentioned previously, Gobet (2005) has eight recommendations that include spending a lot of time on training (so that individuals can acquire basic knowledge), using a variety of exemplars in teaching so as to promote the abstraction of general, underlying principles and pointing out key discriminating features in the material learned so that students learn the proper frameworks essential in the domain and can reuse their knowledge and transfer their skills to conceptually similar domains. In other words, one cannot simply hope that students will pick up the right knowledge, but rather, one has to make sure it is taught and students have the opportunity to learn. (c) Teaching and modelling the use of explanations promotes learning and performance in knowledge-intensive domains. Wellman and Lagattuta (2004) as well as others (e.g., Siegler 2002) have shown that children's ability to explain or try to explain phenomena in a variety of domains enhances their understanding of underlying principles within those domains; this means that creating conditions within the classroom and the home that highlight the definition and importance of understanding a concept and *knowing when something is known* is related to successful performance in knowledge-intensive domains and is most likely the mechanism by which adaptive experts are created.

3. *What key questions are not being answered or asked? What new ways of framing the issues might be worth exploring?* The key questions that are being asked but, as yet, not being answered interface with educational, sociological and health interests:

(i) Using micro-level quasi-experimental and experimental research designs, are educational interventions able to improve children's learning and performance during a child's critical period for intellectual development? What are the specific subject topics that are most complementary to early instruction during a child's critical period for intellectual development?

(ii)   What are the best methods to follow in maximizing the use of exemplars in teaching students so that they will learn underlying, explanatory principles about the domain?

(iii) Do large-scale assessments such as the PISA include test items that attempt to measure adaptive expertise and, if so, what are the effects of student characteristics on their performance?

(iv)   What family or school characteristics promote or hinder the development of adaptive expertise?

(v)   How does socio-economic status (SES) moderate the development of adaptive expertise? Does a low SES minimize the variety of educational experiences required to abstract underlying, explanatory principles in a domain?

(vi)   Using longitudinal studies, how do prenatal and postnatal health relate to school grades, postsecondary participation and labour market participation and/or occupational outcomes?

(vii) What are the effects of early educational and psychological interventions on postnatal health, school grades, postsecondary participation and labour market participation/occupational outcomes?

Other key questions interface with social-organizational and economic interests, such as:

(i)   What are the effects of credentialing (versus education) in today's colleges and universities on innovative, adaptive expert thinking?

(ii)   If knowledge creation and innovation respond to economic incentives, what are the incentives that could be offered to educational systems in experimenting with more inventive approaches to student education?

4. *How can we look beyond conventional disciplinary boundaries? Where could those boundaries be breached in the most interesting, creative and useful manner, in terms of subject matter, methodology, or in any other respect?* At least in some Canadian jurisdictions, there are few opportunities to engage in the kind of research that might begin to seriously answer some of these key questions. In part, this is the case because in order to answer some of these questions, psychologists must have access to children and student populations in classroom settings. None of this research is possible without the full help of school districts and personnel. However, access to schools and children is increasingly more difficult to obtain because research takes time and teachers and other school

officials, for understandable reasons particularly pertaining to the need to cover curriculum and other activities, are unwilling to provide the necessary time and conditions to conduct intervention studies and other studies examining pedagogy. However, unless we are able to bridge this gap, these studies will not be conducted by Canadian researchers and instead will be conducted by others (e.g., Americans) who have access to what are known as partnership programs between schools and universities (also known as university laboratory schools). For example, through the National Network of Partnership Schools at Johns Hopkins University, researchers, educators, parents, students and community members work together to develop and maintain effective academic and other programs at the elementary, middle and high school level to study and modify student learning and success.

The research findings reported in this paper provide compelling evidence for introducing valued forms of thinking such as theory-based reasoning at earlier ages in the individual lifespan and emphasizing deliberate and sustained practice with the effort to improve working memory and performance for individuals of varying levels of intelligence across the lifespan. In sum, these research findings suggest that, across the lifespan, we can improve the odds for developing human capital. Ideally, we should start early in a child's life and continue our efforts. However, to be successful in our aims we must shift our standards and our expectations of students, increasing and widening what we see as possible for all members of society. Initiatives to understand and develop human capital must aim also to bring together those individuals who teach future workers and those individuals who can apply systematic methods for examining the best way to teach thinking, skilled performance and adaptive expertise. Otherwise, we cannot successfully address ways to develop what Davenport (2005) calls the single most important capability for knowledge workers: the management of personal information and the knowledge environment.

Notes

1. This is the field of psychology established by Sir Francis Galton, which focuses on all the behavioural and cognitive differences between people, including individual differences in personality, intellect and physical characteristics. Differences in intellect are often believed to be fixed and stable

characteristics and, therefore, differential psychology is sometimes referred to as trait psychology.

2.   Unless otherwise stated, the term "intelligence" in this paper refers to general intelligence or *g* measured by psychometric tests, which happen to be associated with the bulk of factor analytic research (Sternberg and Pretz 2005). Terms such as *traditional, psychometric, general,* and *measured* intelligence are used interchangeably to denote intelligence measured by tests of intelligence. The term *intelligence quotient* (IQ) is used to denote a score on an intelligence test. Crystallized and fluid intelligence are dimensions of general intelligence.

3.   Another body of literature, which is outside the scope of this paper, but relevant and worthy of mention is focused on the observed competition between neural systems in the management of impulsive behaviour, including perception of immediate versus delayed rewards (e.g., McClure *et al.* 2004). Portions of the limbic system have been shown to be implicated in decisions involving immediate rewards, whereas the lateral prefrontal cortex and posterior parietal cortex weigh in on decisions requiring greater deliberation and cognitive control.

References

Adams, M.J., R. Treiman and M. Pressley. 1998. "Reading, Writing, and Literacy," in *Handbook of Child Psychology,* Vol. 4, *Child Psychology in Practice,* ed. W. Damon, I. Sigel and K. Renninger. New York: Wiley, pp. 275-355.

Adey, P.S. and M. Shayer. 1994. *Really Raising Standards: Cognitive Intervention and Academic Achievement.* New York: Routledge.

Albert, R.S. 1978. "Observations and Suggestions Regarding Giftedness, Familial Influence and the Achievement of Eminence," *The Gifted Child Quarterly* 22:201-11.

Alexander, P.A., C.T. Sperl, M.M. Buehl, H. Fives and S. Chiu. 2004. "Modeling Domain Learning: Profiles from the Field of Special Education," *Journal of Educational Psychology* 96:545-57.

Allard, F. and J.L. Starkes. 1991. "Motor-Skill Experts in Sports, Dance, and Other Domains," in *Toward a General Theory of Expertise: Prospects and Limits,* ed. K.A. Ericsson and J. Smith. New York: Cambridge University Press, pp. 126-52.

Anderson, J.R. 1983. *The Architecture of Cognition.* Cambridge, MA: Harvard University Press.

Baddeley, A.D. 2000. "The Episodic Buffer: A New Component of Working Memory?" *Trends in Cognitive Sciences* 4:417-23.

— 2003. "Working Memory and Language: An Overview," *Journal of Communication Disorders* 36:189-208.

Barnett, S.M. and S.J. Ceci. 2002. "When and Where Do We Apply What We Learn? A Taxonomy for Far Transfer," *Psychological Bulletin* 128:612-37.

— 2005. "The Role of Transferable Knowledge," in *Cognition & Intelligence*, ed R.J. Sternberg and J.E. Pretz. Cambridge: Cambridge University Press, pp. 208-24.

Barnett, S.M. and B. Koslowski. 2002. "Adaptive Expertise: Effects of Type of Experience and the Level of Theoretical Understanding It Generates," *Thinking and Reasoning* 8:237-67.

Barrett, G.V. and R.L. Depinet. 1991. "A Reconsideration of Testing for Competence Rather than Intelligence," *American Psychologist* 46:1012-24.

Barrett, P.T., I. Daum and H.J. Eysenck. 1990. "Sensory Nerve Conduction and Intelligence: A Methodological Study," *Journal of Psychophysiology* 4:1-13.

Beckmann, J.F. and J. Guthke. 1995. "Complex Problem Solving, Intelligence, and Learning Ability," in *Complex Problem Solving: The European Perspective*, ed P.A. Frensch and J. Funke. Hillsdale, NJ: Erlbaum, pp. 3-25.

Bloom, B.S. 1984. "The 2-Sigma Problem: The Search for Methods of Group Instruction as Effective as One-to-One Tutoring," *Educational Researcher* 13:4-16.

Bransford, J.D. and B.S. Stein. 1984. *The Ideal Problem Solver: A Guide for Improving Thinking, Learning, and Creativity*. New York: Freeman.

Brown, A.L. 1989. "Analogical Learning and Transfer: What Develops?" in *Similarity and Analogical Reasoning*, ed. S. Vosniadou and A. Ortony. Cambridge: Cambridge University Press, pp. 369-412.

Carpenter, P.A. and M. Just. 1975. "Sentence Comprehension: A Psycholinguistic Processing Model of Verification," *Psychological Review* 82:45-73.

Carpenter, P.A., M.A. Just and P. Shell. 1990. "What One Intelligence Test Measures: A Theoretical Account of Processing in the Raven's Progressive Matrices Test," *Psychological Review* 97:404-31.

Carroll, J.B. 1993. *Human Cognitive Abilities*. Cambridge: Cambridge University Press.

Catrambone, R. and K.J. Holyoak. 1989. "Overcoming Contextual Limitations on Problem-Solving Transfer," *Journal of Experimental Psychology: Learning, Memory, and Cognition* 15:1147-56.

Cattell, R.B. 1971. *Abilities: Their Structure, Growth, and Action*. Boston: Houghton Mifflin.

Ceci, S. J. 2000. "So Near and Yet so Far: Lingering Questions about the Use of Measures of General Intelligence for College Admission and Employment Screening," *Psychology, Public Policy, and Law* 6:233-52.

Ceci, S.J. and J. Liker. 1986a. "A Day at the Races: IQ, Expertise, and Cognitive Complexity," *Journal of Experimental Psychology: General* 115:255-66.

— 1986b. "Academic versus Non-Academic Intelligence: An Experimental Separation," in *Practical Intelligence: Nature and Origins of Competence in the Everyday World*, ed. R.J. Sternberg and R.K. Wagner. New York: Cambridge University Press, pp. 119-42.

Ceci, S.J. and A. Ruiz. 1992. "The Role of General Ability in Cognitive Complexity: A Case Study of Expertise," in *The Psychology of Expertise*, ed. R. Hoffman. New York: Springer-Verlag, pp. 218-30.

— 1993. "Transfer, Abstractness, and Intelligence," in *Transfer on Trial: Intelligence, Cognition, and Instruction*, ed. D.K. Detterman and R.J. Sternberg. Norwood, NJ: Ablex, pp. 168-91.

Charness, N. and R.S. Schultetus. 1999. "Knowledge and Expertise," in *Handbook of Applied Cognition*, ed. F.T. Durso, R.S. Nickerson, R.W. Schvaneveldt, S.T. Dumais, D.S. Lindsay and M. Chi. Chichester, NY: Wiley, pp. 57-81.

Chase, W.G. and H.A. Simon. 1973. "Perception in Chess," *Cognitive Psychology* 4:55-81.

Cheng, P.W. and K.J. Holyoak. 1985. "Pragmatic Reasoning Schemas," *Cognitive Psychology* 17:391-416.

— 1989. "On the Natural Selection of Reasoning Theories," *Cognition* 33:285-313.

Chi, M.T.H., N. de Leeuw, M.H. Chiu and C. LaVancher. 1994. "Eliciting Self-Explanations Improves Understanding," *Cognitive Science* 18:439-77.

Chi, M.T.H., P. Feltovich and R. Glaser. 1981. "Categorization and Representation of Physics Problems by Experts and Novices," *Cognitive Science* 5:121-52.

Chi, M.T.H., R. Glaser and M.J. Farr, eds. 1988. *The Nature of Expertise*. Hillsdale, NJ: Lawrence Erlbaum Associates.

Cosmides, L. 1989. "The Logic of Social Exchange: Has Natural Selection Shaped How Humans Reason? Studies with the Wason Selection Task," *Cognition* 31:187-276.

Cosmides, L. and J. Tooby. 1996. "Are Humans Good Intuitive Statisticians after All? Rethinking Some Conclusions from the Literature on Judgement under Uncertainty," *Cognition* 58:1-73.

Cummins, D.D. 1992. "Role of Analogical Reasoning in the Induction of Problem Categories," *Journal of Experimental Psychology: Learning, Memory, and Cognition* 18:1103-24.

Davenport, T.H. 2005. *Thinking for a Living*. Cambridge, MA: Harvard Business School Press.

Deary, I.J. and P.G. Caryl. 1993. "Intelligence, EEG, and Evoked Potentials," in *Biological Approaches to the Study of Human Intelligence*, ed. P.A. Vernon. Norwood, NJ: Ablex, pp. 259-315.

de Groot, A.D. 1965. *Thought and Choice in Chess*. The Hague: Mouton.

Dunbar, K. 1995. "How Scientists Really Reason: Scientific Reasoning in Real-World Laboratories," in *The Nature of Insight*, ed. R.J. Sternberg and J.E. Davidson. Cambridge, MA: MIT Press, pp. 365-95.

Dunn, J., J. Brown, C. Slomkowski, C. Tesla and L. Youngblade. 1991. "Young Children's Understanding of Other People's Feelings and Beliefs: Individual Differences and their Antecedents," *Child Development* 62:1352-66.

Duncan, J., P. Burgess and H. Emslie. 1995. "Fluid Intelligence after Frontal Lobe Lesions," *Neuropsychologia* 33:261-68.

Duncan, J., R.J. Seitz, J. Kolodny, D. Bor, H. Herzog, A. Ahmed, F.N. Newell and H. Emslie. 2000. "A Neural Basis for General Intelligence," *Science* 289:457-60.

Engle, R.W., S.W. Tuholski, J.E. Laughlin and A.R.A. Conway. 1999. "Working Memory, Short-Term Memory, and General Fluid Intelligence: A Latent Variable Approach," *Journal of Experimental Psychology: General* 128:309-31.

Ericsson, K.A. 1996. "The Acquisition of Expert Performance," in *The Road to Excellence*, ed. K.A. Ericsson. Mahwah, NJ: Lawrence Erlbaum Associates, pp. 1-50.

Ericsson, K.A. and N. Charness. 1994. "Expert Performance: Its Structure and Acquisition," *American Psychologist* 49:725-47.

Ericsson, K.A. and W. Kintsch. 1995. "Long-Term Working Memory," *Psychological Review* 102:211-45.

Ericsson, K.A. and H.A. Simon. 1993. *Protocol Analysis: Verbal Reports as Data*. Cambridge, MA: MIT Press.

Ericsson, K.A. and J. Smith, eds. 1991. *Toward a General Theory of Expertise: Prospects and Limits*. New York: Cambridge University Press.

Ericsson, K.A., R.T. Krampe and C. Tesch-Romer. 1993. "The Role of Deliberate Practice in the Acquisition of Expert Performance," *Psychological Review* 100:363-406.

Fiez, J.A. 2001. "Bridging the Gap between Neuroimaging and Neuropsychology: Using Working Memory as a Case Study," *Journal of Clinical and Experimental Neuropsychology* 23:19-31.

Funke, J. 1995. "Experimental Research on Complex Problem Solving," in *Complex Problem Solving. The European Perspective*, ed. P.A. Frensch and J. Funke. Hillsdale, NJ: Erlbaum, pp. 243-68.

Garlick, D. 2002. "Understanding the Nature of the General Factor of Intelligence: The Role of Individual Differences in Neural Plasticity as an Explanatory Mechanism," *Psychological Review* 109:116-36.

Gentner, D. 1999. "Analogy," in *The MIT Encyclopedia of the Cognitive Sciences*, ed. R.A. Wilson and F.C. Keil. Cambridge, MA: MIT Press, pp. 17-19.

Gick, M.L. and K.J. Holyoak. 1983. "Schema Induction and Analogical Transfer," *Cognitive Psychology* 15:1-38.

Gigerenzer, G. and K. Hug. 1992. "Domain-Specific Reasoning: Social Contracts, Cheating, and Perspective Change, *Cognition* 43:127-71.

Gigerenzer, G., P.M. Todd and the ABC Research Group, eds. 1999. *Simple Heuristics That Make Us Smart*. New York: Oxford University Press.

Girotto, V. 2004. "Task Understanding," in *The Nature of Reasoning*, ed. J.P. Leighton and R.J. Sternberg. New York: Cambridge University Press, pp. 103-28.

Gladwell, M. 2005. *Blink: The Power of Thinking without Thinking*. New York: Little Brown.

Gobet, F. 1997. "A Pattern-Recognition Theory of Search in Expert Problem Solving," *Thinking and Reasoning* 3:291-313.

— 2005. "Chunking Models of Expertise: Implications for Education," *Applied Cognitive Psychology* 19:183-204.

Gobet, F. and H.A. Simon. 1996. "Templates in Chess Memory: A Mechanism for Recalling Several Boards," *Cognitive Psychology* 31:1-40.

Haier, R.J. 1993. "Cerebral Glucose Metabolism and Intelligence," in *Biological Approaches to the Study of Human Intelligence*, ed. P.A. Vernon. Norwood, NJ: Ablex, pp. 317-32.

Haier, R.J., B.V. Siegel, A. MacLachlan, E. Soderling, S. Lottenberg and M.S. Buchsbaum. 1992. "Regional Glucose Metabolic Changes after Learning a Complex Visuospatial/Motor Task: A Positron Emission Topographic Study," *Brain Research* 570:134-43.

Haier, R.J., B.V. Siegel, K.H. Nuechterlein, E. Hazlett, J.C. Wu, J. Paek, H.L. Browning and M.S. Buchsbaum. 1988. "Cortical Glucose Metabolic Rate Correlates of Abstract Reasoning and Attention Studied with Positron Emission Tomography," *Intelligence* 12:199-217.

Haier, R.J., B. Siegel, C. Tang, L. Abel and M.S. Buchsbaum. 1992. "Intelligence and Changes in Regional Cerebral Glucose Metabolic Rate Following Learning," *Intelligence* 16:415-26.

Hambrick, D.Z., M.J. Kane and R.W. Engle. 2005. "The Role of Working Memory in Higher-Level Cognition," in *Cognition & Intelligence*, ed. R.J. Sternberg and J.E. Pretz. Cambridge: Cambridge University Press, pp. 104-21.

Hansen, K.T., J.J. Heckman and K.J. Mullen. 2004. "The Effect of Schooling and Ability on Achievement Test Scores," *Journal of Econometrics* 121:39-98

Hatano, G. 1982. "Cognitive Consequences of Practice in Culture Specific Procedural Skills," *The Quarterly Newsletter of the Laboratory of Comparative Human Cognition* 4:15-18.

— 1988. "Social and Motivational Bases for Mathematical Understanding," in *Children's Mathematics*, ed. G.B. Saxe and M. Gearhart. San Francisco: Jossey-Bass, pp. 55-70.

Hatano, G. and K. Inagaki. 1984. "Two Courses of Expertise," *Research and Clinical Center for Child Development (Annual Report)* 83:27-36.

— 1986. "Two Courses of Expertise," in *Child Development and Education in Japan,* ed. H.W. Stevenson and H. Azuma. New York: W.H. Freeman & Co., pp. 262-72.

Haverty, L., K.R. Koedinger, D. Klahr and M.W. Alibali. 2000. "Solving Inductive Reasoning Problems in Mathematics: Not-So-Trivial Pursuit," *Cognitive Science* 24:249-98.

Holding, D.H. 1992. "Theories of Chess Skill." *Psychological Research* 54:10-16.

Holyoak, K.J. 1991. "Symbolic Connectionism: Toward Third-Generation Theories of Expertise," in *Toward a General Theory of Expertise: Prospects and Limits,* ed. K.A. Ericsson and J. Smith. New York: Cambridge University Press, pp. 301-35.

Horn, J.L. and J. Noll. 1994. "A System for Understanding Cognitive Capabilities: A Theory and the Evidence on which It Is Based," in *Current Topics in Human Intelligence,* Vol. 4, *Theories of Intelligence,* ed. D. Detterman. Norwood, NJ: Ablex, pp. 151-204.

Hunt, E. 2005. "Information Processing and Intelligence," in *Cognition & Intelligence,* ed. R.J. Sternberg and J.E. Pretz. Cambridge: Cambridge University Press, pp. 1-25.

Jensen, A.R. 2005. "Mental Chronometry and the Unification of Differential Psychology," in *Cognition & Intelligence,* ed. R.J. Sternberg and J.E. Pretz. Cambridge: Cambridge University Press, pp. 26-50.

Johnson, A. 2003. "Procedural Memory and Skill Acquisition," in *Experimental Psychology,* ed. A.F. Healy and R.W. Proctor, in *Handbook of Psychology,* Vol. 4, ed. I.B. Weiner. New York: Wiley, pp. 499-523.

Johnson, P.E., F. Hassebrock, A.S. Duran and J.H. Moller. 1982. "Multimethod Study of Clinical Judgement," *Organizational Behavior and Human Decision Processes* 30:201-30.

Johnson-Laird, P.N. 1999. "Deductive Reasoning," *Annual Review of Psychology* 50:109-35.

Kessels, R.P.C., A. Postma, E.M. Wijnalda and H.F. de Haan. 2000. "Frontal-Lobe Involvement in Spatial Memory: Evidence from PET, fMRI, and Lesion Studies," *Neuropsychology Review* 10:101-13.

Kuhn, D. 2001. "How Do People Know?" *Psychological Science* 12:1-8.

Kyllonen, P.C. 1996. "Is Working Memory Capacity Spearman's *g*?" in *Human Abilities: Their Nature and Measurement,* ed. I. Dennis and P. Tapsfield. Mahwah, NJ: Erlbaum, pp. 49-75.

Kyllonen, P.C. and R.E. Christal. 1990. "Reasoning Ability Is (Little More Than) Working-Memory Capacity?" *Intelligence* 14:389-433.

Leighton, J.P. 2004. "The Assessment of Logical Reasoning," in *The Nature of Reasoning*, ed. J.P. Leighton and R.J. Sternberg. New York: Cambridge University Press, pp. 291-312.

— 2006. "Teaching and Assessing Deductive Reasoning Skills," *Journal of Experimental Education* 74:109-36.

Leighton, J.P. and G.L. Bisanz. 2003. "Children's and Adults' Knowledge and Models of Reasoning about the Ozone Layer and Its Depletion," *International Journal of Science Education* 25(1):117-39.

Leighton, J.P. and R.J. Sternberg. 2003. "Reasoning and Problem Solving," in *Experimental Psychology*, ed. A.F. Healy and R.W. Proctor, in *Handbook of Psychology*, Vol. 4, ed. I.B. Weiner. New York: Wiley, pp. 623-48.

— 2004. *The Nature of Reasoning*. New York: Cambridge University Press.

Liberman, N. and Y. Klar. 1996. "Hypothesis Testing in Wason's Selection Task: Social Exchange, Cheating Detection, or Task Understanding," *Cognition* 58:127-56.

Loewenstein, J., L. Thompson and D. Gentner. 1999. "Analogical Encoding Facilitates Knowledge Transfer in Negotiation," *Psychonomic Bulletin & Review* 6:586-97.

Manktelow, K. I. and D.E. Over. 1991. "Social Roles and Utilities in Reasoning with Deontic Conditionals," *Cognition* 39:85-105.

Manktelow, K.I., N. Fairley, S.G. Kilparick and D.E. Over. 2000. "Pragmatics and Strategies for Practical Reasoning," in *Deductive Reasoning and Strategies*, ed. W. Schaeken, G. De Vooght and G. d'Ydewalle. Mahwah, NJ: Lawrence Erlbaum Associates, pp. 23-48.

McClure, S.M., D.I. Laibson, G. Loewenstein and J.D. Cohen. 2004. "Separate Neural Systems Value Immediate and Delayed Monetary Rewards," *Science* 306:503-07.

Meins, E., C. Fernyhough, R. Wainright, M.D. Gupta, E. Fradley and M. Tuckey. 2003. "Maternal Mind-Mindedness and Attachment Security as Predictors of Theory of Mind Understanding," *Child Development* 73:1715-26.

Miller, E.M. 1994. "Intelligence and Brain Myelination: A Hypothesis," *Personality and Individual Differences* 17:803-32.

Nairne, J. 2003. "Sensory and Working Memory, in *Experimental Psychology*, ed. A.F. Healy and R.W. Proctor, in *Handbook of Psychology*, Vol. 4, ed. I.B. Weiner. New York: Wiley, pp. 423-44.

Neubauer, A.C. 1997. "The Mental Speed Approach to the Assessment of Intelligence," in *Advances in Cognition and Educational Practice: Reflections on the Concept of Intelligence*, ed. J. Kingma and W. Tomic. Greenwich, CT: JAI Press, pp. 149-74.

Neubauer, A.C. and A. Fink. 2003. "Fluid Intelligence and Neural Efficiency: Effects of Task Complexity and Sex," *Personality and Individual Differences* 35:811-27.

— 2005. "Basic Information Processing and the Psychophysiology of Intelligence," in *Cognition & Intelligence*, ed. R.J. Sternberg and J.E. Pretz. Cambridge: Cambridge University Press, pp. 68-87.

Neubauer, A.C., A. Fink and D.G. Schrausser. 2002. "Intelligence and Neural Efficiency: The Influence of Task Content and Sex on the Brain-IQ Relationship," *Intelligence* 30:515-36.

Neubauer, A.C., H.H. Freudenthaler and G. Pfurtscheller. 1995. "Intelligence and Spatio-Temporal Patterns of Event-Related Desynchronization," *Intelligence* 20:249-67.

Neubauer, A.C., G. Sange and G. Pfurtscheller. 1999. "Psychometric Intelligence and Event-Related Desynchronization During Performance of a Letter Matching Task," in *Event-Related Desynchronization (ERD) and Related Oscillatory EEG Phenomena of the Awake Brain. Handbook of EEG and Clinical Neurophysiology*, Revised Series, ed. G. Pfurtscheller and F.H. Lopes da Silva. Amsterdam: Elsevier, pp. 219-31.

Newell, A. and H.A. Simon. 1972. *Human Problem Solving*. Englewood Cliffs, NJ: Prentice-Hall.

Newstead, S.E. and J.St.B.T Evans. 1993. "Mental Models as an Explanation of Belief Bias Effects in Syllogistic Reasoning," *Cognition* 46:93-97.

Nickerson, R. 2004. "Teaching Reasoning," in *The Nature of Reasoning*, ed. J.P. Leighton and R.J. Sternberg. New York: Cambridge University Press, pp. 410-42.

Norris, S.P., J.P. Leighton and L.M. Phillips. 2004. "What Is at Stake in Knowing the Content and Capabilities of Children's Minds? A Case for Basing High Stakes Tests on Cognitive Models," *Theory and Research in Education* 2:283-308.

Parks, R.W., D.A. Loewenstein, K.L. Dodrill, W.W. Barker, F. Yoshii, J.Y. Chang, A. Emran, A. Apicella, W.A. Sheramata and R. Duara. 1988. "Cerebral Metabolic Effects of a Verbal Fluency Test: A PET Scan Study," *Journal of Clinical Experimental Neuropsychology* 10:565-75.

Perkins, D.N. 1995. *Outsmarting IQ: The Emerging Science of Learnable Intelligence*. New York: The Free Press.

Pfurtscheller, G. and A. Aranibar. 1977. "Event-Related Cortical Desynchronization Detected by Power Measurements of Scalp EEG," *Electroencephalography and Clinical Neurophysiology* 42:817-26.

Pfurtscheller, G. and F.H. Lopes da Silva. 1999. "Event-Related EEG/EMG Synchronization and Desynchronization: Basic Principles," *Clinical Neurophysiology* 110:1842-57.

Pine, K.J. and R.S. Siegler. 2003. "The Role of Explanatory Activity in Increasing the Generality of Thinking." Paper presented at the Biennial Meeting of the Society for Research in Child Development, Tampa, FL.

Pollard, P. and J.St.B.T. Evans. 1987. "Content and Context Effects in Reasoning," *American Journal of Psychology* 100:41-60.

Prabhakaran, V., J.A.L. Smith, J.E. Desmond, H. Glover and J.D.E. Gabrieli. 1997. "Neural Substrates of Fluid Reasoning: An fMRI Study of Neocortical Activation during Performance of the Raven's Progressive Matrices Test," *Cognitive Psychology* 33:43-63.

Priest, A.G. and R.O. Lindsay. 1992. "New Light on Novice-Expert Differences in Physics Problem Solving," *British Journal of Psychology* 83:389-405.

Rattermann, M. and D. Gentner. 1998. "More Evidence for a Relational Shift in the Development of Analogy: Children's Performance on a Causal-Mapping Task," *Cognitive Development* 13:453-78.

Reed, T.E. and A.R. Jensen. 1991. "Arm Nerve Conduction Velocity (NCV), Brain NCV, Reaction Time, and Intelligence," *Intelligence* 15:33-48.

— 1992. "Conduction Velocity in a Brain Nerve Pathway of Normal Adults Correlates with Intelligence Level," *Intelligence* 16:259-72.

Roberts, M.J. and E.J. Newton, eds. 2005. *Methods of Thought: Individual Differences in Reasoning Strategies.* New York: Psychology Press.

Salomon, G. and D.N. Perkins. 1989. "Rocky Roads to Transfer: Rethinking Mechanisms of a Neglected Phenomenon," *Educational Psychologist* 24:113-42.

Schmidt, F.L. and J. Hunter. 2004. "General Mental Ability in the World of Work: Occupational Attainment and Job Performance," *Journal of Personality and Social Psychology* 86:162-73.

Siegler, R.S. 2002. "Microgenetic Studies of Self-Explanation," in *Microdevelopment: Transition Processes in Development and Learning,* ed. N. Granott and J. Parziale. New York: Cambridge University Press, pp. 31-58.

Sperber, D., F. Cara and V. Girotto. 1995. "Relevance Theory Explains the Selection Task," *Cognition* 57:31-95.

Stanovich, K.E. and R.F. West. 1998. "Individual Differences in Rational Thought," *Journal of Experimental Psychology: General* 127:161-88.

— 2000. "Individual Differences in Reasoning: Implications for the Rationality Debate?" *Behavioral and Brain Sciences* 23:645-726.

Stanovich, K.E., W.C. Sá and R.F. West. 2004. "Individual Differences in Reasoning," in *The Nature of Reasoning*, ed. J.P. Leighton and R.J. Sternberg. New York: Cambridge University Press, pp. 375-409.

Stenning, K. and P. Yule. 1997. "Image and Language in Human Reasoning: A Syllogistic Illustration," *Cognitive Psychology* 34:109-59.

Sternberg, R.J. 1999. "Intelligence As Developing Expertise," *Contemporary Educational Psychology* 24:359-75.

Sternberg, R.J. and T. Ben-Zeev. 2001. *Complex Cognition: The Psychology of Human Thought*. New York: Oxford University Press.

Sternberg, R.J. and E.L. Grigorenko, eds. 2002. *The General Factor of Intelligence*. Mahwah, NJ: Erlbaum.

Sternberg, R.J. and J.E. Pretz, eds. 2005. *Cognition and Intelligence*. New York: Cambridge University Press.

Sternberg, R.J., C. Nokes, P.W. Geissler, R. Prince, F. Okatcha, D.A. Bundy and E.L. Grigorenko. 2001. "The Relationship between Academic and Practical Intelligence: A Case Study in Kenya," *Intelligence* 29:401-18.

Tomlinson-Keasey, C. and T.D. Little. 1990. "Predicting Educational Attainment, Occupational Achievement, Intellectual Skill, and Personal Adjustment among Gifted Men and Women," *Journal of Educational Psychology* 82:442-55.

Vernon, P.A., ed. 1987. *Speed of Information Processing and Intelligence*. Norwood, NJ: Ablex.

Wason, P.C. 1966. "Reasoning," in *New Horizons in Psychology*, ed. B.M. Foss. Oxford: Penguin.

Wellman, H.M. and K.H. Lagattuta. 2004. "Theory of Mind for Learning and Teaching: The Nature and Role of Explanation," *Cognitive Development* 19:479-97.

Wenke, D., P.A. Frensch and J. Funke. 2005. "Complex Problem Solving and Intelligence," in *Cognition & Intelligence*, ed. R.J. Sternberg and J.E. Pretz. Cambridge: Cambridge University Press, pp. 160-87.

6

Human Capital Development and Education

ROBERT CROCKER

Economic research yields good evidence of positive economic and social returns to education. This paper examines the evidence on the returns to educational resource inputs. This research has not yielded many consistent results useful for policy development. However, there are indications that resource use is more important than resource allocations. It is also clear that the main value of higher achievement is not directly on economic returns but on access to higher education. A number of suggestions are made for a more systematic research agenda on resource use and on the mediating effects of school and classroom practices on outcomes.

Introduction

Overview of Human Capital Theory

Human capital theory holds that the well-being of a society is a function not only of the traditional stocks of financial capital, labour and natural resources but also of the knowledge and skills of individuals. This "human capital" can be used like any other asset to generate outcomes of value to individuals and society. In particular, the theory predicts that increased knowledge and skill will yield improved economic outcomes for both individuals and societies. This idea has attained increased prominence in the past couple of decades because of the widely held view that we are in a "knowledge economy," in which knowledge and skill convey a greater premium than in the past.

Sweetland (1996) traces the origins of human capital theory to the work of Adam Smith in the eighteenth century and John Stuart Mill in the nineteenth. However, the modern formulation of human capital as part the overall economic production function is generally traced to mid-twentieth century Nobel Prize winning works by Schultz and Becker. Both of these works have had fairly recent updates (Schultz 1993; Becker 1993). Earlier works by Freidman and Kuznets (1945) and Robert Solow (cited in Sweetland 1996) were also major contributors to development of the theory. The primary concern of these economists was why economic development has advanced faster than the growth of the stocks of traditional capital and labour and, more specifically, how to explain the large residual component in traditional economic production functions. Human capital theory locates this explanation in knowledge and skill and particularly in education and work experience as the primary source of these attributes.

Human Capital Theory and Education

Education is a key element of human capital theory because it is viewed as the primary means of developing knowledge and skill and because level of education is a way of quantifying the quality of labour. Mincer (1974) is generally credited with developing the core model designed to explain differences in individual income as a function of level of education and work experience. Mincer's *human capital earnings function* has income as the dependent variable and years of education the main independent variable.[1] Work experience is also typically included in the model as a proxy for unobserved sources of acquisition of knowledge and skill.

Much subsequent human capital research, especially that conducted by economists, can be seen mainly as attempts to refine and extend the Mincer model. A large number of specific issues have been investigated. Of particular interest is the effect of gains in income through education relative to the opportunity costs in lost work time in attaining higher education levels. There is also the question of whether education is of value because it contributes to knowledge and skill or whether education is merely a proxy for underlying ability. This view leads to the competing concept that education is not a cause of economic outcomes but is more of a screening device used by employers to select those most likely to have the desired abilities. For example, it may be argued that those most likely to persist in schooling are those who possess other attributes most valuable to employers. The requirement for specific credentials for access to many high-level occupations may be seen as an extreme example of the screening idea. This is illustrated by studies of *sheepskin effects,* or the additive effects of possessing a credential over that of years of education (Ferrer and Riddell 2002).

A broader issue is the extent to which public or private educational expenditures represent investment rather than consumption. The private return on educational expenditures has been widely investigated and is now rarely questioned. The return to society is less well-established and more difficult to model because of the myriad of possible causes (and effects if we go beyond economic outcomes). This issue is at the heart of the debate over the proportions of educational costs that should be borne by individuals versus governments. Larger individual benefits lead to an argument for individuals bearing a larger proportion of the cost. Larger societal outcomes present an argument for greater public investment. This issue is also linked to policies in which education is considered a means of reducing poverty and of moving individuals from reliance on income support to self-reliance.

Focus of this Paper

Almost all of the research on the place of education in human capital development has been concerned with the economic returns to education. Most of this research has taken the form of attempts to estimate the individual wage premiums associated with higher levels of education and, more recently to separate the causal effects of education from those of other confounding factors. Societal returns have generally been inferred from individual returns, although some comparative studies have focused more specifically on country-level returns. Because another paper in this series is specifically concerned with economic returns, this area of research receives only brief treatment here. In effect, the first two of the above questions are left to the economics paper and we focus on the remaining questions. More specifically, this paper focuses on human capital theory as a driving force for recent research and policy-making in education. Thus, rather than using the conventional model of education as input and economic return as outcome, we examine education policies and practices, and particularly resource allocations as inputs with educational attainment and achievement as outcomes.

Aside from the contribution of education to the overall economic production function, human capital theory also underlies studies of the impact of specific forms of investment in education and of differing uses of the resources available to education. Under this approach, educational attainment becomes the proximate dependent variable and educational resource allocations and uses the independents. The underlying issue here is not the economic return to education but the cost-effectiveness of uses of educational resources. Ideally, an argument can be made that the preferred educational structures and strategies are those that yield the greatest attainment or achievement for the least cost. For example, the desired balance of expenditures at different levels of education (early childhood, elementary/secondary, postsecondary, lifelong learning, skills training) can be related to the relative returns to these levels. Unfortunately, this kind of cost-benefit analysis is not easy to carry out and is not necessarily widely supported in a political environment which considers any form of educational expenditure to be desirable and where, until fairly recently, educational expenditures have been viewed as outcome rather than input.

While comprehensive cost-benefits analyses continue to elude educational researchers, there have been many studies of the allocation and use of educational resources. Many recent large-scale cross-national and, in Canada, cross-provincial comparative studies are concerned with the relative performance of various jurisdictions, as measured by a wide variety of indicators. More specific studies have examined such factors as school size, class size, overall expenditures, teachers' salaries and the like as contributors to improved performance, all under the implicit assumption that higher educational performance is a societal good and that the goal is to determine how best to use the resources available to education.

Figure 1 gives a simplified schematic model designed to capture the distinctions made here. For economists and other social researchers, the main focus is on the bottom two layers of the model. For educational researchers the main interest is on teaching and learning processes. The usual end points for the educational researcher, namely attainment and achievement, are the starting points for the economist.

It is important to note that this model is intended to capture the thrust of research on human capital development as it relates to formal education. Other sources of knowledge and skill such as work experience itself and informal and non-formal learning, are not included here as these have not been the subject of much research. Similarly, the concept of lifelong learning, which has become a prominent feature of many educational policy and mission statements, is not strictly a part of the model, again because there is much advocacy and sentiment but little research around this idea.

Figure 1. Conceptual Model of Education and Human Capital Development

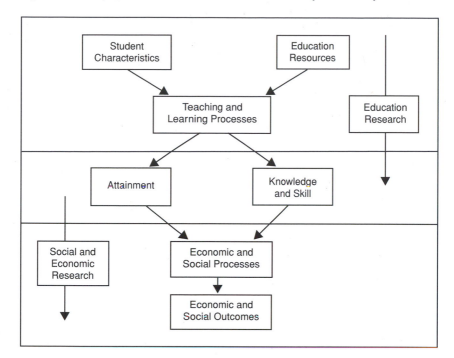

This paper does not address the large body of research on the relationships among student characteristics, teaching and learning processes and outcomes. While this represents a core area of educational research in its own right, the theoretical basis for most of the research in this area is found mainly in the psychology of learning, and not in human capital theory. An argument will be made later in this paper for the need for convergence of resource-outcome and process-outcome research. However, a review of the latter is beyond the scope of the paper.

Human Capital Development and Educational Policy

Whatever the level of empirical support for human capital theory, it is not difficult to document the extent to which this theory forms the basis for educational policy. Virtually all major policy statements in education begin with reference to the knowledge society and the importance of education for individual, state or provincial prosperity.

Indeed, even though a case can be made that education has other important goals, it is difficult to imagine that the current high level of both individual and public financial commitment to education could be sustained without an abiding faith in the economic value of education.

On an international level the economic significance of education is a focus of research by the Organisation for Economic Co-operation and Development (OECD). A few statements from recent OECD publications illustrate the extent to which one of the world's foremost economic policy organizations has taken the importance of education to economic development as given.

> Educational attainment is becoming increasingly important, relative to other factors, in shaping young people's life chances. Changing economic and social conditions — information and communication technologies, the globalisation of economic activity, greater personal responsibility and autonomy in all aspects of life — have given knowledge and skills an increasingly central role in the economic success of individuals and nations. In addition to the growing economic importance of human capital, the social returns to learning, in the form of enhanced personal well-being and greater social cohesion, are also significant (OECD 2005*a*).

> Education is an investment that can help foster economic growth, contribute to personal social development and reduce social inequality. Like any investment, it involves both costs and returns. Some of the returns are monetary, and directly related to the labour market, while others are personal, social, cultural or more broadly economic. Some returns accrue to the individual while others benefit society in general, for example, in the form of a more literate and productive population (OECD 1996).

The periodic OECD *Education at a Glance* (OECD 2005*a*) reports have become standard references on educational inputs and outcomes. Comparative statistics on educational inputs, processes and outcomes are taken seriously as measures of educational quality. The underlying assumption is that all of this does have something to do with economic productivity. Indeed, such indicators as postsecondary expenditures or participation rates are sometimes taken as outcomes in themselves, on the apparent assumption that these are proxies for economic prosperity.

Within Canada, although education is under provincial jurisdiction, a large federal government presence can be found in areas in which education touches on labour market development. Traditionally, this has been confined to the postsecondary level, where skills development has been a major element in successive federal economic development strategies. However, there is increased evidence of a federal presence in early childhood, K–12, literacy and adult basic education, albeit in ways intended not to raise too many jurisdictional red flags.[2] It is not difficult to identify an explicit human capital development focus in federal agencies concerned with education and labour market development.

To illustrate the point, the federal government's 2004 budget included provision for a new "workplace skills strategy." The description of this strategy opens with the following statement:

> At present, the Canadian economy is being transformed by global, technological, and demographic shifts, each of which has serious skills implications. In the emerging knowledge-based and globalized economy, a nation's primary competitive advantage will lie in the strategic use of human resources. Improving Canada's competitive position means ensuring that Canadian workers have the skills, knowledge and supportive environment needed to excel, to contribute to innovation, and to remain flexible and resilient in the face of ever-changing work demands.

> Human capital development is a shared responsibility of both public and private sectors, with the Government of Canada helping to play a leadership and partnership role (www.hrsdc.gc.ca/en/ws/initiatives/wsi/WSI_proposal_overview.shtml).

In a similar vein, the mission statement of the National Literacy Secretariat begins with the following statement:

> Forty-two percent of Canadians aged 16–65 do not have the literacy skills required for full participation in the knowledge economy. The National Literacy Secretariat (NLS) works to promote literacy as an essential component of a learning society and to make Canada's social, economic and political life more accessible to people with weak literacy skills (www.hrsdc.gc.ca/en/hip/lld/nls/About/aboutus.shtml).

Similar statements can be found in the documentation for dozens of other federal government programs providing support to students, workers, schools and researchers.

The situation is no different at the provincial level. For example, New Brunswick has recently developed a "prosperity plan" which places education at the forefront of a range of strategies to increase economic activity in that province. This plan states:

> New Brunswick will have a quality education system that fosters a culture of lifelong learning for citizens from the earliest moment, aspires to excellence and achievement at all times, and ensures graduates have the knowledge and are well prepared to successfully participate in today's knowledge economy (Government of New Brunswick 2002).

A similar sentiment can be found in the most recent business plan of the Alberta Ministry of Advanced Education.

Alberta's vision

> A vibrant and prosperous province where Albertans enjoy a superior quality of life and are confident about the future for themselves and their children.

Mission of the Ministry of Advanced Education

> In support of Alberta's vision, Advanced Education's mission is for Alberta to be a learning society where all Albertans have access to the opportunity to develop the learning, work and life skills they need to achieve their aspirations and maximize their potential to the benefit of themselves and Alberta (www.advancededucation.gov.ab.ca/department/businessplan/bp2005-08.pdf).

A similar thrust can be found in ministerial statements, curriculum documents, accountability reports and other sources, to the point where there is little doubt that human capital development is one of the primary drivers of educational policy. Indeed, it may be argued that much of the increase in efforts at accountability and outcome assessment in education is driven by the need for the system to be seen as productive in achieving the outcomes that are key to human capital development.

Of course, this perspective is not without its critics. Aside from researchers who continue to cast doubt on the empirical validity of human capital theory, there are many who believe that education is about more than providing a ready supply of skilled workers, and that the system has responded too much to government and corporate labour market demands. Critics of the accountability movement are particularly vocal in decrying what they believe is a "corporate agenda" now pervading educational policy and the resulting homogenization of the system (Puk 1999; Wien and Dudley-Marling 1998). Some have even called on teachers to actively resist this movement (Hyslop-Margison 2000)

Research on Human Capital Development and Education

Economic Returns to Attainment, Credentials and Performance

The classic human capital function takes the form of a regression equation with wages as the outcome and years of education (attainment) and work experience as predictors. However, some fairly recent studies have attempted to include knowledge and skill directly into the model. Since this research has not received the same amount of attention as the research on levels of education, and since some Canadian studies can be found, this area is examined briefly here.

Krahn and Lowe (1998) used data from the International Adult Literacy Study (IALS) to examine the match between literacy skills possessed by Canadian adults and their use in the workplace. The study showed that almost three-quarters of Canadian workers are employed in a job appropriate to their literacy skills. Of the one-fourth of workers exhibiting a mismatch, almost four times more have higher literacy levels than are demanded by their jobs (literacy surplus), than are in jobs requiring higher skills than possessed by the worker (literacy deficit). Literacy surplus was found to be more common among women and younger workers. The study also provided some evidence that literacy skills may be lost if not used.

In a follow-up study, Krahn and Bolby (1999) used data from the National Graduates Surveys of 1990 and 1995 to examine the match between education and job skills using a traditional fit between educational credentials and jobs and a generic skills approach based on reported use of skills derived from the Employability Skills Profile (Conference Board of Canada 2000). Results showed that graduates from professional programs, as well as those having advanced degrees experienced a better education-job skills match on both the "credential fit" and "generic skills" measures. On the other hand, humanities and social sciences graduates experienced a better match of generic skills than of credentials to their jobs. Further analysis revealed that leadership and teamwork skills are less likely to be developed in postsecondary programs than cognitive, communications and new-technology skills. Finally, the results indicated that a significant minority of graduates do not have the opportunity to use all of their employment-related skills in their jobs.

In two further papers based on IALS data, Osberg (2000) and Green and Riddell (2001) investigated the hypothesis that literacy can have an impact on earnings beyond that which is associated with educational credentials. Osberg's concern was mainly with measurement issues, particularly with various ways of scaling the literacy scores. Nevertheless, he found that literacy had a significant impact on earnings no matter how the scores were scaled, accounting for about 30 percent of the economic return from education. The same result was found by Green and Riddell. These authors found that educational attainment has a larger impact than work experience on earnings. The study also provided some support for the view that literacy skills may play a role in how well immigrants adjust to the labour market.

Charette and Meng (1998) used Canadian data from the earlier Statistics Canada *Survey of Literacy Skills Used in Daily Activities* to examine the returns on literacy. These authors found that including literacy and numeracy measures in the income equation increases the return to education for males but decreases it for females. Similar results were found by Osberg (2000) and Dalton (2004). These results suggest that performance is more important for males and years of education more important for females.

A review by Walters (2004) presents the competing arguments of credentialism versus human capital theory. In particular, Walters examined the work of Collins and others who argue that a "credential society" has emerged in which education is valued less for its ability to create knowledge and skill than for its ability to sort individuals in convenient ways to create a hierarchy in job selection and advancement. Walters also cites the work of Livingstone and others as providing evidence that the premium on education has been declining and that the system is now producing many overqualified workers. While not inconsistent with the evidence on positive individual returns to education, the credentialist perspective suggests the possibility that higher education is a zero-sum game or worse at the societal level.

Walters used results from the 1997 National Graduates study to investigate the education-job match and, in particular, whether those with higher levels of education reported a better fit to their work than those at lower levels. After controlling for a number of background factors, graduates of professional programs had the highest probabilities of a close match, followed by Master's and Doctorate graduates. Despite the conventional wisdom which holds that trades and college graduates obtain education that is more directly job-related than typical university undergraduate programs, only small differences in job match were found among these three groups. These results were reinforced by an analysis of fields of study, which showed much higher probabilities of close match for those in specific fields of study such as education, health and engineering than for humanities, fine arts or social science graduates. This latter result was obviously related to requirements for specific credentials for entry to many jobs in these fields.

The relationship between academic achievement (as opposed to attainment or credential) and economic outcomes gained attention when Hernstein (1971) argued that labour market outcomes were predictable from test scores. The premium on school-based achievement seems to have been an explicit component in only a few studies of economic impact. Jencks *et al.* (1979) examined this relationship using data from seven countries, and estimated that a one-standard deviation increase in test scores accounts for an increase of between 3 percent and 27 percent in earnings.[3] Hanushek (2004) and Altonji and Blank (1999) reached the same conclusions, after controlling for other factors such as work experience, labour market conditions and individual characteristics.

In the United Kingdom, Dolton and Makepeace (1990), using a survey of university graduates, concluded that post-graduation earnings were higher for those with first- or second-class degrees. Blackburn and Neumark (1993) found increased wages to be associated with higher levels of academic ability. A further UK study by Naylor, Smith and McKnight (2000) also found significant increases in earnings with degree class. Specifically, a 5.5 percent premium was associated with a first-class degree, a 2.6 percent premium for a second-class degree and a 2.6 percent deficit for a third-class degree. These same authors, in a 2002 study, found that the premium on a first-class degree increased between 1985 and 1998 to 9.4 percent for males and 11.2 percent for females. Hernstein and Murray (1994) argued that the rising return to education is attributable to a rising return to ability. Grogger and Eide (1995) and Murname, Willett and Levy (1995) also found positive returns to performance.

Dalton (2004) examined the question of whether there is a premium on the grades achieved in university, controlling for the effects of credentials, individual characteristics and labour market effects. Dalton was able to match the results from about 1,800 respondents to a 2002 follow-up survey of university graduates with the academic records of these same students. She was also able to extend the dataset by incorporating labour market information on a variety of occupations from the 2003 edition of the *Job Futures* report published by Human Resources Development Canada.

Dalton found that, on average, there is a return on grades. This return is small relative to the premiums on education level and credential, but they persist even when these factors are controlled. The size of the return is particular to specific groups and contexts; in particular, inclusion of separate grades for mathematics and English in the model results in a positive return for mathematics and a negative return for English. The return to academic major is positive in a bivariate model but becomes negative in a model with controls for individual and labour market characteristics and credential. The return to English in high-unemployment-rate occupations is negative for females and positive for males. The return to grades is stable across credential groups but varies across low- and high-unemployment groups.

The most obvious area in which a premium on grades can be found is not directly in the economic return to grades but in the use of grades as the means of access to higher levels of education. However, this seems not to have been considered in the research. This is most apparent in the transition between secondary and postsecondary education. Since postsecondary education is not (yet) universal, high-school grades are the main selection device for entry to postsecondary institutions, and especially to universities.[4] The well-established premium on postsecondary education clearly depends on the student achieving at a sufficient level, first to gain access to a postsecondary institution and second to continue to achieve at a level sufficient to graduate. In addition, undergraduate grades are the major determinant of entry to the "high level" professional schools and to graduate studies. This, of course, means that the premium on grades is likely to mirror that on credentials. As far as we can tell, there have been no studies of the effects of grades within credential areas. We do not know, for example, if engineers or business graduates with high grades do better than those with the same credentials but lower grades.

The Return to Educational Resource Inputs

While the existence of an individual premium on education is well-established, it does not follow that this has a positive impact on society as a whole. Nevertheless, the dominant belief is clearly that the aggregate of individual benefits is a societal benefit. More directly, the belief is that education has a causal effect on overall economic activity, presumably through increasing the supply of those workers most in demand, creating a climate of entrepreneurship or more generally increasing the productivity of the workforce. As pointed out earlier, this belief is a strong driving force for public expenditures on education.

On the surface, the most obvious way to study the returns to society is by applying the human capital earnings function to cross-national or cross-system (systems could be schools, districts or states/provinces) data. Alternatively, it is possible to examine time-series data, and particularly the effects of deliberate shifts in educational policy designed to yield higher education levels for larger numbers of people. Again, this area of research belongs more properly to the economics paper. For now, we follow the policy thrust and assume that there is a societal benefit and that some level of expenditure (or investment) of public resources is necessary to achieve this benefit. This leads to the main contribution of educational research to the human capital development issue, that of the impact of different levels of resources and of different ways of using these resources. Most such research is based, at least implicitly, on a variation of the human capital function which we may call the *education production function*. In this model, the dependent variable is educational attainment or achievement and the independent variables are educational expenditures or proxies for expenditures, such as class size, teacher qualifications or program interventions of various kinds.

Studies in the United States

Most of the research on the education production function comes from the United States. This work is generally thought of as having its origins in the Coleman study of educational equality (Colemen *et al.* 1966). This study has been widely interpreted as indicating that most of the differences in educational achievement are due to home and family circumstances, exacerbated in the US by race, and that the effects of schooling (and by implication of educational expenditures) are minimal. Jencks *et al.* (1972) used a re-analysis of the Coleman data to argue that individual differences are about hereditary and environment equally, with a large residual, but that, among environmental factors, increasing equality in school resources would contribute little to increasing equality in economic outcomes. This early work stimulated a debate that continues to this day. Educators quite naturally challenge the proposition that schools make no difference and governments continue to devote substantial resources to education on the assumption that they do.

A common thrust of such research involves the use of national time-series data on resource inputs and outcomes. Resources are typically expressed as per-pupil expenditures or as cost-intensive resource uses such as class size, teacher salaries or teacher qualifications. Typically, these resource measures are correlated with either NAEP results or results on the Scholastic Aptitude Test (SAT), although use of the latter measure has been criticized because of differential participation rates over time and across states.

Perhaps the most influential work of this nature is that of Eric Hanushek. In a series of individual studies and syntheses extending over 20 years, Hanushek (1981, 1986, 1989, 1991, 1997, 1999) has consistently concluded that the research evidence is insufficient to support any strong or consistent relationship between resource inputs and student achievement. Although Hanushek's work remains influential, it is perhaps a measure of the controversial nature of this work, and the existence of countervailing arguments, that there is little indication of policymakers using this work to keep resources constant or to justify decreases.

A strong challenge to Hanushek's conclusions has been presented by Greenwald, Hedges and Laine (1996). These authors were critical of Hanushek for using simple vote counting (counting the number of statistically significant effects) in his synthesis work. Using the techniques of meta-analysis to combine effects across many studies, these authors found positive effects for a variety of resource variables including per-pupil expenditures, pupil-teacher ratio, school size (higher achievement in smaller schools) and teacher ability, education and experience. Estimates were made of the effect on achievement of a change of $500 per student. These ranged from 0.04 of a standard deviation for pupil-teacher ratio to 0.22 for teacher education. Despite their general conclusion, however, these authors pointed out that there are large variations in effects across studies, and especially across different methods (e.g., cross-sectional versus longitudinal).

In a response to Greenwald, Hedges and Laine, Hanushek (1996) pointed out that meta-analysis can point only to the possibility that some resource effects are positive, a point consistent with his argument that what matters is not resources but how they are used. Hanushek was also critical of the selection method used by Greenwald, Hedges and Laine, arguing that this method excludes too many useful results. For example, Hanushek (1996) presented data showing large increases in these resource inputs from the 1960s to the 1990s, but only small increases in achievement on the National Assessment of Educational Progress (NAEP), arguing that this presents a *prima facie* case for minimal resource effects. Hanushek also examined the common arguments that much of the increased funding has gone into reducing racial disparities and other special programs for the disadvantaged and that students are coming to school less prepared than in earlier years. Hanushek concluded that, on balance, student input characteristics have improved rather than deteriorated and that changes in student inputs cannot account for the lack of achievement gains.

A comprehensive literature review by Grissmer *et al.* (2000) examined the issue of disproportionate spending on the disadvantaged, arguing that this should result in larger increases in achievement for the targeted groups. This, indeed, has been the case, with the largest gains in NAEP scores being found for black, Hispanic and lower achieving white students. This has been interpreted as evidence that targeted use of resources yields the desired payoff. However, this seems to have had little impact on overall average performance.

Grissmer *et al.* (2000) also examined the results of more recent reviews and, while concluding that there is now general support for positive resource effects, variation across study methods, levels of aggregation and analytical approaches continue to plague the field. There seems to be no consensus on methods of analysis, other than that measurement at lower levels of aggregation (e.g., student or school) yields better results than those at higher levels (e.g., state or country) and that some of the inconsistencies can only be resolved by using experimental or quasi-experimental studies.

The Tennessee STAR study of class size has been widely cited as one of the few significant attempts at experimentation using a resource variable.[5] In that experiment, the State of Tennessee randomly assigned about 6,000 kindergarten students in 79 schools to class sizes of approximately 15 and 23. These class sizes were maintained through Grade 3. Additional students entering the experimental schools were also randomly assigned, giving a total of about 12,000 students having some exposure to the experiment. Class sizes then reverted to normal (larger and variable) class sizes up to Grade 8.

The results of this experiment showed statistically significant positive achievement effects from smaller classes at all grades and for all subjects up to Grade 8 (Finn and Achilles 1999). The long-term effects seem confined to students who had been in the small classes for all four years (Nye, Hedges and Konstantopoulos 1999). Short-term effects were greater for black and other disadvantaged students. Although questions have been raised about departures from the experimental design that inevitably occur in a large-scale implementation (Hanushek 1999), these have been addressed and not found to have been significant sources of bias.

A more recent similar study was conducted in Wisconsin (Molnar *et al.* 1999). This study used a slightly different, quasi-experimental, design and focused more explicitly on disadvantaged students. The one-year results were similar to those for the Tennessee experiment but with smaller effect sizes. As far as we can determine, no longer-term results have yet been reported.

A further thrust is found in studies of differences across states in resource allocation and use. Grissmer *et al.* (2000) justified the use of comparative state-level data on the grounds that states are the primary policy-making bodies, that there is substantial variation among states in resources allocated and that states have implemented a large variety of reforms over the past couple of decades, many of which have been explicitly directed at improving achievement. The existence of state-level scores on the NAEP assessment also provides a valid and comparable dependent variable.[6] In effect, state differences may be viewed as a "natural experiment" on the effects of resource variation. Grissmer and his colleagues at the RAND Corporation set out to examine state-level effects, controlling for other factors known to influence achievement. In particular, it was argued that developing state-level family background indicators from census and other data provided a more accurate picture than using student self-reported data for NAEP questionnaires. The Grissmer study was also unique in attempting to estimate the cost-effectiveness of various resource utilizations.

The results indicated, as expected, that family characteristics account for most of the variance across scores within states. However, there were also significant state-specific effects for students with similar family backgrounds. Some of these can be explained by characteristics of state educational systems, and particularly by variations in per-pupil expenditures and how these expenditures are allocated. In particular, higher levels of participation in public pre-kindergarten programs, lower pupil-teacher ratios in lower grades, higher reported adequacy of teacher resources, and lower levels of teacher turnover showed positive effects on achievement. Higher teacher salaries, higher teacher education levels and increased teacher experience beyond three years did not show significant effects. Wide variations in the cost-effectiveness of expenditures were also found, depending on grade level, programs and the SES levels of students. The most cost-efficient use of resources were providing K–8 teachers with more teaching resources, expanding pre-kindergarten programs in low-SES states and implementing low student-teacher ratios in lower grades in lower-SES states.

Although the results for the impact of reform were considered preliminary, there were several indications that reform initiatives have yielded some payoff. In particular, a case study of the two states — Texas and North Carolina — which had the highest achievement gains, revealed that similar reforms, involving increased accountability, standards and assessments, had occurred in both states to a greater degree than elsewhere. In general, these results suggested that the way in which resources are allocated is more important than simply increasing resources and that resources are more effective when targeted at the most disadvantaged students. More specifically the authors suggested that targeting resources to improved teacher working conditions, including smaller class sizes, would be more effective than using the same resources to increase teacher salaries.

In his more recent work, Hanushek has continued to challenge other studies on resource effects. In a critique of the Tennessee STAR experiment, Hanushek (1999) questioned some of the design features of STAR, suggesting that these bias the results upward. More important, he argues that the results are predicated on unrealistically large reductions in class size, beyond what could be implemented on a system-wide scale. Indeed, the STAR results are consistent with the earliest well-known review of class size (Glass and Smith 1979), which concluded that little benefit is derived until class size is reduced to around 15 students. Hanushek has also argued that large-scale survey results, which tend to show either no class size effects or effects in favour of larger classes, cannot be ignored because, despite their correlational nature, they are more representative of the real world and more generalizable across systems and countries than any experiments that have been done.

Finally, Hanushek argued that class size reduction is one of the costliest of educational reforms and that the observed effects are clearly not sufficient to justify the costs involved in implementing general class size reductions.

International Achievement Studies

Hanushek and Luque (2003) used results from international large-scale assessments to present a broader argument about the effects of resources. A general summary of results from six international mathematics and science assessments from 1970 to 1995 is presented as indicating no systematic pattern, at the country level, between resources and test results. The coefficients associated with per-student expenditures, student-teacher ratio and the ratio of total expenditures on education to GDP all show these resource indicators as having negative impact. Hanushek and Luque argue that organizational features of education systems are more likely than resources to influence outcomes.

Building on these results, Hanushek and Luque used data from the Third International Mathematics and Science Study (TIMSS). This study involved achievement measures of 9, 13 and 17-year-olds in more than 40 countries, along with extensive student, teacher and school questionnaires. In this case, the country-level results yielded slightly greater evidence of resource effects than earlier studies. However, school-level analyses within countries yielded few consistent effects for class size, teacher education and teacher specialization. In particular, Hanushek and Luque argue that there is no clear support for the hypothesis that resources have a greater effect in developing than in developed countries. School effects explain substantial variance in achievement in the absence of controls for family factors, but the explanatory power of school variables is substantially attenuated once family factors are controlled. Hanushek and Luque acknowledge that the results depend on whether family factors are considered precursors to schooling or the other way around. Nevertheless, although the order of entry of variables into a regression equation is mathematically arbitrary, it is logically difficult to think of a model that places school variables ahead of family variables in a causal sequence since children are exposed to family influences long before they enter school.

Finally, it is useful to examine results of the Programme for International Student Assessment (PISA), a new periodic assessment being conducted by the OECD. The PISA assessment was administered in 32 countries in 2000 with reading as the core subject and in 41 countries in 2003 with mathematics as the core subject. Like the IEA studies, PISA uses a sophisticated design that is capable of producing reasonably accurate country-level statistics on a variety of student and school characteristics, as well as achievement. While the PISA data have not yet been fully exploited to examine the education production function, this database offers considerable potential for such analysis.

The school resource factors available from PISA 2000 were student-teacher ratio, school size and levels of teacher qualifications. School size has not typically been examined, but an argument can be made that larger schools should offer some economies of scale and hence should be more efficient. These variables were available at the school level for all participating countries. Variations across countries and within countries could thus be examined.

While the PISA report (OECD 2001) noted that student-teacher ratio is not the same as class size, this is perhaps a better resource indicator than class size since it is not confounded with issues of teacher deployment. On average, a ten-point increase (or 0.10 standard deviation on the PISA scale) in reading performance was associated with having 3.3 fewer students per teacher. However, this relationship was non-linear, with both the smallest and the largest being associated with lower performance than the mid-range ratios. The results at the low end were attributed to the practice of having smaller ratios in schools with low achieving students. Those at the high end were consistent with the conventional view that larger ratios are detrimental to achievement.

On average, a ten-point gain in achievement was associated with having just over 200 more students in a school. However, this relationship was also non-linear, with little gain being seen for schools with over 1,000 students. Finally, a ten-point gain was associated with 27 percent more teachers in the school having a tertiary level qualification with a major in the subject being taught.

Within countries, most of the effects were statistically non-significant, with substantial differences in their values across countries. An argument can thus be made that the significance of the overall effects is more a consequence of the large sample size (of schools) or, alternatively, that the small sample of schools within countries leads to instability in the results.

The PISA report also examined the relative effects of school and family factors on achievement. As in most other studies, resource and other school-level effects were found to be attenuated in the presence of family factors. One effect that seems to be unique to PISA is student use of school resources. This was found to have a positive influence on performance, but was also related to family background. It may be argued from this that students from higher SES families may make better use of school resources, thereby adding to the advantage already available. On the other hand, using a broader range of school indicators, it was also found that schools can help mitigate the adverse effects of low SES. Indeed, a few countries, including Canada, seem to have been able to combine high levels of performance with relatively low impacts of SES on performance.

PISA 2003 (OECD 2004), which focused on mathematics, took a slightly different approach to resources. While retaining student-teacher ratio and school size, an overall index of school resources was developed by combining responses to several questionnaire variables. A more sophisticated multi-level modelling approach was also taken. For the mathematics scale, school size and the index of quality of school resources were statistically significant overall but student-teacher ratio was not. Within countries, very few of the effects were significant. Again, the report noted the possibility that the absence of an effect for student-teacher ratio may be related to the placement of weaker students in smaller classes. This possibility was also observed for other resource-related variables such as tutoring and out-of-class lessons in mathematics. Both of these were negatively correlated with mathematics performance, but it was not possible to separate the effects of these activities on "like" students from the broader likelihood that weaker students are more likely to be exposed to these activities.

Canadian Evidence

No Canadian studies were found that directly addressed the effects of resources on outcomes. However, it is possible to identify some effects from the international studies and the Student Achievement Indicators Program (SAIP). The most recent edition of the report *Education Indicators in Canada* (Statistics Canada 2003) also contains some comparative information.

Looking first at PISA, Tables 1 and 2 give the effect sizes for Canada and the overall effect for all OECD countries for the resource variables discussed earlier, plus some others included in the tables but not addressed in detail in the report.

Table 1. PISA 2000: Canadian and OECD Resource Effects for Reading

Resource Indicator	Unit	Change in Reading Score per Unit on Resource Variable	
		Canada	OECD
Student-teacher ratio	20–25 compared to less than 20	**22.86**	−0.73
Student-teacher ratio	25–30 compared to less than 20	−7.70	−10.03
Student-teacher ratio	More than 30 compared to less than 20	**−40.71**	**−22.48**
Percent of computers available to 15-year-olds	1% increase	**−0.51**	**−0.69**
Teachers with tertiary qualification in subject of test	1% increase	**0.39**	**0.30**
Quality of school infrastructure	one standard deviation increase	**2.41**	2.26
Student use of school resources	one standard deviation increase	**8.44**	**16.18**

Note: Statistical significance of OECD effects inferred from reported standard errors.
Source: OECD (2001, Table 8.5a).

Table 2. PISA 2003: Canadian and OECD Resource Effects for Mathematics

Resource Indicator	Unit	Change in Reading Score per Unit on Resource Variable	
		Canada	OECD
School size	increase of 100 students	1.83	**4.7**
Student-teacher ratio	one student increase	**3.57**	0.7
Preschool attendance	one or more years at a pre-kindergarten program	**13.74**	**8.0**
Quality of school resources	one standard deviation increase	**5.92**	2.4
Teacher shortage	one standard deviation greater shortage	**−5.59**	**−3.7**

Source: OECD (2004, Tables 5.20 and 5.21).

The 2000 effects are based on models controlling for SES. The 2003 effects are based on multi-level models, controlling for a wider range of variables.

The non-linear effects of student-teacher ratio in reading are more apparent for Canada than for OECD as a whole. Being in schools with mid-range student-teacher ratios is clearly advantageous. Again, on the low end, the result is likely related to the assignment of low achieving students to smaller classes. The results at the high end seem to support an argument for reducing the size of the largest classes, rather than a general reduction. The student-teacher data are not broken down by categories for mathematics, but the overall relationship shows a performance advantage for higher student-teacher ratios.

Both quality of school infrastructure (reading) and quality of instructional resources (mathematics) show positive effects on performance. This is also true for student use of resources. What is less clear is whether high-quality resources or increased use are a consequence of higher expenditures. On the other hand, student access to computers, a relatively expensive resource that schools have been struggling to provide, shows a negative effect for reading.

Teacher specialization was positively related to reading scores. However, this index is not available for mathematics. Instead, an index of teacher shortage was used. This also showed an effect in the expected direction, with a greater reported shortage being associated with lower achievement.

The School Achievement Indicators Program (SAIP) is a pan-Canadian assessment operated by the Council of Ministers of Education since the early 1990s. Samples of 13-year-old and 16-year-old students in all jurisdictions (including separate English and French samples in some jurisdictions) have been assessed in mathematics, reading and writing and science on a cyclic basis. The last three assessments, mathematics in 2001, writing in 2002 and science in 2003 have included comprehensive student, teacher and school questionnaires, allowing some analysis of the kinds of relationships of interest here. The public reports have included comparative data on a large number of variables but correlational results on only a few. Although some ongoing research is attempting to develop more comprehensive models of achievement from the SAIP data, results of these projects are not yet widely available.

Only a small number of correlations in the public reports touch on resource variables. These are summarized in Table 3. The effects noted are those showing statistically significant effects across most jurisdictions. Although these results are based on bivariate correlations, with no control for student characteristics, the pattern is generally consistent with what has been found in other studies. The result for parents helping to raise funds seems unique to this study. The actual impact of such fund-raising efforts on the overall school budget and on outcomes is unknown but warrants study in light of the controversial nature of school fund-raising activities. In particular the prevalent view seems to be that schools must engage in fund-raising to make up for shortfalls from government sources. If so, there is a further link to socioeconomic status, with schools in more affluent areas likely being capable of raising larger amounts in this way.

Table 3. SAIP Correlations Between Resource Variables and Achievement

Positive	Negative
Mathematics 2001	
School size Mathematics class size (larger classes)	Percentage of students with learning problems
Writing 2002	
School size Language arts class size (larger classes) Parents help raise funds	Percentage of students with learning problems Shortage of specialized teachers Shortage or inadequacy of instructional materials, space, infrastructure
Science 2004 No consistent patterns for any variables	

Sources: CMEC (2003*a*, *b*, 2005).

The *Education Indicators in Canada* Report (Statistics Canada 2003) gives total per-capita and per-student expenditures on education along with trends in these expenditures for Canada and the provinces. In principle, it should be possible to use these in conjunction with SAIP performance to develop relationships similar to the state-level patterns found in American studies. In practice, this does not yield significant effects for several reasons. To begin with, variations in expenditures across provinces are not as large as those found across states in the US, nor are the variations in achievement. Also, the small number of jurisdictions would require very high correlations to reach statistical significance. Finally, the results depend strongly on whether or not the territories are included since these jurisdictions have both exceptionally high expenditures and exceptionally low achievement.

Nevertheless, it is interesting to note that the two provinces, Alberta and Quebec, which have consistently outperformed others on SAIP and PISA, have tended to have expenditures slightly below the Canadian average, while the two with the highest expenditures per student, Ontario and Manitoba, have tended to show mid-level performance. The Atlantic provinces have had expenditures considerably below the Canadian average and have tended to have among the lowest achievement levels. While this may be suggestive of a non-linear relationship between expenditures and performance, the data are inadequate to infer a clear pattern.

The Mediating Effects of Teaching and Learning Processes

The conceptual model indicates that resources can be expected to exert effects on outcomes only indirectly, through their effects on teaching and learning processes. This is consistent with the position taken by Hanushek and others that resource use, not resource magnitude, is the key factor in outcomes.

Even though a large body of research exists on processes and outcomes (often referred to as process-product research) this generally does not intersect with resource-outcome studies. Researchers who spend their time looking at resources and outcomes have tended to rely on secondary analysis of existing data sources, rather than getting closer to schools and classrooms. Process-outcome researchers tend to be more interested in the more micro world of classrooms and generally are not concerned with the resources that must be brought to bear to make classrooms function.

A recent study by Elliott (1998) exemplifies the kind of work needed both to get inside the process black box and to link what is inside to both resource inputs and outcomes. Elliott linked data on resource inputs based on US census data with process and outcome data (mathematics and science achievement scores) from the National Education Longitudinal Survey of 1988. The main resource variable was school district expenditures. This was conceptualized as purchasing services, such as teacher qualifications, smaller class sizes, and availability and condition of equipment, which were hypothesized as contributing to "opportunity to learn." The latter, in turn, were hypothesized as being related to processes such as emphasis on higher order thinking and inquiry skills, emphasis on math computations and memorizing facts and emphasis on the relevance of mathematics and science, which are related to achievement. The model is thus one of direct resource effects and indirect mediating effects based on the translation of resources into processes. Thus, rather than simply being proxies for resources, variables such as class size and teacher qualifications were viewed as the consequence of resource inputs but related to the processes used and hence to opportunity to learn.

Elliott found small but significant direct expenditure and process effects. However, the mediating effect between expenditures and teaching practices was found only for science. Part of the positive effects of expenditures on achievement was accounted for by the mediating effects of teacher education and experience. The effects for science were stronger, with expenditures affecting classroom processes which, in turn, influence achievement. Elliott attributed this to both the existence of more variance in science than in mathematics achievement and to the greater demands of science teaching on resources and on teacher capabilities.

Elliott concluded that the results support the use of resources to hire more qualified teachers but that the effectiveness of these teachers depends on their use of effective teaching strategies. Elliot also argued that research is needed to more precisely pinpoint how resources are being used. In this respect, Elliott's work supports the position consistently taken by Hanushek that the key to resource effects lies in resource use.

In a similar, vein, Wenglinsky (1997) proposed a more elaborate mediating model, with expenditures broken down into teacher, per-student instructional, administrative and capital components. Different cost components were hypothesized to affect teacher-student ratio (the reciprocal of the usual student-teacher ratio), teacher qualifications and aspects of the school environment. In this study, the NAEP database was combined with a national database of cost components. Using structural equation modelling,[7] Wenglinsky examined the effects of cost components on the teacher-student ratio, student behaviour in the classroom, and mathematics achievement in Grades 4 and 8.

Wenglinsky concluded that expenditures affect the achievement of Grade 4 students in two stages. First, expenditures on instruction and school district administration increase teacher-student ratios (effectively making classes smaller). Increased teacher-student ratios, in turn, increase average achievement in mathematics. For Grade 8 students, there is an additional stage, in which increased teacher-student ratios lead to a reduction in problem behaviours which, in turn, result in increased achievement. In addition, Wenglinsky found that achievement was not associated with variations in capital spending, school-level administrative expenditures or teacher-education levels. While showing opposite results to many other studies on the teacher-student ratio issue, this study does help identify areas of expenditure that seem to be productive or non-productive.

Effective Schools

Paralleling, but rather independent of, research on classroom teaching and learning process and achievement is a body of literature on "school effectiveness." This literature is concerned mainly with school climate, leadership styles, school improvement planning and similar issues where the focus is the whole school rather than the teacher or classroom. The recent preoccupation in some quarters with school choice may be seen as an offshoot of the school effectiveness literature.

Research on school effectiveness identified a number of school factors related to achievement, including high expectations, positive teacher role models, feedback on student performance, student acceptance of school norms, strong leadership of the principal, an orderly school environment, frequent assessments of student performance and emphasis on mastery of basic skills (Levin 1995). According to Levin, this body of research has been subject to a number of methodological criticisms and has tapered off in more recent years.

That is not to say that school improvement initiatives can no longer be found. Indeed, many jurisdictions now seem to have produced ways to encourage schools to develop school improvement plans. A prominent Canadian example is the Alberta Initiative for School improvement (at www.education.gov.ab.ca/k_12/special/aisi/whatisaisi.asp). However, it appears as if such initiatives are now less research-based and more grounded in total quality management (TQM) and other management theories (Levin 1995). In reality, this research is not particularly useful in attempting to elaborate the education production function because few of the factors, which seem to be identified with school improvement, are related to school resources or, more likely, no efforts have been made to examine the impact of resources on school climate and leadership factors.

Postsecondary Education

Much of the attention in human capital studies has been focused on the value of postsecondary education. Indeed, most of the studies reviewed in the section on the economic returns involved the individual returns of postsecondary education.

That sector enjoyed substantial expansion from the 1960s to the 1980s, before a period of retrenchment in the 1990s as government financial constraints reduced the levels of available funding. This expansion was clearly related to human capital development and particularly to labour market demands and outcomes. Although calls are beginning to emerge for greater accountability, there is a dearth of research on societal returns and particularly on the relationship of postsecondary resources to outcomes.

The recent CPRN review (Finnie and Usher 2005) on measuring postsecondary quality has proposed a sequential model which closely resembles the production function schematic, presented earlier in this report. This model may be depicted as follows:

beginning characteristics → learning inputs → learning outputs → outcomes

The authors go on to identify several approaches to measuring quality, including periodic internal or external reviews of units or institutions, ranking systems, accreditation systems and student surveys. None of these seem to have been used to estimate the relationships suggested by the model. In particular, most quality measures use inputs and processes as if these were the outcomes. For example, the *Maclean's* system for ranking Canadian universities (*Maclean's* 2005) places substantial emphasis on the number of faculty with PhDs, entry averages of students, expenditures, class sizes and a host of other input measures in developing their composite rankings. This represents an explicit attempt to treat inputs as if they were outcomes. Only a couple of indicators, such as the "reputational survey," look at all like outcomes and these suffer from significant methodological difficulties.

Without a clear measure of outcome, it is difficult to conceptualize how a more detailed production function for postsecondary education could be estimated. Some of the studies cited earlier illustrate the point. Basic literacy measures or perceptions of the education-job skills match are not a substitute for the kind of achievement measures found in studies of elementary / secondary education. Outcomes in postsecondary education are much more differentiated by program and it is not at all clear how this diversity could be captured by any form of exit test. Many professions (accounting, medicine, law and engineering to name a few) use an elaborate system of examinations as part of the credentialling process, with the appropriate university degree serving only as an initial and not a final credential. However, none of these systems seem to have been used to measure the quality of the university experience in the form of differences in institutional success rates on the qualifying examinations or other such comparisons. Even an obvious matter such as class size, which varies enormously across programs and institutions, and which is a clear point of contention, has not received the research scrutiny in postsecondary education that it has in elementary and secondary.

One area in which a small amount of work is emerging is that of the cost-effectiveness of new approaches to teaching, particularly distance methods such as correspondence or Web-based courses. While this area has not been reviewed in any detail, there are indications that cost-effectiveness, as well as access, is a consideration in institutional decisions to offer such programs (e.g., Oslington 2004; Jung 2005).

Conclusions

The Human Capital Earnings Function

The individual economic return to higher levels of education has been so widely studied that there is now little dispute over the existence of positive effects. Education conveys an individual advantage additional to that conveyed by the overall economy or by family and other background factors. There seems to be little risk to an individual in making a decision to invest time, effort and money in pursuing higher levels of educational attainment.

Although there is some research, including a number of Canadian studies, on the place of ability, knowledge and skill in individual economic outcomes, debate continues over whether the education advantage is a matter of acquiring marketable attributes or whether it is mainly a screening device or a proxy for underlying ability. In reality, it would be difficult to argue that credentials are acquired independently of knowledge and skill acquisition. Also, ways in which knowledge and skills have been measured (basic literacy, perceptions of skill match) are likely inadequate to represent the specific competencies required in many high-level professions or even trades or technology occupations.

Attempts to apply the human capital earnings function at the societal level have been less successful. While, in general, societies with higher levels of education are among the most economically advanced, it is not clear that this situation is driven by education or by other factors independent of or acting together with education. Aside from questions of whether the sum of individual economic gains is zero (some lose and some gain in the overall distribution of education and earnings), the overall economy is driven by many factors that have not been fully incorporated into the equation.

The Education Production Function

There is little doubt that human capital theory is having a profound impact on educational policy. Belief that we are in a knowledge economy that places an ever higher premium on education is firmly entrenched and certainly is a strong driver of educational policy. Most broad statements of educational aims refer to the knowledge economy or the importance of education for economic prosperity. A major thrust of educational accountability, reform and expansion initiatives, at all levels, is to improve the economic circumstances of individuals and to ensure the prosperity and competitiveness of societies.

In light of this, and especially in the face of limited resources for education, it might be expected that research would have something to say about the efficient use of educational resources. Unfortunately, the research on resource effects had not yielded many consistent results. This area remains controversial and there is little specific advice that can be given to policymakers on whether there is payoff from added resources or on how resources should be prioritized. In particular, there is little in the research that would tell us about the value of high cost initiatives or of major reallocations of resources. Some areas of cost increase, such as allocation of additional resources to the lowest achieving students, have been driven by human rights arguments and have not been investigated from a cost-effectiveness perspective.

As an example, although the class-size evidence seems reasonably clear, the results are not particularly helpful for policy. In an experimental context, smaller classes in the primary grades yield higher achievement levels that seem sustained over several years. However, large reductions in class size are required to yield the desired effects. Moreover, broader studies of the place of class size among a variety of other factors affecting achievement, smaller class size generally shows either zero or negative effects, likely because the effects are so small as not to be detectable by the models used and because all sources of confounding cannot be removed.

What should policymakers make of these results? Obviously, a public appetite exists for class size reductions regardless of what the research says. However, since it would be a costly proposition to bring average class sizes down to the levels at which payoff can be expected, the politically acceptable solution tends to be one of trying to achieve modest class size reductions, satisfying some of the demand while keeping costs to a minimum.

To take a second example, although teacher qualifications (years of education and experience) is a major driver of teacher salaries, the results for these factors are also not clear enough to permit any strong policy statement on the value of continued use of the current salary grid. There is some evidence that at least a few years of experience counts and that specialization is an advantage. However, there is almost no value to having higher degrees, even though this has significant salary implications. The problem here is that some means have to be found to create a career ladder for teachers, even if this has no relationship to outcomes. In the absence of performance indicators, education and experience take on a practical value as proxies for performance.

At the postsecondary level, we know even less about the effects of resources on outcomes. Most of the indicators data available on postsecondary education focus on inputs and participation almost as if these were outcomes. Although studies of the human capital earnings function have focused mainly on higher education, to the extent that outcomes are measured at all this is done in highly generic ways such as through years of education, credentials, basic literacy skills or self-reported education-job match. The small amount of work that looks directly at performance is based on the earnings function and does not look at educational resources or processes.

Where Do We Go from Here?

Human capital theory has clearly shown itself to be a useful foundation for research on the value of education. This theory may also be seen as a primary force in educational policy development. While it is possible to give other reasons for public support for mass education, it is difficult to imagine the system sustaining itself at ever-expanding levels without its participants believing that there is economic benefit. What is interesting here is that this belief can be held even in the absence of evidence or in the presence of only weak evidence. This illustrates how policy can be, and usually is, influenced by many forces other than empirical evidence.

From an empirical research perspective, the ideal study of resource effects would be an experiment on the effects of schooling versus no schooling. Such an experiment is impossible in elementary and secondary education for obvious reasons. Virtually all children in the developed world are now exposed to a substantial period of schooling, at least through to secondary school (though not to secondary graduation). It is possible only to look at differences between schools or systems. Since substantial efforts have long been made to minimize these differences, the variation in schooling available to study is thus quite small compared, for example, to the variability in family backgrounds or other characteristics that students bring to school. Comparative studies across systems, particularly countries, with widely varying resources are possible, but this is also fraught with problems of confounding and of relatively few data points.

Comparative studies are possible at the senior secondary and postsecondary levels because individuals can be found with widely varying levels of exposure to higher education, including no exposure. Indeed, this is the thrust of most research under the human capital earnings function. However, the selective nature of the postsecondary system, and the further selection factors in getting postsecondary education to the workplace, introduce confounding factors that have not yet been well enough sorted out to determine the causal effects of higher education and especially the causal effects of what has been learned, as opposed to having earned a credential. Again, one could imagine an ideal experiment in which individuals are randomly assigned to postsecondary programs and the effects measured over time. However, it seems unlikely that any system or institution could be persuaded to conduct such an experiment.

In the absence of the "definitive" experiment, what can be done to advance our understanding of the economic effects of education and particularly of the cost-effectiveness of particular resource allocations? In an earlier paper (Crocker 2002), the author prepared a "wish list" of needed research on the education production function. The remainder of this section draws heavily from that paper.

Outcomes Definition and Measurement

First, almost all of the resource effect studies have used achievement in core subjects, typically reading mathematics and science as the outcome. While there may be considerable debate over what constitutes valid outcomes, the school curriculum extends well beyond these areas. For example, there would likely be agreement that skills contribution to health and citizenship should be taught. A current example is renewed emphasis on physical fitness, in light of the health risks associated with childhood obesity.

> There is need for public and professional validation of outcomes, for priority-setting among outcomes and for research designed to assess public and professional views on the range of outcomes to be measured.

Once some broader outcomes are clear, these can be measured and research can be directed to the effects of resources designed to achieve these outcomes.

This type of work needs to be extended to the postsecondary level, where there seems to be no consensus on core outcomes common to all programs.

> There is a need first to identify and validate a set of common outcomes expected of graduates from core postsecondary programs.

A good starting point for this might be the employability skills profile developed by the Conference Board of Canada (2000). Since this originally emerged in the context of a federal government "prosperity initiative" and was developed from extensive consultation with educational and business leaders, this profile has been subjected to a validity process that would be difficult to duplicate. It would not be an overwhelming job to develop an outcome measure based on the elements of this profile and to administer this in settings such as postsecondary graduation, the National Graduates Survey or a survey similar to the International Adult Literacy Survey. Having information on performance on these elements would add significantly to the ability to distinguish the effects of years of education, credentials and skills

Beyond this, it should be possible to:

make greater use of available information on trade and professional credentials to conduct research on the factors contributing to these competencies.

While professional and trade organizations have a proprietary interest in the content and results of credentialling tests, it would not be unreasonable to engage such organizations in studies of the impact of results on these tests on economic outcomes. Indeed, professional organizations are in a position to track and to gather information from their members on a long-term basis.

Use of Large-Scale Surveys

Large-scale surveys have long been used for research on the education/earnings function. Some use is now being made of achievement surveys, particularly NAEP in the United States and TIMSS and PISA internationally, to examine the resource-outcome relationship in elementary and secondary education. These have tended to be of limited use because the focus of these surveys has not been on resources and because of the limitations of what can be gathered from self-report questionnaires. The consequence is the need to use proxies for resources, such as student-teacher ratios or teacher qualifications.

Ideally what would be required is a resource number that could be attached to individual children, along with their achievement results. In practice, the best that could likely be obtained would be school-level data or group data for children in various categories. For example, it might be possible, with the appropriate design, to identify the level of resources attached to special needs children, those in advanced programs or the like. Realistically, there seems to be nothing in the design of current international surveys that would come close to this.

In Canada, several provinces now have more or less comprehensive student assessment programs, many of which are administered to the entire population at a grade level. Provinces also have large amounts of data that could be translated into more precise resource indicators. For example, the ratio of total teacher salaries to enrolment at the school level or per-student expenditures on instructional resources can be computed from available data. Some differentiation of resources expended on students within schools could also likely be made. Using such data would permit assembly of population-level data that would be much more precise on both resource and outcome variables than anything now available.

> There is a need for research specifically designed to develop and test comprehensive models of the factors contributing to achievement. The primary focus of such research should be on the path from resource inputs to processes to outcomes and emphasis should be placed on ways of diminishing the impact of student background and other contextual variables on achievement.

Field Experiments

There is a limit to the yield of survey data in investigating causal relationships, and we appear to be reaching a saturation point in what can be learned from such surveys. No matter how sophisticated the statistical models, there will always be uncontrolled extraneous variables and lack of control over the variables of primary interest.

Education has little tradition of using randomized clinical trials, and those that are found have typically been small scale and somewhat artificial relative to the real world of schools. Nevertheless, examples such as Tennessee STAR illustrate what is possible when a jurisdiction decides that a major issue of resources and outcomes needs to be carefully examined.

There is something of a tradition in introducing new initiatives in education of conducting "pilot projects." These are particularly prevalent in curriculum implementation. However, these usually are biased toward success by trying the initiative first with the best teachers and schools with every intention of implementation regardless of the results. Despite this history, an opportunity exists to implement more rigorous designs in pilot projects. By field experiments we mean simply an experiment or quasi-experiment conducted under realistic school conditions and on a large enough scale to be broadly generalizable.

> There is a need for judicious use of large-scale experiments in advance of major policy changes or program implementations, especially where significant resource allocations or changes in practice are contemplated. Using such designs in the context of pilot projects would be a desirable starting point.

An obvious example of what is meant here is the case of integration of special needs students into regular classrooms. This is a large-scale initiative, being implemented to a significant degree in all Canadian jurisdictions. The driving force behind this approach is human rights legislation and court cases that have entrenched the principle of having children placed in the "least restrictive" environments. Of the large number of studies of children with disabilities, almost none deal with the effectiveness and certainly not with the cost-effectiveness of different placements for such children. Indeed, the prevalent view seems to be that there is no empirical question to be answered here, but simply a human rights question. However, no service is done to these children or to others in moving ahead with an approach, especially a high cost one, that is not established to be effective in achieving desired outcomes.

There are sufficient numbers of precedents for long-term large-scale experiments in areas such as medicine to lead us to believe that experimental research can eventually become the dominant approach to answering questions about the impact of resources. Some indications are emerging that this approach may gain a foothold in education.

Part of the problem with education production function studies is that resource variables are typically measured in an unrefined manner. One of the advantages of experimental or quasi-experimental designs is that they frequently require more careful thought to the "treatment" variable than is possible with survey designs. Class size is a typical example. To begin with, student-teacher ratio may be only a rough proxy for class size. Class size has as much to do with how teachers are deployed in a district or school as with the student-teacher ratio. For example, it is not unusual to see a situation in which many of the teachers in a large school are assigned to various kinds of specialist duties rather than to a regular classroom. One of the advantages of experimental or quasi-experimental designs is that they force us to develop more nuanced definitions of the "treatments" than are typically found in naturalistic studies.

Longer-Term Longitudinal Studies

Most studies under the education/income production function have been of recent graduates, with graduate follow-up surveys being a primary tool. Similarly, most resource/outcome studies rely on resource indicators gathered at a particular point in time, even though outcomes are usually cumulative in nature. Longitudinal studies have the potential of adding considerably to the ability to examine these issues. The beginnings of a longitudinal approach can be found in Canada in such surveys as the Youth in Transition Survey. The question, of course, is whether such studies can be sustained for a long enough period to yield the desired payoff. Again, there is precedent in medicine, where long-term follow-up studies are fairly common.

The Process "Black Box"

Educational resources obviously are not used directly to purchase outcomes. The model shown in Figure 1, and most similar models, shows an intervening "process" component between resource inputs and outcomes. What these models call "teaching and learning processes" represent the goods and services purchased with the resources available. These may be of greater or lesser quality, and we cannot assume that more resources will yield higher quality. Aside from a few elements, such as class sizes or qualified teachers, which have been used as proxies for resources where more direct measures have not been available, the process component has largely been ignored in studies of the education production function.

To again use the class-size example, it is rare to see in studies of class size any reference to differences in what teachers may do in small classes compared to larger ones. To over-simplify the point, an argument can be made that to the extent that teaching practices are relatively fixed, for example, on transmission of knowledge, then class size should not matter. This is the common argument at the postsecondary level, where teaching to ever larger classes can be seen as a matter of technology (i.e., using more sophisticated presentation settings or tools or, more recently, using the Internet). On the other hand, a common argument made by teachers is that smaller classes allow teachers to pay more attention to individuals. This implies that some form of one-on-one teaching is desirable and would be practised if only classes were small enough. This, of course, raises the more direct question of whether more individualized instruction is better than group instruction. Some answers to that question can be found, but these are not generally considered in production function studies.

The time has perhaps come for research on process-outcome relationships and on resource-outcome relationships to converge. Some convergence may be possible in the context of large-scale surveys, where data on both resource and process variables typically exist. Examples of how such work may be conducted are the studies by Elliottt and Wenglinsky cited earlier. Unfortunately, the process information, which can be gathered by survey questionnaires is usually too limited to be of much use. One possible way to achieve such convergence would be to revive the kind of micro-level analysis that was typical of process-product research in the 1970s and to extend this to micro-level analysis of how resources are used. The time now seems to be ripe to move away from reliance on large-scale surveys and global measures of resources and to establish a new research agenda, designed both to get inside the black box and to determine the effects of targeted resource allocations and uses on what goes on in schools and classrooms and how this mediates the education production function.

Prospects for Interdisciplinary Research

Much of the research on the education production function already has an interdisciplinary character. In particular, this is one area in which researchers from another discipline — economics — have put their minds to education. Educators have also used economic concepts, models and analytical techniques in addressing the issue of resource allocation and use. To a lesser degree, work of this nature has also occupied sociologists concerned with issues of equality of educational opportunity. The Coleman study itself, which many would consider the beginnings of research on educational resources, was the work of sociologists.

Despite these links, little of the research can be considered truly interdisciplinary in nature. There are few examples in which the authors of individual studies can be said to cut across disciplines, although some reviews and edited volumes have representation from the various disciplines.

Building an interdisciplinary research agenda has much to recommend it. For example, the tendency for economists to rely on global indicators of resource inputs could be tempered by advice from educators on the specifics of how resources are used. The political climate of policy-making could be addressed by political scientists who can bring to bear insights into why concepts such as human capital development can enjoy such currency, despite limited evidence on the social impacts.[8] Broader measures of outcomes are certainly required, demanding expertise in measurement, whose practitioners are to be found largely in psychology.

It is relatively easy to see the advantages of an interdisciplinary approach to the advancement of research in this area. It is quite another thing, however, to develop the interdisciplinary teams and networks necessary to address the research areas already mentioned. Such things do not just happen, and it is beyond the scope of any individual researcher to establish the needed connections. Nevertheless, there exist in Canada some models for developing interdisciplinary networks. The Networks of Centres of Excellence program, a joint effort of the three major granting councils, is one such example. Itself a model of how agencies involved in disparate disciplines can collaborate, establishing an NCE for interdisciplinary research on human capital development would be one way to develop a Canadian presence in this area and to bring life to some of the needed research on the education production function. This is not the place to bring forward a plan for such a network. However, the field is attracting interest and there is sufficient need to examine issues such as cost-effectiveness and the social impact of education that this would be an attractive area in which to develop a network.

Notes

1. This is an oversimplification of the Mincer model, just as that model is an oversimplification of the real world. Since we do not intend to pursue the issue of economic outcomes in detail here, it is not considered necessary to elaborate this model in either conceptual or mathematical terms.
2. It is notable that federal agencies assiduously avoid using the word "education" in their titles or programs, and that most such programs involve funding or research but not the operation of programs.
3. This section draws heavily on a literature review conducted by Stephanie Dalton as part of her M.Ed. thesis (Dalton 2004). The author is indebted to her for stimulating his interest in the effects of performance on economic outcomes and for permission to draw on her work.
4. High-school grades are less extensively used in the United States than in Canada and other countries because few US jurisdictions have state-wide high-school graduation examinations and because broader aptitude tests such as the SAT are in wide use in the United States. However, this simply alters the measure, not the principle.
5. An early Canadian experiment on class size (Shapson *et al.* 1980) was widely cited in earlier reviews of class size but seems now to have been superseded by the high profile of the Tennessee experiment.

6. Because the publication of state-level NAEP results has been voluntary, not all states are available for all analyses.
7. Structural equation modelling is a generalized version of regression analysis particularly suited to examining the direct and indirect effects of predictors on outcomes.
8. Recent research on social impacts is summarized in the paper by Craig Riddell in this volume.

References

Altonji, J.G. and R.M. Blank. 1999. "The Demand for and Return to Education: When Education Outcomes are Uncertain," *Handbook of Labor Economics* Vol. 3. New York: Elsevier Science.

Blackburn, M.L. and D. Neumark. 1993. "Omitted-ability Bias and the Increase in Return to Schooling," *Journal of Labour Economics* 11(3):521-44.

Becker, G. 1993. *Human Capital: A Theoretical and Empirical Analysis with Special Reference to Education*. Chicago: University of Chicago Press.

Charette, M. and R. Meng. 1998. "The Determinants of Literacy and Numeracy and the Effect of Literacy and Numeracy on Labour Market Outcomes," *Canadian Journal of Economics* 31(3):495-517.

Colemen, J.S. *et al.* 1966. *Equality of Educational Opportunity.* Washington, DC: Government Printing Office.

Conference Board of Canada. 2000. *Employability Skills Profile, 2000+.* Ottawa: Conference Board of Canada. At www.conferenceboard.ca/education/learning-tools/employability-skills.htm.

Council of Ministers of Education, Canada (CMEC). 2003*a. Student Achievement Indicators Program: Mathematics Learning, The Canadian Context.* Toronto: CMEC.

— 2003*b. Student Achievement Indicators Program: Student Writing, The Canadian Context.* Toronto: CMEC.

— 2005. *Student Achievement Indicators Program: Science III.* Toronto: CMEC.

Crocker, R.K. 2002. *Learning Outcomes: A Critical Review of the State of the Field in Canada.* Ottawa: Canadian Education Statistics Council. At www.cesc-csce.ca/ pcera2003E.html.

Dalton, S. 2004. "The Impact of Academic Performance on Post-Graduation Earnings." St Johns, Nfld.: Memorial University of Newfoundland. Unpublished Master's Thesis.

Dolton, P.J. and G.H. Makepeace. 1990. "The Earnings of Economics Graduates," *Economic Journal* 100:237-50.

Elliott, M. 1998. "School Finance and Opportunities to Learn: Does Money Well Spent Enhance Students' Achievement?" *Sociology of Education* 71:232-45.

Ferrer, A.M. and W.C. Riddell. 2002. "The Role of Credentials in the Canadian Labour Market," *Canadian Journal of Economics* 35(4):879-905.

Finn, J.D. and C.M. Achilles. 1999. "Tennessee's Class Size Study: Findings, Implications and Misconceptions," *Educational Evaluation and Policy Analysis*, Special Issue 21(2):S97-109.

Finnie, R. and A. Usher. 2005. *Measuring the Quality of Post-Secondary Education: Concepts, Current Practices and a Strategic Plan*. Ottawa: Canadian Policy Research Networks.

Freidman, M. and S. Kuznets. 1945. *Income from Independent Professional Practice*. New York: National Bureau of Economic Research.

Glass, G.V. and M.L. Smith. 1979. "Meta-analysis of Research on the Relationship of Class Size and Achievement," *Educational Evaluation and Policy Analysis* 1(1):2-16.

Government of Alberta. 2005. *Mission of the Ministry of Advanced Education*. At www.advancededucation.gov.ab.ca/department/businessplan/bp2005-08.pdf.

Government of New Brunswick. 2002. *New Brunswick's Prosperity Plan, 2002–2012*. Fredericton: NB Government.

Green, D.A. and W.C. Riddell. 2001 *Literacy, Numeracy and Labour Market Outcomes in Canada*. Ottawa: Statistics Canada.

Greenwald, R., L.V. Hedges and R.D. Laine. 1996. "The Effects of School Resources on Student Achievement," *Review of Educational Research* 66(3): 345-52.

Grissmer, D., A. Flanagan, J. Kawata and S. Williamson. 2000. *Improving Student Achievement: What State NAEP Scores Tell Us*. Santa Monica, CA: RAND Corporation.

Grogger, J. and E. Eide. 1995. "Changes in College and the Rise of the College Wage Premium," *Journal of Human Resources* 30(2):280-310.

Hanushek, E.A. 1981. "Throwing Money at Schools," *Journal of Policy Analysis and Management* 1:19-41.

— 1986. "The Economics of Schooling: Production and Efficiency in Public Schools," *Journal of Economic Literature* 24:1141-77.

— 1989. "The Impact of Differential Expenditures on School Performance," *Educational Researcher* 18(4):45-65.

— 1991. "When School Finance Reform May Not Be Good Policy," *Harvard Journal on Legislation* 28:423-56.

— 1996. "A More Complete Picture of School Resource Policies," *Review of Educational Research* 66(3):397-409.

— 1997. "Assessing the Effects of School Resources on Student Performance: An Update," *Educational Evaluation and Policy Analysis* 19(2):141-64.

— 1999. "Some Findings from an Independent Investigation of the Tennessee STAR Experiment and from other Investigations of Class Eize Effects," *Educational Evaluation and Policy Analysis,* Special Issue 21(2):S143-63.

— 2004. "Some Simple Analytics of School Quality." NBER Working Paper No. 10229. Cambridge, MA: National Bureau of Economic Research. At www.nber.org/ papers/w10229.

Hanushek, E.A. and J.A. Luque. 2003. "Efficiency and Equity in Schools Around the World," *Economics of Education Review* 22:481-502.

Hernstein, R.J. 1971. "IQ," *Atlantic Monthly,* September, pp. 43-64

Hernstein, R.J. and C. Murray. 1994. *The Bell Curve: Intelligence and Class Structure in American Life.* New York: Free Press.

Human Resources and Skills Development Canada (HRDC). 2004. *Workplace Skills Initiative: Overview.* At www.hrsdc.gc.ca/en/ws/initiatives/wsi/ WSI_proposal_overview.shtml.

Hyslop-Margison, E.J. 2000. "The Market Economy Discourse in Education: Implementation, Impact and Resistance," *Alberta Journal of Educational Research* 46(3):203-13.

Jencks, C. *et al.* 1972. *Inequality: A Reassessment of the Effect of Family and Schooling in America.* New York: Basic Books.

Jencks, C. *et al.* 1979. *Who Gets Ahead? The Determinants of Economic Success in America.* New York: Basic Books.

Jung, I. 2005. "Cost-effectiveness of Online Teacher Training," *Open Learning* 20(2):131-46.

Krahn, H. and J.W. Bolby. 1999. *Education-Job Skills Match: An Analysis of the 1990 and 1995 National Graduates Surveys.* Ottawa: Human Resources Development Canada.

Krahn, H. and G.S. Lowe. 1998. *Literacy Utilization in Canadian Workplaces.* Ottawa: Statistics Canada.

Levin, H.M. 1995. "Raising Educational Productivity," in *The International Encyclopedia of Economics of Education,* ed. M. Carnoy. 2nd edition. Oxford: Pergamon.

Maclean's. 2005. *University Rankings '05,* 14 November.

Mincer, J. 1974. *Schooling, Experience and Earnings.* New York: Columbia University Press.

Molnar, A., P. Smith, J. Zahonik, A. Palmer, A. Halbach and K. Ehrle. 1999. "Evaluating the SAGE Program: A Pilot Program in Targeted Pupil-Teacher Reduction in Wisconsin," *Educational Evaluation and Policy Analysis,* Special Issue 21(2):S165-77.

Murname, R.J., J.B. Willett and F. Levy. 1995. "The Growing Importance of Cognitive Skill in Wage Determination," *Review of Economics and Statistics* 77(2):251-66.

Naylor, R., J. Smith and A. McKnight. 2000. *Occupational Earnings of Graduates: Evidence for the 1993 UK Population.* Warwick, UK. University of Warwick.

Nye, B., L.V. Hedges and S. Konstantopoulos. 1999. "The Long-term Effects of Small Classes: A Five Year Follow-up of the Tennessee Class Size Experimen," *Educational Evaluation and Policy Analysis*, Special Issue 21(2):S127-42.

Organisation for Economic Co-operation and Development (OECD). (1996). *Education at a Glance: OECD Indicators.* Paris: OECD.

— 2001. *Knowledge and Skills for Life: First Results from PISA 2000.* Paris: OECD.

— 2004. *Learning for Tomorrow's World: First Results from PISA 2003.* Paris: OECD.

— 2005a. *Education at a Glance: OECD Indicators.* Paris: OECD.

— 2005b. *From Education to Work: A Difficult Transition for Young Adults with Low Levels of Education.* Paris: OECD.

Osberg, L. 2000. *Schooling, Literacy and Individual Earnings.* Ottawa: Statistics Canada.

Oslington, P. 2004. "The Impact of Uncertainty and Irreversibility on Investments in Online Learning," *Distance Education* 25(2):233-42.

Puk, T. 1999. "Formula for Success According to TIMSS or the Subliminal Decay of Jurisdictional Educational Integrity," *Alberta Journal of Educational Research* 45(3):225-38.

Shapson, S.M., E.N. Wright, G. Eason and J. Fitzgerald. 1980. "An Experimental Study of the Effects of Class Size," *American Educational Research Journal* 17:144-52.

Schultz, T.W. 1993. *Origins of Increasing Returns.* Oxford: Blackwell.

Statistics Canada. 2003. *Education Indicators in Canada.* Ottawa: Statistics Canada.

Sweetland, S.R. 1996. "Human Capital Theory: Foundations of a Field of Inquiry," *Review of Educational Research* 66(3):341-59.

Walters, D. 2004. "The Relationship Between Post-secondary Education and Skill: Comparing Credentialism with Human Capital Theory," *Canadian Journal of Higher Education* 34(2):97-124.

Wenglinsky, H. 1997. *When Money Matters.* Princeton, NJ: Educational Testing Service.

Wien, C.A. and C. Dudley-Marling. 1998. "Limited Vision: The Ontario Curriculum and Outcomes-based Learning," *Canadian Journal of Education* 23(4):405-20.

7

Human Capital Development and the Frontiers of Research in the Sociology of Education

Stephen L. Morgan
Mark W. McKerrow

Family background is universally considered to be the most important determinant of educational achievement and attainment. Compelling research, however, often fails to motivate policymakers and the public to propel policy change. The literature points to policy recommendations in regard to grade retention, ability streaming and social capital development: grade retention does more harm than good; when ability streaming is in place, steps should be taken to eliminate inequities that — while not part of the ideal-type model of streaming — appear to develop in practice; and it is prudent to expand structured opportunities, such as extracurricular activities, to develop students' peer networks.

Introduction

The sociological literature on educational achievement and attainment has contributed substantially to our current understanding of human capital development. Sociologists have examined the determinants of skills and knowledge in adolescence for more than five decades. These skills constitute the majority of the human capital brought into and drawn on in the labour market, and much public policy is devoted to enhancing the educational system's capacities to foster them.

Accordingly, in our synthesis of the sociological literature, we will focus mostly on explanations for motivation and commitment to schooling, learning and preparation for postsecondary education and finally, college entry and subsequent educational attainment. And thus, even though we will at times summarize noteworthy findings from studies of early childhood education as well as adult education, our presentation will be dominated by the core literature from the sociology of education which has covered these areas.[1]

Because our paper is therefore limited in scope, we should note at the outset that more comprehensive summaries of the literature in the sociology of education are available. The 25 chapters in Hallinan (2000) constitute a comprehensive presentation of this sociological literature. The classic reader of Karabel and Halsey (1977), the updated reader Halsey *et al.* (1997), and a recent compilation of state-of-the-art research, Hedges and Schneider (2005), all offer excellent introductions to the field.

In the remainder of our paper, we first summarize the four primary explanatory mechanisms from the sociology of education. These explanations are based, mostly, on empirical research on educational institutions in the United States, rather than Canada, as the literature in the sociology of education is dominated by studies of US institutions. Following this broad accounting of the explanatory mechanisms from the sociology of education, we will narrow the focus to consider what is known about these mechanisms in Canadian education. For this later section, we draw on the non-sociological literature on education in Canada, as the education literature in Canadian sociology is somewhat thin. We conclude with a brief note on recent attempts to assess the effects of lifelong learning, before ending with an appeal for better and more frequent Canada-US comparisons.

Primary Explanatory Mechanisms in the Sociology of Education

In this section, we describe the four most prominent categories of explanation for patterns of educational achievement and attainment. We begin with family background effects and radiate outwards to school-level and neighbourhood-level mechanisms. Intermixed in this paper, we offer definitions and some explanation of the sociological concepts of cultural and social capital, which are often used in sociology when developing explanations for the accumulation of human capital.

We summarize this literature in open-ended fashion, focusing more on the questions and frameworks that have been formulated than on the answers that have been established. We take this strategy for two main reasons: we reserve our summary of findings for the next section which discusses more directly Canadian education; and second, the literature has more effectively formulated questions than answers to its own questions.

Family Background

In the sociology of education, family background — usually defined as some function of parents' education, occupational attainment, family income, and wealth — is universally considered to be the most important determinant of educational achievement and attainment. Two basic explanatory models have dominated the sociological literature: the status attainment model and a radical critique of it. Although these two perspectives were developed alternatively in the United States and in France, the basic position of most sociologists is that they are broadly relevant to all industrial societies.

The status attainment approach is grounded on a specific causal mechanism that relates individuals' expectations and aspirations for the future to the social contexts that generate them. The origins of the model are in structural-functional sociology from the mid-twentieth century. The 1953 article entitled "Educational and Occupational Aspirations of Common Man Boys," written by Joseph A. Kahl, is perhaps the most influential early piece. But, the explanation is most often identified with the so-called "Wisconsin model" of status attainment, which was based on early analyses of the Wisconsin Longitudinal Survey (a random sample of all high-school seniors in the state of Wisconsin in 1957). The full model was first fully specified in two influential articles published in the *American Sociological Review* , Sewell, Haller and Portes (1969) and Sewell, Haller and Ohlendorf (1970), that reported results from both the original 1957 data and the follow-up 1964 data on the educational and early occupational careers of young men.

According to the original Wisconsin model, the joint effects of a high-school student's family background and mental ability on his eventual educational and occupational attainments can be completely explained by the expectations that others hold of him. In particular, significant others — parents, teachers and peers — define expectations that students then internalize as educational and occupational aspirations. Because the underlying theory assumes that students are compelled to follow their own aspirations, the model is powerfully simple and implies that significant others can increase a student's educational and occupational attainment merely by increasing their own expectations of him or her.

Regarding the specific processes of aspiration formation, the principal social psychological theorist, Archibald Haller, maintained that aspirations are formed in three ways: imitation, self-reflection and adoption. Once formed, Haller wrote that aspirations are embedded in "approximately consistent and mutually reinforcing cognitions" which then "have an inertia of their own and are expressed in corresponding behavior" (1982, 5-6). Thus, students' educational and occupational aspirations become stable, abstract, motivational orientations (see Spenner and Featherman 1978), and the measured Wisconsin model variables — college plans and expected future occupation — are merely realistic indicators of these latent status aspirations.

Although the theory underlying the original Wisconsin model was bold, its creators were well aware of its many limitations. Almost immediately upon publication, they began to qualify its basic mechanisms, and in the process they weakened its most parsimonious theoretical claims by allowing for the addition of supplemental direct effects of socio-economic status on all endogenous variables. The addition of paths not predicted by the original socialization theory presented problems for the powerful claims of the 1969 article. In particular, the claim that significant others could raise students' educational and occupational attainments by simply imposing higher expectations on them began to seem less credible. Instead, the revised models of the 1970s and 1980s suggested that, while the expectations of parents, teachers and peers have direct effects on the educational and occupational attainment process, other variables, such as the structure of opportunities in the education system and the labour market, also play an important role.

These revisions were, in part, a response to research critical of the Wisconsin model and its supposed origins in structural-functionalist sociology. Critics argued that structural constraints embedded in the opportunity structure of society should be at the centre of all models of educational attainment, and hence that concepts such as aspirations and expectations offer little or no explanatory power. Most famously, Pierre Bourdieu dismissed the work of sociologists who assert that associations between aspirations/expectations and attainments are causal. Rather, for Bourdieu, the unequal opportunity structures of society "determine aspirations by determining the extent to which they can be satisfied" (Bourdieu 1973, 83). And, as such, aspirations and expectations have no autonomous explanatory power, as they are nothing other than alternative indicators of attainment.

Critiques such as these helped to bring an end to the brief dominance of status attainment theory in the study of social inequality. Accordingly, a more radical conflict approach to explaining educational achievement and attainment was then developed in the 1970s and 1980s. The perspective is best captured by the work of Pierre Bourdieu, as most widely read in his early 1973 article and in Bourdieu and Passeron (1977). For Bourdieu, sociologists of education should focus on the reproduction of inequality. In the past education literature, too much attention was given to studies of mobility; much more research should be devoted to uncovering the mechanisms that generate immobility. More deeply, Bourdieu assumed that the education system, while projecting an ethos of class neutrality, in fact serves primarily to reproduce the class structure.

Bourdieu's most celebrated theoretical mechanism is based on the concept of cultural capital — the possession of cultural knowledge that signifies membership in the dominant social classes. This cultural capital is transmitted in the home, and schools then reward students based on the generalized cultural competence that working-class students do not, by definition, possess. Bourdieu writes: "By doing away with giving explicitly to everyone what it implicitly demands of everyone, the educational system demands of everyone alike that they have what it does not give" (1973, 58). Accordingly, he writes that "the negative predispositions toward the school which result in the self-elimination of most children from the most culturally unfavored classes and sections of a class ... must be understood as an anticipation, based upon the unconscious estimation of the objective probabilities of success possessed by the whole category, of the sanctions objectively reserved by the school for those classes or sections of a class deprived of cultural capital" (ibid., 58). In relation to the status attainment model, and in particular the Wisconsin model described earlier, the claim here is that significant others have no real individual-level effects; instead, they respond mechanically to cultural capital endowments. Students rebel (or have low aspirations) because they subconsciously recognize this reality.

Both forms of family background scholarship are still prominent in the sociological literature, and each has received updates and embellishments since the 1970s. Lareau used Bourdieu's basic framework to model the behaviour of parents, arguing for "the importance of class and class cultures in facilitating or impeding children's (or parents') negotiation of the process of schooling" (Lareau 1987, 289). Morgan (2005) takes the expectations and aspirations tradition of explanation and builds a new stochastic decision-tree model of commitment. The goal of this work is to integrate sociological and economic approaches by building a model where educational achievement and subsequent attainment are sensitive to the exogenous impact of shifts in costs and benefits but also independent belief formation processes that can over-whelm expected utility calculations. The ultimate goal is to transcend both the status attainment perspective and its radical critique in the work of scholars such as Bourdieu in order to determine how struc-tural dynamics should be incorporated into models of educational at-tainment — that is, as structure that is imposed from the outside as the rigid constraints maintained by institutions or via individual responses to perceived structural constraints (see also Breen and Goldthorpe 1997; and Gambetta 1987).

The Impact of Race

Explanations that consider the racial identification of students are an important set of mechanisms that are inextricably related to the family-background-based explanations presented in the last section. This re-search tradition is dominated by studies of the gaps that exist between the achievement and attainment of white and black students in the US, although there is a vast literature on different contrasts in the US and in other countries. Their relevance to the Canadian education system is unclear at present, although immigration patterns and the renewed consideration of access for Canadian Aboriginals prompts us to include some discussion of this literature.

A primary source for these explanations is the 1998 volume by Christopher Jencks and Meredith Phillips, *The Black-White Test Score Gap*.[2] This volume, which grew out of a conference on the topic, repre-sents most of the major explanations for race differences (although pre-sented only as explanations for the black-white gap in the US). In their summary chapter, Jencks and Phillips set the background for race-specific differences by noting that the black-white test-score gap in the US has declined over the course of the twentieth century. Comparable standardized tests show, however, that the rapid convergence of scores since the 1960s slowed in the late 1980s. Jencks and Phillips then show that family background explains some of the gross difference between whites and blacks. But an unexplained portion remains, and differences across siblings suggest that test scores cannot be explained entirely by family background. They note that there is no evidence that there is any genetic basis for the black-white differences (i.e., there is evidence of a genetic basis for intelligence and test-score differences, but not any evidence that genetic differences explain any of the black-white gap). They show that early childhood differences have been found, especially in vocabulary, but the gaps widen throughout childhood and adolescence. And, as we will discuss more broadly later, they claim that there is no evidence that levels of per pupil expenditures across schools explain much of the gap, but secondly, average class size may matter.

Against this background, the volume includes updated (and sometimes confirmatory) positions on the following race-specific explanations. Fordham and Ogbu (1986) are credited with developing the claim that black adolescents underachieve in schooling because they maintain a disproportionately oppositional student culture. Based on ethnographic evidence — drawn primarily from observations of students in predominantly black schools — Ogbu and his colleagues argue that, for the most part, blacks in the US are descendants of involuntary immigrants who were brought to the US as slaves. This history breeds fictive kinship that leads to a rejection of the dominant culture. School success is thereby regarded as "acting white," and loyalty to a fictive kin group prompts black students to apply sanctions to their high-achieving peers. As a result, relatively high-achieving black students reduce their effort in school, and average test scores among black students decline.

Although frequently cited, this tradition of scholarship has foundered. The most recent survey-based research has shown that blacks and whites do not differ to the degree emphasized by Ogbu and his colleagues (see Ainsworth-Darnell and Downey 1998; Cook and Ludwig 1997). These results have now been corroborated by ethnographies, including Carter (2005).

A more recent and increasingly prominent explanation for black-white differences is Claude Steele's two-part theory of stereotype threat and disidentification (see Steele 1992, 1997). According to Steele and his colleagues, black students from all levels of the socio-economic spectrum are haunted by the specter of confirming stereotypes of inherent black inferiority. These threatening stereotypes interfere with everyday educational performance in school, especially on important tests, because black students try too hard to avoid the low performance that "makes the stereotype more plausible as a self-characterization in the eyes of others, and perhaps even in one's own eyes" (Steele and Aronson 1995, 797). Stereotype threatened test-takers spend "more time doing fewer items more inaccurately — probably as a result of alternating their attention between trying to answer the items and trying to assess the self-significance of their frustration" (ibid., 808). Stereotypes do not directly lower the motivation or performance expectations of test-takers. Instead, stereotypes activate a subconscious mechanism wherein stereotype anxiety, which is manifest in self-evaluative pressure, impairs test-taking efficiency.

Over time, Steele surmises, black students adapt to their predicament, and this adaptation results in disidentification. In order to maintain positive self-images, they inoculate their global self-esteem against performance evaluations in schooling. In so doing, they disidentify with educational achievement in general in order to claim a psychic victory, which preserves self-worth. Unfortunately, however, disidentification does not offer a costless victory because it undermines the motivation and commitment that are necessary for continued educational achievement. Thus, unlike stereotype threat, disidentification directly lowers motivation and one's own performance expectations, further depressing future achievement.

This two-part explanation is widely discussed in the literature now for two primary reasons. First, the experimental results on stereotype threat effects on test performance have been widely replicated (see Steele, Spencer and Aronson 2002 for citations). Second, it offers a new explanation for the existence of an oppositional culture, reinterpreted as widespread disidentification, which emerges from widespread and current stereotypes.[3] For those who find the oppositional culture mechanism promising, it is useful to have contemporary sources for it that do not have to be justified by a history of involuntary immigration status.

The Structure of Opportunities to Learn

In contrast to Bourdieu's efforts to discredit the status attainment perspective, since the 1970s other scholars have attempted to work within (or alongside) the status attainment tradition by giving greater emphasis to the structure of schools and the mechanisms by which students are allocated to different positions within this structure. Alan Kerckhoff argued that status attainment explanations focused too narrowly on socialization processes in which parents, teachers and peers influence a student's aspirations, which subsequently influences their educational attainment. More attention should be paid to allocation processes in which students are placed into different positions within the school (e.g., different ability streams) according to "externally imposed criteria" (Kerckhoff 1976, 369).

This perspective resulted in a new wave of studies that focused on the effects of exposure to alternative opportunities to learn, as structured by the configurations of schooling institutions. Much of the early literature addressed curriculum tracking and streaming. The more recent literature has looked at the consequences of age-grading of classes, as well as promotion and retention policies.

In the United States, age-graded classrooms within levels of grammar and secondary schooling were institutionalized in the early twentieth century (see Tyack 1974; Tyack and Cuban 1995). This organizational form has arisen in other countries, and a good deal of important research has shown how it spread through institutional imitation as countries have expanded access to schooling (see Meyer, Ramirez and Soysal 1992). But, in spite of the surface-similarity of age-grading within schools, tremendous variation exists in how instructional material, or opportunities to learn, is distributed across students.

Consider first-grade reading instruction. Students are most commonly gathered together into small reading groups, with assignments to reading groups based on recommendations from kindergarten teachers. In an early article, Eder (1981) showed how kindergarten teachers' recommendations were based on perceptions of ability and maturity, with the latter defined as ability to maintain attention. Because most children enter the first grade with little or no ability to read, assignments to reading groups are almost entirely a function of behavioural maturity. The result is that the lowest reading groups are characterized by the largest number of behaviour problems throughout first grade, operationalized as reading turn violations where students interrupt each other. As a consequence, more material can be presented in the highest reading groups, which creates a self-fulfilling prophecy out of the initial group assignments (see also Hallinan and Sørensen 1983).

Although ability grouping in the first grade represents a pure-type example of how opportunities to learn can be differentially and consequentially distributed, most attention has focused on later grades. The educational systems of most industrialized nations employ some form of curriculum tracking or streaming, usually where students are sorted into entirely different classes based on perceived ability.

In an extraordinary set of studies, much has been learned about these processes in the US. Prior academic ability is the strongest determinant of track placement, but family background is related to track placement beyond what would be expected based on academic ability alone (Lucas 1999; Gamoran and Mare 1989). This relationship may emerge because of the decisions of teachers and guidance counselors (Rosenbaum 1976), as well as the deliberate intervention of highly-educated parents (Useem 1992). This is of potential consequence to class reproduction because many studies find track placement to have independent effects on learning and educational attainment. Barr, Dreeben and Wiratchai (1983) carefully analyze the curriculum-management process as it interacts with group assignments. Gamoran (1992) assessed the reasons for variation in tracking across types of schools, and Hallinan (1996) then modelled movement between tracked classes.

Even though much has been learned about tracking policies and practices, no definitive study of the causal effect on achievement of having been assigned to one track rather than another has achieved a consensus. Even the best available study, where Gamoran and Mare (1989) assessed the consequences of high-school tracking for achievement on standardized tests, has failed to generate a consensus. As a result, debate proliferates (see Hallinan 1994; Oakes 1994), as no one has been able to effectively challenge the traditional claims that one, learning is easiest when material is presented at a comfortable pace; and two, students differ in their ability to absorb new material.

Nonetheless, in the past 30 years, a de-tracking movement emerged in the United States, partly in response to some of this early scholarship (i.e., Oakes 1985; Rosenbaum 1976). This reform movement effectively eliminated the broad cross-subject secondary school tracks of the mid-twentieth century. The college preparatory, general and vocational tracks were broken down into sequences of courses, allowing, for example, for students to take advanced math but general English. Although some scholars believe these organizational changes have been helpful in a variety of ways (see Wellner and Oakes 2000), others have argued that the little has changed other than administrative procedures (see Lucas 1999).

Nonetheless, the most recent literature seems to support some forms of tracking, at least insofar as the school-to-work transition could be better managed. In comparison to German and Japanese secondary schools, de-tracked (or ostensibly de-tracked) comprehensive secondary schools in the United States do not prepare non-college-bound students for entry into the labour force (see Rosenbaum 2001). Increasingly, scholars have advocated for new vocational programs that provide skills that are demanded in the labour market, as well as novel apprenticeship programs that provide on-the-job training and employment contacts for non-college-bound youth.

In the United States, debates over the distribution of opportunities to learn are now dominated by discussion of promotion and retention policies, especially as they now interface with the Bush administration's federal legislation *No Child Left Behind*. Most of the literature here notes that retention policies have no substantial benefits and instead produce substantial harm (see Hauser 2004*a, b*; Hauser, Simmons and Pager 2004; Shepard and Smith 1989; Walberg, Reynolds and Wang 2004). The mechanisms are unclear, but a strong stigma may be attached to failing; failing may lead to lower effort and aspirations because it causes students to distance their school performance from their identity and self-esteem; and failing may break up social networks. The issue is not completely settled, however. Orfield and Kornhaber (2001) provide a collection of essays that debate the benefits of these policies, and Alexander, Entwisle and Dauber (2003) use unique data on Baltimore City Schools to generate some support for the relative attractiveness of retention policies. Promoters of strict retention policies generally argue that high-stakes tests and retention threats motivate students while forcing teachers to maintain consistently high expectations for all students. Detractors argue that motivational responses are in the opposite direction, and they lead at-risk students to withdraw further from schooling. As a result, more students drop out of high school (see Jimerson, Anderson and Whipple 2002).

What has not been discussed sufficiently is the relationship between tracking and retention policies within a more general opportunities-to-learn framework. To the extent that the students who are promoted are placed in low tracks with the least-skilled teachers, the relative harm of retention policies may be lessened for particular students. And, if age-grading of classes were abandoned, then the distinction between retention and tracking practices would disappear.

Social Capital, School and Neighbourhood Effects

In the government report, *Equality of Educational Opportunity* (Coleman and US Office of Education 1966) — now known simply as the Coleman Report — James S. Coleman argued that school resources had surprisingly small independent effects net of the effects of family background. Perhaps the largest and most famous piece of educational research ever undertaken, the Coleman Report has become the touchstone of research on school effects. The most famous claim of the report — that school resources only very weakly predict educational achievement — is still debated, although mostly within the field of economics (see Card and Krueger 1996; Hanushek 2001). (Also see Crocker in this collection.)

Less than two decades later, however, Coleman and a new set of colleagues then presented evidence that schools may matter a great deal net of family background (see Coleman, Hoffer and Kilgore 1982; Hoffer, Greeley and Coleman 1985; Coleman and Hoffer 1987). In particular, Coleman and his colleagues presented evidence that private Catholic schools in the United States are more effective than public schools, even though they spend comparably less money on each pupil. Their findings were challenged immediately by other researchers (see Morgan 2001 for a summary of the debate).

Coleman then developed a social capital explanation for educational achievement, focusing on the functional communities within which Catholic schools are situated. Given the importance of types of capital to this human capital development project, some detail on the sociological origins of the term social capital is appropriate before describing how social capital research is relevant to human capital development (and the Catholic school effect in particular).[4]

Foundational definitions of social capital are most frequently attributed to Bourdieu (1986[1983]) and Coleman (1988). For Bourdieu, capital is created and sustained through struggle in relevant fields of competition. It exists in three "guises" — economic, social and cultural capital.[5] Although embodied in everyday behavioural practices, the three types of capital are only readily observable when objectified and institutionalized as money, credentialed cultural competence and titles that signify social advantage. The network ties through which social capital is accumulated and institutionalized must be activated through symbolic exchanges. The ties are therefore irreducible to measures of spatial proximity or associations that are devoid of content. Nonetheless, Bourdieu's definition of social capital is usually paraphrased as: a stock of social resources that confer advantages on those who are able to access it.

For Coleman, social capital is any feature of social structure that a purposive actor uses to their advantage when pursuing their interests.

Beyond this broad definition, Coleman preferred to present the term by providing vignettes of the positive and negative returns yielded by different forms of social capital — primarily sets of network ties, specific norms that sanction proscribed behaviour and implicit shared expectations. This allowed him to present the term social capital as a broad concept of nearly limitless power and utility.[6]

Now, recall that the Catholic school research began in 1983, before Coleman is commonly thought to have developed the term "social capital" for his 1988 piece "Social Capital in the Creation of Human Capital." This is simply a misreading of the literature, as Coleman had already been heavily engaged in debating the unique advantages that social capital provided to Catholic schools in educating their students. His enthusiasm for the concept was, in fact, created out of the conflict over his results on Catholic schools, and it has origins in his community resources work from the 1960s and 1970s.

The Catholic schools research then led to two strands of subsequent survey research in the sociology of education: effective schools research and a new generation of social capital research (Carbonaro 1998; Lee and Smith 1993, 1995; Lee, Smith and Croninger 1997; Morgan 2000, 2001; Morgan and Sørensen 1999*a, b*).[7] And, in the end, it has come to be fairly widely accepted that Catholic schools (and other effective public schools) achieve their comparative success through at least one of several complementary explanations: strict discipline, a normative view that all children can learn, communal organizational practices that build trust between teachers and principals, a supportive community outside the school imbued with productive social capital that helps parents to enforce norms of academic diligence (see Bryk, Lee and Holland 1993; Bryk and Schneider 2002). The main criticism of these narratives is one of selection bias: effective schools attract the best students, net of observable characteristics of students and their families.[8]

Even though this research initially had few connections to market models of school competition — which advocate the decoupling of public funding of schools from traditional administrative structures by giving students vouchers to spend at schools of their choice (see Chubb and Moe 1990; Hoxby 1996, 2003) — the Catholic schools research was soon co-opted to it. School choice advocates claimed that the primary benefits of Catholic schooling could be fostered within the public school sector by enabling parents to choose schools. The resulting elective communities would become fictive functional communities where like-minded adults monitor peer groups and the performance of teachers similarly. Subsequent analysis of school choice programs have not shown large gains, or the creation of functional communities, even though there are claims that school choice creates learning benefits (Howell and Peterson 2002; Peterson and Hassel 1998).

Although the social capital literature in education is deeply connected to school effects research, there is also an important individual-level tradition of analysis. Focusing on peer group affiliations and associational opportunities, this type of social capital research interfaces with sociologists' longstanding interest in extracurricular activities and school outcomes (see Holland and Andre 1987; and Feldman and Matjasko 2005 for reviews). Here, it has been argued that participation in extracurricular activities is positively related to academic achievement, high-school completion and various measures of psychological well-being such as self-esteem and general life satisfaction (Gilman 2001). The most powerful predictor of outcomes is participation in extramural sports, with academic, music and arts clubs more weakly related to outcomes. Some claim that the effects appear to be strongest for at-risk students (Mahoney 2000; Mahoney and Cairns 1997).

Most explanations for these relationships posit that extracurricular activities develop some form of social capital that is used to create human capital. McNeal (1999) argues that extracurricular activities generate social capital in the form of supportive networks of friends and adults. Because participants in extracurricular activities tend to have high educational aspirations and achievement, and because participation develops new networks (Dworkin, Larson and Hansen 2003), engaging in extracurricular activities can lead to networks with school-supporting norms. Case studies (e.g., Reis and Diaz 1999) find that high-achieving females report that their extracurricular activities worked in just this way for them. Extracurricular activities may also be important in developing social capital — not just because they provide exposure to different people — but also because they provide a different setting in which members work cooperatively in activities of shared interest.

Although not forms of social capital narrowly conceived (Coleman 1988), other explanations for the apparent effects of extracurricular activities focus on social networks as well. Exposure to networks of high achievers may also lead some extracurricular participants to accept and adopt pro-school values. Extracurricular activities may be a source of recognition and respect (Coleman 1961) that provide incentives to retain contact with school, rather than drop out prior to graduation (Finn 1989). Extracurricular activities can lead to a simple increase in the number of friends at school, which could itself increase attachment to schooling. This point is especially important with respect to dropping out because high-school dropouts are found to be more likely to have been rejected by their school peers and have friendships with people who have already dropped out (Parker and Asher 1987). Many suggest that extracurricular activities are also a site of informal learning related to teamwork, communication and other social skills, but this is not well documented.

Research on extracurricular activities has currently undergone "proliferation through segmentation," in which the trend has been to segment students into sex, race and ethnic groups, as well as to further segment extracurricular activities themselves — e.g., activities can be either "structured" or "unstructured" (McHale, Crouter and Tucker 2001); intramural or extramural (Broh 2002); affiliated with or independent of the school (Jordan and Nettles 2000). All studies on extracurricular activities suffer from potentially serious selection problems. Most studies attempt to deal with selection by adjusting for observed variables in regression analyses, which reduces estimates of the effects of extracurricular participation, but these models are not complete solutions to the concerns. Accordingly, there is a clear need for additional research.

Research on Canadian Education

Before describing the literature that has engaged these four broad themes to study educational outcomes in Canada, we first note two important reasons why we will not be able to construct a tight synthesis of the sociology of education literature in four sections parallel to those just offered.

First, we have had to go beyond the Canadian sociology literature in search of education research that engages these four explanations. It seems that a greater proportion of Canadian sociologists adopt a critical epistemological stance and focus on aspects of social institutions that maintain or worsen social inequalities, especially across class, sex, race and ethnicity. This criticism includes institutions whose purported aim is to build human capital and reduce inequality. Much of this literature seems conjectural to us in the sense that facts are too readily interpreted as evidence of unfair practices or contemptible motives. More importantly, it offers little practical guidance on how to develop human capital. In fact, it often takes a critical position on the human capital paradigm itself, arguing that it is an ideology that justifies — rather than explains — unequal outcomes. Although the following positions on the state of Canadian sociology may well be too alarmist, they are not appreciably inaccurate. Ogmundson claims that "Marxist and feminist schools of thought have established hegemony.... quantitative studies, in particular, are weak and getting weaker" (2002, 68). McLaughlin writes that the "Canadian case shows what can happen when this critical edge of our disciplinary culture is taken too far" (2004, 96). And Michael Smith laments that Canadian sociology's dominant perspective has led to the "relative marginalization of sociology with respect to policy choice" (2000, 251).

This dominant epistemological stance shapes the sociological study of education in Canada. Bourdieu's perspective on the reproduction of class receives a great deal of attention, and the "hidden curriculum" — which is the transfer of knowledge, tastes and so on that is not part of the official curriculum — is also a common theme (e.g. Baldus and Kassam 1996). Conversely, the equally (or more) established status attainment perspective is discounted and ignored. The leading Canadian textbook on the sociology of education explicitly takes a critical perspective (Wotherspoon 1998, 2004).[9]

Second, although Canadian data are generally high quality, they have not permitted the range of analysis reported in our last section on findings from the US. Canada lacks a nationally-representative, school-based, longitudinal survey such as those that have been used extensively in quantitative research in the sociology of education in the United States.[10] Perhaps as a consequence of this data shortage, there is considerably less quantitative research on issues related to the structure of opportunities to learn and general school effects on achievement. Much of the outcomes-based analysis of education that we found is based on the cross-provincial-focused School Achievement Indicators Program (SAIP) (see Crocker 2002). These data are limited in the sense that they do not allow for the measurement of outcomes for the same students over time in school, and they lack both substantial classroom-level characteristics and students' subsequent labour-market experiences. Even so, by looking broadly across the literature on Canadian education inside and outside sociology, we have been able to find relevant empirical research that engages the same four explanatory mechanisms detailed in the last section.

Family Background in Canadian Education

For research on primary and secondary education, the role of family background has, of course, been well analyzed in Canada. Even so, the literature lacks depth, as we now explain. In the major Canadian sociology journals, articles that consider the relationship between family background and educational achievement are often framed with Bourdieu's theory of social reproduction (Beagan 2001; Lehmann 2005; Maxwell and Maxwell 1995; Nakhaie and Curtis 1998), as summarized in the last section. Education journals are similarly dominated by critical perspectives. Wotherspoon and Schissel (2001), for example, raise objections to "at-risk" labelling of students, thereby undermining what we would see to be well-intentioned efforts to improve skill acquisition among disadvantaged youth. They write that "as with many educational ideologies, an uncritical adoption of practices associated with at-risk discourses may also contain potential to reinforce the problems that they seek to address or to produce new dangers" (Wotherspoon and Schissel 2001, 321).

What this research lacks, in general, is empirical content. Bourdieu's cultural capital thesis is invoked as an explanation, but not evaluated for its explanatory power relative to other perspectives. Thus, there is an opportunity for better empirical research in Canadian sociology, and some recent literature has shown the promise of studying specific family-background-based mechanisms in Canada. For example, Davies (1995b) shows that claims of a working-class oppositional culture in Canada are relatively weak and do not account for a substantial proportion of the social reproduction of inequalities in educational outcomes. The importance of family background for early childhood outcomes has been studied effectively (see Peterson 1994), and a good deal is now known about how family-background origins determine the child-rearing practices to which children are exposed (see Sayer, Gauthier and Furstenberg 2004).

Willms' (2002) edited volume based on the National Longitudinal Survey of Children and Youth (NLSCY) examines the relationship between family background and childhood vulnerability (measured with cognitive ability test scores and behaviours), as well as the mechanisms that may mediate the relationship. It shows that the relationship between family background and vulnerability is evident even among young infants; it grows with age, and this can possibly be explained by a variety of predictors of vulnerability, such as parenting style, child care, family structure, parental education and so on.

On balance, however, the main findings call into question the attention often given to family background. Family background is not strongly related to the most important predictors of childhood outcomes, such as parenting practices, and family background is a poor predictor of childhood vulnerability. Therefore, there is little support for policies targeting children from poor families in particular. Universal programs, or targeted programs using more specific indicators of vulnerability are more advisable.

It would seem that the majority of the research on the relationship between family background and education is conducted by employees or affiliates of Statistics Canada. However, many of these papers are primarily descriptive in nature, and they effectively highlight the basic facts concerning issues of importance without making strong causal claims. The recent work of de Brouker (2005) is a case in point. He masterfully presents the facts on secondary school completion in Canada and in international perspective, and he poses a challenge to policy advocates. However, by focusing on students' economic reasoning and available economic incentives, he does not identify the range of underlying mechanisms that lead some students to drop out of high school.[11]

In studies of higher education, more specific research on the effects of family background is available. Recent concerns that increasing tuition at postsecondary institutions will exacerbate educational disparities related to family background have been studied. Some research in this area finds that the relationship between postsecondary attendance and tuition has changed little over the 1990s (Drolet 2005; Corak, Lipps and Zhao 2003). However, this is strongly at odds with research relating specifically to the University of Guelph, which found a marked change in composition of family background over the 1990s (Quirke and Davies 2002). Also, large increases in the tuition of professional programs do appear to change the distribution of family background of graduates as measured by parental education (Frenette 2005a).[12]

The Impact of Race in Canadian Education

Canadian sociology has been concerned to a great degree with the impact of ascriptive characteristics such as birthplace, race and ethnicity, which is perhaps a consequence of the legacy of John Porter's landmark sociological study of stratification in Canada, *The Vertical Mosaic*

(1965). Porter argued that the English and the French were given "charter status" as the founding peoples of Canada and that all others tacitly accepted a lower status in the distribution of socio-economic position.

Although test-score gaps across racial or ethnic divisions do generate some descriptive research in Canada, research on race as a predictor of educational outcomes focuses on the particularities of the Canadian situation. Although perhaps this could be seen as a weakness of the Canadian scholarship, we would argue the opposite, since the pressure to improperly extrapolate from patterns in other countries has been avoided. As shown by Guppy and Davies (1998, 105-10), Canada is very different from the US in that, conditional on immigration status, most visible minority groups, including blacks, have higher educational attainment than other Canadians.

A distinctive feature of this research tradition is the concern given to developing and then analyzing "anti-racist" educational practices (see Bonnett and Carrington 1996; Carrington and Bonnett 1997; Dei 1996), under the presumption of that pre-existing curricula unintentionally disadvantage minority students. Although to us this research is more normative than explanatory, it has helped to frame some important empirical research, which has led in turn to fruitful examination of how immigrant children and their families compare to other majority and minority subpopulations (e.g., Dyson 2001; Maxwell, Maxwell and Krugly-Smolska 1996), how non-white teachers cope with their own felt disadvantage (e.g., Carr and Klassen 1997), and the special challenges posed by the incorporation of Canadian Aboriginals (e.g., Ryan 1989).[13]

The Structure of Opportunities to Learn in Canadian Education

Although the opportunities-to-learn framework is used infrequently in the Canadian literature, there are some reliable empirical analyses of tracking, streaming, ability grouping and the consequences of retention.[14] Crocker (2002) uses the SAIP data to demonstrate that streaming and ability grouping are common in Canada, although more common among 16-year-olds than among 13-year-olds. He also shows that there is substantial variation across jurisdictions. Using the TIMSS, Frempong and Willms (2002) find that grade 7 and 8 classrooms with less ability grouping tend to have better average performance, conditional on a range of covariates. Davies (1994) finds that placement in non-ability streams predicts dropping out of high school in an Ontario sample. As in the de-tracking movement in the US, there are similar efforts to de-stream schools in some jurisdictions in Canada. Although little research exists that assesses the consequences of such de-streaming for student outcomes, Ross, McKeiver and Hogaboam-Gray (1997) argue that teachers initially lose confidence in their abilities to produce learning immediately after de-streaming but eventually recover as they work through the challenges of implementation.

The largest area of inquiry concerns the effectiveness of vocational education, which is generally considered the lowest track in the tracking literature. Lyons, Randhawa and Paulson (1991) provide an historical account of the devaluation of vocational education in Canada, which is common in most advanced industrialized countries. They argue, however, that it is high time for Canada to improve its offerings to non-college-bound youth. Taylor (2005) has, accordingly, studied school-to-work policy in Ontario, and finds it wanting with respect to the adequacy of workplace placements for students; she calls for greater effort on the part of governments, educators and unions to ensure allocation opportunities. Lehmann (2005) studied youth apprenticeships in Canada and Germany, and he argues that these show considerable promise. His research is notable for its analytic focus and consideration of the stratification literature in sociology, which leads him to a nuanced position on the degree to which vocational education merely reproduces inequality. He claims that while some forms of vocational education may be limiting for those who prematurely commit to them (as such students therefore usually eliminate themselves from the pursuit of postsecondary education), he finds that apprenticeships are viewed by apprentices as useful choices, which allow them to make the most of their occupational futures. The extent to which this finding is consistent with the older findings of Richer (1974) — that Canadian students in pure technical high schools have higher aspirations than those in high schools with both technical and college-prep students — deserves examination in contemporary Canada.

Finally, unlike in the US, there appears to be little research on the effects of retention on later student outcomes. Janosz *et al.* (1997) and Westbury (1994) demonstrate that retention effects appear to be largely negative in Canada, but Westbury laments the lack of other research on the topic to corroborate the findings. Indeed, she notes that few school boards in Canada collect consistent over-time data on rates of retention and promotion. The literature on the vicissitudes of Canadian educational policy suggests that this will be an area of growing research, as common educational policies tend to spread across industrialized societies. For work on this broader policy context, see especially Davies (2002), Davies and Guppy (1997), and Guppy and Davies (1999).[15]

Social Capital, School and Neighbourhood Effects in Canadian Education

Although some quantitatively-oriented studies of school effects on learning outcomes can be found in the Canadian literature, such as Ma and Klinger (2000), Ma (2001), and Frempong and Willms (2002), it appears that the paucity of longitudinal, school-based survey data limits this type of research in Canada, and the range of grades over which data are available. Consistent with research on the US, Ma and Klinger (2000) and Frempong and Willms (2002) find that:

- the mean SES of a school (or a classroom in the case of Frempong and Willms) is associated with lower achievement scores for individual students, conditional on background variables and
- a "liberal" disciplinary climate is associated with higher achievement.

There is substantial case-study-based research which is similar to the effective schools research from the US, and it focuses, for example, on the effectiveness (and attractiveness) of common schools (Callan 1995) as well as the impact of effective cooperation between district-level and school-level administrators (Coleman, Mikkelson and LaRocque 1991). If policy implications are to emerge from these sorts of studies, replication across multiple sites is needed until appropriate, widespread survey data are available to sustain their conjectures.

Although the impact of school financial resources on student outcomes is not commonly studied in the Canadian education literature, some attention is given to the particular consequences of the finance system (e.g., Sale and Levin 1991). This attention dovetails with a major emergent issue in Canadian education and Canadian sociology of education: the marketization — broadly conceived — of education. Scott Davies and his colleagues have begun a research program on school choice. One focus is on the growth of small, non-élite private schools in Canada. Contrary to expectations, these new private schools (and the educators who work at them) are not generally motivated by neoliberal ideology (Davies and Quirke 2005); instead, their interest is in providing education that is tailored to different students' needs. Another focus is the increasing use of private tutoring (Davies 2004; Aurini 2005), which Davies (2004) argues is a substitute for school choice that may be in higher demand because of the Canadian public's growing dissatisfaction with public education (see Guppy and Davies 1999 for a discussion of the declining confidence in public education). Aurini and Davies (2005) look at home-schooling and conclude that it is on the rise and has attained new levels of legitimacy among the mainstream. They also conclude that home-schooling is not motivated by parental concern over human capital development but by a concern for individualized instruction (every child is different) and the preciousness of their children.

Canadian research on social capital and peer networks reaches the same conclusions as the US research, but it appears to focus more narrowly on the issue of dropping out of high school.[16] Ellenbogen and Chamberland (1997) find that students at-risk for dropping out (as measured by a combination of self-reported attitudes and students' records) tend to have fewer friends at school than those not at-risk, and also tended to have more friends who were already dropouts and who had jobs. Janosz *et al.* (1997) find that the number of friends, the level of involvement with one's friends, and being a "leader" in your network are all negatively related to dropping out. Although their sample is somewhat small, they add to the debate by adjusting for an unusually rich set of personality variables obtained from several test batteries. Davies' (1994) findings confirm the importance of friends who are dropouts in the dropout process.

Although not focusing on the effects of peers on schooling in particular, Craig, Peters and Willms (2002) show that involvement with peers who are frequently in trouble is strongly related to behavioural problems in early adolescence. Young adolescents' self-reported lack of social competence, which attempts to capture number of friends and ease of friendship formation, also strongly predicts emotional and behaviour problems.

Research Unique to Canada: Lifelong Learning

The acquisition of skills and knowledge among adults is rarely studied by sociologists of education. As we noted at the outset, sociologists by and large assume that most of the crucial skill acquisition that is relevant for labour market performance occurs in childhood and adolescence. However, a large-scale, multi-method, collaborative Canadian undertaking focuses on lifelong learning. The project began as *New*

Approaches to Lifelong Learning (NALL), which included a national survey and set of interviews conducted in 1998, as well as several case studies. Data collection has continued with *The Changing Nature of Work and Lifelong Learning: National and Case Study Perspectives* (WALL), which allows longitudinal analysis by revisiting case studies, replicating many parts of the survey, and re-interviewing many respondents of the first survey five years later. Much of the longitudinal analysis is incomplete, so the focus here will be on earlier work from NALL.[17]

The NALL survey was the first extensive survey of informal learning practices in Canada, and the first anywhere in over 25 years. The project is also novel — from a sociology of education perspective — because it covers a range of types of learning (e.g., formal schooling, informal learning) as well as a range of sites of learning. For example, the survey asks about learning in paid employment, volunteer work, leisure activities, care and household activities. The case studies cover these different sites of learning, as well as examining paid employment across a range of occupations and industries.

A major NALL finding is that informal learning is widespread: estimates suggest that adults are engaged in about 15 hours per week (much more than formal learning), and that informal learning occurs across the range of activities outlined above, not just at the workplace. Even these basic findings suggest that informal learning is potentially a major part of human capital development, and that a greater understanding of informal learning is an important step in the development of effective human capital development policy. For example, if informal learning is better understood this has obvious implications for introducing new technology and designing workplace training.

What bearing do the mechanisms of sociology of education and the NALL research have on one another? One of the main findings of the NALL research is that, unlike formal schooling, informal learning is unrelated to personal characteristics such as sex, race, ethnicity and age (Livingstone 2000); it is also unrelated to formal education. This equity of adult learning could be the basis for the amelioration of human capital differences across groups that develop over the course of formal schooling as measured by achievement tests and completed years of schooling. There may be smaller group differences in the willingness to learn among adults, even if there are large group differences in the willingness to attend formal schooling in adolescence. Policy interventions that boost adult learning for those with weaker workplace skills may have more potential than has been claimed (e.g., Heckman 1998).

It is also possible to interpret equity in informal learning across sex, race, ethnicity and education groups as evidence of inequality in the returns to human capital across these same groups. In other words, as many have suggested, conventional indicators of human capital such as test scores and completed education may be much more strongly related to family background, race, etc. than human capital itself. Because formal academic credentials are held in such high regard compared to practical knowledge obtained outside academic institutions (Collins 1979), it will be difficult to argue this case without a convincing demonstration that the content of informal learning enhances productivity. Some programs attempt to measure the content of non-credentialed knowledge (e.g., Prior Learning Assessment and Recognition, PLAR), but the NALL research to date mostly addresses the duration of informal learning.[18]

Insofar as informal learning takes the form of learning from others, the literature on social capital and school effects seems highly relevant to the study of adult informal learning because it suggests that features of the workplace can affect learning. One possibility is to connect the informal learning literature and research with network analysis on information channels in the workplace (e.g., Burt 2004), which attempts to understand the properties of interpersonal networks that facilitate the goals of workers and/or their firms via information flows and social support.

The NALL/WALL research may also influence how we think about the learning that goes on in schools. It is possible that by bringing in styles of learning that occur away from the school into the school, the learning disparities observed across family background and race can be more effectively addressed. In the opposite direction, however, by bringing informal learning practices into the classroom, some pitfalls of particular forms of informal learning will be identified.

Most obviously, if learning goes on in a greater variety of activities than is normally acknowledged, then some of these activities can be incorporated into the formal schooling process (Schugurensky and Mündel 2005). This would serve to broaden the types of skills learned at school because respondents cited a broad range of personal and social skills developed that are not the focus of academic education. The recognition that learning takes place during a diversity of activities also suggests that student apathy could be reduced by introducing material and activities of a more obviously practical nature than purely academic material.

Policy Implications

The literature review demonstrates that there are few consensus positions in the sociology of education because thoughtful studies can generally be found to cast doubt on most conclusions; consequently, the state of the literature is such that unqualified support for one specific policy over another is rarely justified on empirical grounds. Nonetheless, the literature points to policy recommendations for grade retention, ability streaming and social capital development.

Grade retention is almost certainly a poor policy choice insofar as retained students' outcomes are concerned. It is intuitively obvious to most people that the threat of grade retention stimulates student effort and that poorly performing students could benefit from revisiting material that they have not mastered; however, the weight of the evidence is that grade retention does more harm than good for the performance of retained students. They appear to learn no more when retained, and they are far more likely to drop out of high school.

The evidence on the net effects of ability streaming is not as compelling, and we advocate neither ability streaming nor de-streaming. However, when ability streaming is in place, steps should be taken to eliminate inequities that, while not part of the ideal-type model of streaming, appear to develop in practice. Deviations from the meritocratic ideal of placement on the basis of academic and mental ability appear to follow a class-biased pattern in which higher-class students obtain higher-track placements, conditional on conventional measures of academic achievement and cognitive ability. Higher-track classes typically are taught by more experienced teachers and use more engaging teaching materials.

Social capital development also warrants policy consideration. Although the findings are plagued by selection-bias complications, it is difficult to see how trying to develop new forms of social capital could cause substantial harm. How best to develop social capital is unknown, however. With respect to social capital in the form of peer networks, perhaps the most obvious strategy would be to expand structured opportunities, such as extracurricular activities, to develop students' peer network. However, the literature suggests that many students are uninterested in structured activities, and that the uninterested often have low achievement and are the most vulnerable to dropping out. Perhaps these students can be better reached with mandatory activities, or expanded unstructured opportunities to develop their peer networks.

Although these sorts of interventions may have positive effects for those with pre-existing weak attachments to schooling, they should not be permitted to interfere with time devoted to instruction. And, the possibility that such interventions could backfire (e.g., by creating an opportunity for the cultivation and reinforcement of anti-schooling norms in some associational groups) must be recognized and prevented by school officials.

Recommendations for Further Research

There are many unanswered questions, but in this concluding section we focus on research topics relevant mostly to education in Canada that are not obvious from our prior summary of the literature.

Provocative Comparative Methodology

A fundamental problem faced in the research-policy nexus is that compelling research findings often fail to motivate policymakers and the public in a way that propels policy change because research that carefully attends to causal inference through statistical control fails to generate public interest in the way that narrative does (Levin 2002). Policy-oriented research should be, where it is sensible, designed at the outset to be provocative while at the same time attending carefully to the importance of control in causal inference. These goals can be met by employing comparative methods, in which one criterion for the selection of comparison cases is that their juxtaposition will generate interest.

Research that compares Canada to the US could be useful, and this possibility has guided the way in which we have structured our synthesis of the literature. As others have noted, Canada and the US serve well as each other's comparison case (Lipset 1990; Card and Freeman 1993; Ogmundson 2002) because they are very similar, and this is especially true for education systems. Each of the four types of explanations we have focused on could be motivated directly by Canada-US comparisons, perhaps particularly well when aligning provinces and US states with comparable populations.

These points may be obvious, but when considering how well each country could serve as the other's comparison case, there is surprisingly little Canada-US comparative work in sociology. Part of the process of encouraging this type of research could be an effort to accumulate information on dataset comparability. This could involve compiling a list of existing comparative Canada-US research. We believe that such an effort would substantially increase the volume of comparative research; if researchers knew which US datasets were compatible with which Canadian datasets on which issues, then the time-consuming and frustrating initial explorations into compatibility issues, and even into what datasets exist, would be greatly reduced.

Of course, one need not cross international borders to generate interest. Interprovincial comparisons in Canada may be more sensible in many cases because of their greater specificity. What we advocate here is that specificity and closeness of comparison cases not be the only criteria for choice; provocative comparisons should be pursued where possible. Deliberate attempts to compare "have" and "have-not" provinces, or to compare provinces with informal rivalries (e.g., Alberta and Ontario) could generate research of public interest. The policy implications of such research may then command greater public support.

Substantive Topics of Particular Interest in Canada

Two topics of research appear to be of particular interest in the present Canadian policy context: high-school completion and postsecondary institutional flatness. First, Audas and Willms (2001) have proposed that the NLSCY be used to study dropping out of high school from a lifecourse perspective. We propose that this project be pursued with comparative methods. Similarly, the NLSCY is well-suited to the study of postsecondary entry. One could study why high-ability students from disadvantaged backgrounds do not complete secondary school (or complete secondary school but do not pursue postsecondary education at expected rates). Research on high-ability students from disadvantaged backgrounds is also sensible because policies are most likely to have effects on them, and because there should be broad support for policies intended to encourage fairness and educational success for disadvantaged but talented students. For example, these policies should be supported even by those who believe that education acts primarily as a signal, as well as by those who think that promoting high-school completion for all necessarily involves lowering standards.

Second, research suggests that Canadian postsecondary education is becoming more institutionally hierarchical. As such, it is beginning to resemble postsecondary education in the United States. It seems sensible to study the causes and effects of this convergence, and it is therefore a natural topic for Canada-US comparisons. We do not claim that this is a novel proposal: the Canada-US comparison offered by Davies and Hammack (2005), for example, is exemplary and serves as a fine model for more widespread work.

Notes

We thank Kyle Siler and an anonymous reviewer for stimulating and helpful comments.

Direct correspondence to Stephen L. Morgan (slm45@cornell.edu) or Mark W. McKerrow (mwm22@cornell.edu) at Department of Sociology, 323 Uris Hall, Cornell University, Ithaca, NY 14853.

1. Our relative inattention to human capital development in adulthood is also consistent with the findings of some recent literature in economics, such as Heckman's conclusion that "adults past a certain age ... make poor investments" (1998,117) (see Krueger 2003, 42-55 for a contrary position). Moreover, Neal and Johnson (1996) conclude that most of the differences in wages between blacks, Hispanics, and non-Hispanic whites can be attributed to differences in cognitive skills that are formed by age 18. See our penultimate section where we discuss efforts to model lifelong learning in Canada.
2. See also the review paper of Hallinan (2001).
3. But see Morgan and Mehta (2004) for a dissenting view on disidentification.
4. Coleman, Hoffer and Kilgore (1982) also suggested that non-academic tracks are more demanding and have more academic courses in Catholic schools. Catholic schools also place a higher proportion of students in academic tracks conditional on students' background characteristics (Hoffer, Greeley and Coleman 1985).
5. See the *Family Background* section for some detail on Bourdieu's usage of cultural capital.
6. Definitions of social capital are often criticized for their generality. The expansive literature that now exists is testament to the appeal that such loose conceptualizations offer (see Burt 2000; Portes 1998; Sandefur and Laumann 1998; and Woolcock 1998 for reviews of the literature). And, ironically, the more specific ways in which Coleman used the concept of social capital have attracted little attention. Although almost never recognized, social capital has a more specific place in Coleman's formal theoretical system — the linear system of action (see Coleman 1990). In this system, social capital is any feature of social structure that actors use to facilitate exchange in order to reach an equilibrium that improves the welfare of all

engaged actors. For the simple system with which he introduces the framework, the relationship that two brothers have with their parents can be
used as social capital to facilitate the exchange of football and baseball
cards in order to improve the welfare of both traders.

7.   There is a large literature on neighbourhood effects on education, health
      and crime (e.g., Jencks and Mayer 1990; see Sampson, Morenoff and
      Gannon-Rowley 2002 for a review). It is strangely disconnected from the
      literature on school effects.

8.   In Morgan and Sørensen (1999*a*), the first author examined whether or not
      the network density of parents surrounding Catholic schools creates a
      norm-enforcing environment that is especially conducive to student learn-
      ing. In this paper, we found that this was generally the case, but alterna-
      tive relationships were present within the public school sector. Here,
      schools embedded in dense networks showed net lower levels of achieve-
      ment, suggesting that these communities were reinforcing norms not as
      clearly linked to student achievement.

9.   Its perspective is tellingly summarized in the textbook's publicity mate-
      rial: "Throughout the book, formal education is presented as a contested
      and contradictory endeavour that contributes to the reproduction of so-
      cial inequality at the same time it offers possibilities for social justice and
      change" (Wotherspoon 1998). See Davies (1995*a*) for a somewhat subver-
      sive summary of critical perspectives in the sociology of education.

10.   These datasets are produced by the *National Center for Education Statistics*,
      which has no direct counterpart in Canada. Canada also lacks a tradition
      of long-term, household-based longitudinal datasets, which are also widely
      used to study education in the United Sates. The data produced by Statis-
      tics Canada, however, is beginning to develop such a tradition. Even so,
      Canadian datasets, in general, are comparatively more difficult to access
      than those in other countries, because of confidentiality issues and resource
      barriers.

11.   Warren (2002) actually contests both the opportunity-cost and time-
      allocation explanations of the paid work-dropout relationship. He makes
      a strong case that the majority of the relationship between paid work and
      dropping out represents pre-existing disengagement from school. He also
      finds that paid employment detracts minimally from academically-oriented
      activities because working adolescents also spend less time with friends,
      watching television and so on.

12.   Frenette (2005*b*) also examines the issue of equity of postsecondary access
      by comparing the relationship between parental income and postsecond-
      ary attendance in Canada to the relationship in the US, concluding that

access is decidedly more equitable in Canada. However, Wanner (1993) finds that educational and occupational mobility are similar across the two countries.

13. We do not summarize research on francophone-anglophone differences, or on bilingualism issues.

14. Nagy (1996) emphasizes the need to consider variation in opportunities to learn when comparing results on standardized achievement tests across students who have been exposed to alternative curricula. He uses this argument, in particular, to argue that Canadian education is better in comparison to the educational systems of other countries, contrary to some of the alarmist literature.

15. See also Eisenberg (1995), Elliott and Maclennan (1994), and Lanning (1994) for related work.

16. For example, Janosz *et al* (1997) include extracurricular activities as a predictor, but pay it little attention.

17. The national survey for WALL was fielded in the winter of 2003/04, and results are expected to be released soon. Many working papers can be found at the WALL Web site, but they largely consist of literature reviews and the development of analytic typologies.

18. Eichler (2005) suggests that we should consider some form of remuneration for what is now unpaid house and care work. It seems unreasonable to expect that this would come into effect any time soon, but she and others are amenable to the quantification of the value of unpaid work (see also Schugurensky and Mündel 2005).

References

Ainsworth-Darnell, J.W. and D.B. Downey. 1998. "Assessing Racial/Ethnic Differences in School Performance," *American Sociological Review* 63:536-53.

Alexander, K.L., D.R. Entwisle and S.L. Dauber. 2003. *On the Success of Failure: A Reassessment of the Effects of Retention in the Primary Grades*. Cambridge: Cambridge University Press.

Audas, R. and J.D. Willms. 2001. "Engagement and Dropping out of School: A Life Course Perspective." Applied Research Branch Working Paper No. W-01-1-10E. Ottawa: Human Resources and Development Canada.

Aurini, J. 2005. "Educational Entrepreneurialism in the Private Tutoring Industry: Balancing Profitability with the Humanistic Face of Schooling," *Canadian Review of Sociology and Anthropology* 41(4):475-91.

Aurini, J. and S. Davies. 2005. "Choice Without Markets: Homeschooling in the Context of Private Education," *British Journal of Sociology of Education* 26(4):461-74.

Baldus, B. and M. Kassam. 1996. "'Make Me Truthful, Good, and Mild': Values in Nineteenth-Century Ontario Schoolbooks," *Canadian Journal of Sociology* 21(3):327-58.

Barr, R., R. Dreeben and N. Wiratchai. 1983. *How Schools Work*. Chicago: University of Chicago Press.

Beagan, B. 2001. "Micro Inequities and Everyday Inequalities: 'Race,' Gender, Sexuality and Class in Medical School," *Canadian Journal of Sociology* 26(4):583-610.

Bonnett, A. and B. Carrington. 1996. "Constructions of Anti-Racist Education in Britain and Canada," *Comparative Education* 32:271-88.

Bourdieu, P. 1973. "Cultural Reproduction and Social Reproduction," in *Knowledge, Education, and Cultural Change: Papers in the Sociology of Education*, ed. R.K. Brown. London: Tavistock Publications, pp. 71-112.

— 1986[1983]. "The Forms of Capital," in *Handbook of Theory and Research for the Sociology of Education*, ed. J.G. Richardson. New York: Greenwood Press, pp. 241-58.

Bourdieu, P. and J.C. Passeron. 1977. *Reproduction in Education, Society and Culture*. London, Beverly Hills: Sage Publications.

Breen, R. and J.H. Goldthorpe. 1997. "Explaining Educational Differentials: Towards a Formal Rational Action Theory," *Rationality and Society* 9:275-305.

Broh, B.A. 2002. "Linking Extracurricular Programming to Academic Achievement: Who Benefits and Why?" *Sociology of Education* 75:69-95.

Bryk, A.S. and B.L. Schneider. 2002. *Trust in Schools: A Core Resource for Improvement*. New York: Russell Sage Foundation.

Bryk, A.S., V.E. Lee and P.B. Holland. 1993. *Catholic Schools and the Common Good*. Cambridge, MA: Harvard University Press.

Burt, R.S. 2000. "The Network Structure of Social Capital," in *Research in Organizational Behavior*, Vol. 22, ed. R.I. Sutton and B.M. Staw. Greenwich, CT: JAI Press.

— 2004. "Structural Holes and Good Ideas," *American Journal of Sociology* 110(2):349-99.

Callan, E. 1995. "Common Schools for Common Education," *Canadian Journal of Education* 20:251-71.

Carbonaro, W.J. 1998. "A Little Help from My Friend's Parents: Intergenerational Closure and Educational Outcomes," *Sociology of Education* 71:295-313.

Card, D. and R.B. Freeman. 1993. *Small Differences that Matter: Labor Markets and Income Maintenance in Canada and the United States*. Chicago: The University of Chicago Press.

Card, D. and A.B. Krueger. 1996. "School Resources and Students Outcomes: An Overview of the Literature and New Evidence from North and South Carolina," *Journal of Educational Perspectives* 10:31-50.

Carr, P.R. and T.R. Klassen. 1997. "Different Perceptions of Race in Education: Racial Minority and White Teachers," *Canadian Journal of Education* 22:67-81.

Carrington, B. and A. Bonnett. 1997. "The Other Canadian 'Mosaic' – 'Race' Equity Education in Ontario and British Columbia," *Comparative Education* 33:411-31.

Carter, P.L. 2005. *Keepin' It Real: School Success Beyond Black and White*. New York: Oxford University Press.

Chubb, J.E. and T.M. Moe. 1990. *Politics, Markets, and America's Schools*. Washington, DC: The Brookings Institution.

Coleman, J.S. 1961. *The Adolescent Society: The Social Life of the Teenager and its Impact on Education*. New York: Free Press of Glencoe.

— 1988. "Social Capital in the Creation of Human Capital," *American Journal of Sociology* 94:S95-S120.

— 1990. *Foundations of Social Theory*. Cambridge, MA: Harvard University Press.

Coleman, J.S. and T. Hoffer. 1987. *Public and Private Schools: The Impact of Communities*. New York: Basic Books.

Coleman, J.S. and United States Office of Education. 1966. *Equality of Educational Opportunity*. Washington, DC: US Dept. of Health, Education, and Welfare.

Coleman, J.S., T. Hoffer and S. Kilgore. 1982. *High School Achievement: Public, Catholic, and Private Schools Compared*. New York: Basic Books.

Coleman, J.S., S.B. Kilgore, T. Hoffer. 1982. "Public and Private Schools," *Society* 19(2):4-9.

Coleman, P., L. Mikkelson and L. LaRocque. 1991. "Network Coverage: Administrative Collegiality and School District Ethos in High-Performing Districts," *Canadian Journal of Education* 16:151-67.

Collins, R. 1979. *The Credential Society*. New York: Academic Press.

Cook, P.J. and J. Ludwig. 1997. "Weighing the "Burden of 'Acting White'": Are There Race Differences in Attitudes toward Education?" *Journal of Policy Analysis and Management* 16:256-78.

Corak, M., G. Lipps and J. Zhao. 2003. *Family Income and Participation in Post-Secondary Education*. Analytic Studies Branch Research Paper Series. Catalogue No. 11F0019MIE - No. 210. Ottawa: Statistics Canada. At www.statcan.ca/cgi-bin/downpub/listpub.cgi?catno=11F0019MIE.

Craig, W.M., R. D. Peters and J.D. Willms. 2002. "The Role of the Peer Group in Pre-Adolescent Behavior," in *Vulnerable Children: Findings from Canada's National Longitudinal Survey of Children and Youth*, ed. J.D. Willms. Edmonton: University of Alberta Press, pp. 317-27.

Crocker, R.K. 2002. "A Decade of SAIP: What Have We Learned? What Do We Need to Know?" in *Towards Evidence-Based Policy for Canadian Education*, ed. P. de Broucker and A. Sweetman. Montreal and Kingston: McGill-Queen's

University Press and John Deutsch Institute for the Study of Economic Policy, Queen's University, pp. 207-25.

Davies, S. 1994. "In Search of Resistance and Rebellion among High School Dropouts," *Canadian Journal of Sociology* 19(3):331-50.

— 1995*a*. "Leaps of Faith: Shifting Currents in Critical Sociology of Education," *American Journal of Sociology* 100:1448-78.

— 1995*b*. "Reproduction and Resistance in Canadian High Schools: An Empirical Examination of the Willis Thesis," *The British Journal of Sociology* 46:662-87.

— 2002. "The Paradox of Progressive Education: A Frame Analysis," *Sociology of Education* 75:269-86.

— 2004. "School Choice by Default? Understanding the Demand for Private Tutoring in Canada," *American Journal of Education* 110(3):233-55.

Davies, S. and N. Guppy. 1997. "Globalization and Education Reforms in Anglo-American Democracies," *Comparative Education Review* 41:435-59.

Davies, S. and F.M. Hammack. "The Channeling of Student Competition in Higher Education: Comparing Canada and the US," *Journal of Higher Education* 76(1):89-106.

Davies, S. and L. Quirke. 2005. "Providing for the Priceless Student: Ideologies of Choice in an Emerging Private School Market," *American Journal of Education* 111(4):523-47.

de Brouker, P. 2005. *Without a Paddle: What to Do about Canada's Drop-outs.* CPRN Research Report No. W/30. Ottawa: Canadian Policy Research Networks. At www.cprn.org/en/doc.cfm.

Dei, G.J.S. 1996. "The Role of Afrocentricity in the Inclusive Curriculum in Canadian Schools," *Canadian Journal of Education* 21:170-86.

Drolet, M. 2005. *Participation in Post-Secondary Education in Canada: Has the Role of Parental Income and Education Changed over the 1990s?* Analytic Studies Branch Research Paper Series. Catalogue No. 11F0019MIE - No. 243. Ottawa: Statistics Canada. At www.statcan.ca/cgi-bin/downpub/listpub.cgi?catno=11F0019MIE.

Dworkin, J.B., R. Larson and D. Hansen. 2003. "Adolescents' Accounts of Growth Experiences in Youth Activities," *Journal of Youth and Adolescence* 32(1):17-26.

Dyson, L.L. 2001. "Home-School Communication and Expectations of Recent Chinese Immigrants," *Canadian Journal of Education* 26:455-76.

Eder, D. 1981. "Ability Grouping as a Self-Fulfilling Prophecy," *Sociology of Education* 54:151-62.

Eichler, M. 2005. "The Other Half, or More of the Story: Unpaid Household and Care Work and Lifelong Learning," in *International Handbook of Educational Policy,* ed. N. Bascia, A. Cumming, A. Datnow, K. Leithwood and

D. Livingstone. Vol. 13 of *Springer International Handbooks of Education*. Dordrecht: Springer.

Eisenberg, J. 1995. "The Limits of Educational Research: Why Most Research and Grand Plans in Education Are Futile and Wasteful," *Curriculum Inquiry* 25:367-80.

Ellenbogen, S. and C. Chamberland. 1997. "The Peer Relations of Dropouts: A Comparative Study of at-Risk and not at-Risk Youths," *Journal of Adolescence* 20:355-67.

Elliott, B. and D. Maclennan. 1994. "Education, Modernity, and Neo-Conservative School Reform in Canada, Britain and the US," *British Journal of Sociology of Education* 15:165-85.

Feldman, A.F. and J.L. Matjasko. 2005. "The Role of School-Based Extracurricular Activities in Adolescent Development: A Comprehensive Review and Future Directions," *Review of Educational Research* 75(2):159-210.

Finn, C. 1989. "Withdrawing from School," *Review of Educational Research* 59:117-42.

Fordham, S. and J.U. Ogbu. 1986. "Black Students' School Success: Coping with the Burden of Acting White," *The Urban Review* 18:1-31.

Frempong, G. and J.D. Willms. 2002. "Can School Quality Compensate for Socioeconomic Disadvantage?" in *Vulnerable Children: Findings from Canada's National Longitudinal Survey of Children and Youth*, ed. J.D. Willms. Edmonton: University of Alberta Press, pp. 277-303 .

Frenette, M. 2005a. *The Impact of Tuition Fees on University Access: Evidence from a Large-Scale Price Deregulation in Professional Programs*. Analytic Studies Branch Research Paper Series Catalogue No. 11F0019MIE - No. 263. Ottawa: Statistics Canada. At www.statcan.ca/cgi-bin/downpub/listpub .cgi?catno= 11F0019MIE.

— 2005b. *Is Post-Secondary Access More Equitable in Canada or the United States?* Analytic Studies Branch Research Paper Series. Catalogue No. 11F0019MIE - No. 244. Ottawa: Statistics Canada. At www.statcan.ca/cgi-bin/downpub/ listpub.cgi?catno=11F0019MIE.

Gambetta, D. 1987. *Were they Pushed or Did they Jump? Individual Decision Mechanisms in Education*. Cambridge: Cambridge University Press.

Gamoran, A. 1992. "The Variable Effect of High School Tracking," *American Sociological Review* 57:812-28.

Gamoran, A. and R.D. Mare. 1989. "Secondary School Tracking and Education Inequality: Compensation, Reinforcement, or Neutrality?" *American Journal of Sociology* 94:1146-83.

Gilman, R. 2001. "The Relationship Between Life Satisfaction, Social Interest, and Frequency of Extracurricular Activities among Adolescent Students," *Journal of Youth and Adolescence* 30(6):749-67.

Guppy, N.L. and S. Davies. 1998. *Education in Canada: Recent Trends and Future Challenges*. Ottawa: Statistics Canada.

— 1999. "Understanding Canadians' Declining Confidence in Public Education," *Canadian Journal of Education* 24:265-80.

Haller, A.O. 1982. "Reflections on the Social Psychology of Status Attainment," in *Social Structure and Behavior: Essays in Honor of William Hamilton Sewell, Studies in Population*, ed. R.J. Hauser, D. Mechanic, A.O. Haller and T.S. Hauser. New York: Academic Press.

Hallinan, M.T. 1994. "Tracking: From Theory to Practice," *Sociology of Education* 67:79-84.

— 1996. "Track Mobility in Secondary School," *Social Forces* 74:983-1002.

—, ed. 2000. *Handbook of the Sociology of Education*. New York: Kluwer Academic/Plenum Publishers.

— 2001. "Sociological Perspectives on Black-White Inequalities in American Schooling," *Sociology of Education* (Special Issue):50-70.

Hallinan, M.T. and A.B. Sørensen. 1983. "The Formation and Stability of Instructional Groups," *American Sociological Review* 48:838-51.

Halsey, A.H., H. Lauder, P. Brown and A.S. Wells, eds. 1997. *Education: Culture, Economy, and Society*. Oxford: Oxford University Press.

Hanushek, E.A. 2001. "Spending on Schools," in *A Primer on America's Schools*, ed. T.M. Moe. Stanford, CA: Hoover Institution Press, Stanford University, pp. 69-88.

Hauser, R.M. 2004a. "Progress in Schooling," in *Social Inequality*, ed. K.M. Neckerman. New York: Russell Sage, pp. 271-318.

— 2004b. "Schooling and Academic Achievement in Time and Place," *Research in Social Stratification and Mobility* 21:47-65.

Hauser, R.M., S.J. Simmons and D.I. Pager. 2004. "High School Dropout, Race-Ethnicity, and Social Background from the 1970s to the 1990s," in *Dropouts in America: Confronting the Graduation Rate Crisis*, ed. G. Orfield. Cambridge, MA: Harvard Education Press, pp. 85-106.

Heckman, J.J. 1998. "What Should Be Our Human Capital Investment Policy?" *Fiscal Studies* 19(2):103-19.

Hedges, L.V. and B.L. Schneider, eds. 2005. *The Social Organization of Schooling*. New York: Russell Sage Foundation.

Hoffer, T., A.M. Greeley and J.S. Coleman. 1985. "Achievement Growth in Public and Catholic Schools," *Sociology of Education* 58:74-97.

Holland, A. and T. Andre. 1987. "Participation in Extracurricular Activities in Secondary School: What is Known, What Needs to be Known?" *Review of Educational Research* 57(4):437-66.

Howell, W.G. and P.E. Peterson. 2002. *The Education Gap: Vouchers and Urban Schools*. Washington, DC: The Brookings Institution Press.

Hoxby, C.M. 1996. "The Effects of Private School Vouchers on Schools and Students," in *Holding Schools Accountable: Performance-Based Reform in Education*, ed. H.F. Ladd. Washington, DC: The Brookings Institution, pp. 177-208.

—, ed. 2003. *The Economics of School Choice*. Chicago: University of Chicago Press.

Janosz, M., M. LeBlanc, B. Boulerice and R.E. Tremblay. 1997. "Disentangling the Weight of School Dropout Predictors: A Test on Two Longitudinal Samples," *Journal of Youth and Adolescence* 26(6):733-62.

Jencks, C. and S.E. Mayer. 1990. "The Social Consequences of Growing up in a Poor Neighborhood," in *Inner-City Poverty in the United States*, ed. L.E. Lynn and M.G.H. McGreary. Washington, DC: National Academy Press, pp. 111 86.

Jencks, C. and M. Phillips, eds. 1998. *The Black-White Test Score Gap*. Washington, DC: The Brookings Institution Press.

Jimerson, S.R., G. E. Anderson and A.D. Whipple. 2002. "Winning the Battle and Losing the War: Examining the Relation between Grade Retention and Dropping out of High School," *Psychology in the Schools* 39(4):441-57.

Jordan, W.J. and S.M. Nettles. 2000. "How Students Invest their Time Outside of School: Effects on School-Related Outcomes," *Social Psychology of Education* 3:217-43.

Kahl, J. 1953. "Educational and Occupational Aspirations of Common Man Boys," *Harvard Educational Review* 23:186-203.

Karabel, J. and A.H. Halsey, eds. 1977. *Power and Ideology in Education*. New York: Oxford University Press.

Kerckhoff, A.C. 1976. "The Status Attainment Process: Socialization or Allocation?" *Social Forces* 55:368-81.

Krueger, A.B. 2003. "Inequality, too Much of a Good Thing," in *Inequality in America: What Role for Human Capital Policies?* ed. B.M. Friedman. Cambridge, MA: MIT Press, pp. 1-75.

Lanning, R. 1994. "Education and Everyday Life: An Argument against 'Educational Futures'," *Canadian Journal of Education* 19:464-78.

Lareau, A. 1987. "Social Class Differences in Family-School Relationships: The Importance of Cultural Capital," *Sociology of Education* 60:73-85.

Lee, V.E. and J.B. Smith. 1993. "Effects of School Restructuring on the Achievement and Engagement of Middle-Grade Students," *Sociology of Education* 66:164-87.

— 1995. "Effects of High School Restructuring and Size on Early Gains in Achievement and Engagement," *Sociology of Education* 68:241-70.

Lee, V.E., J.B. Smith and R.G. Croninger. 1997. "How High School Organiza-tion Influences the Equitable Distribution of Learning in Mathematics and Science," *Sociology of Education* 70:128-50.

Lehmann, W. 2005. "Choosing to Labour: Structure and Agency in School-Work Transitions," *Canadian Journal of Sociology* 30:325-50.

Levin, B. 2002. "Knowledge and Action in Educational Policy and Politics," in *Towards Evidence-Based Policy for Canadian Education*, ed. P. de Broucker and A. Sweetman. Montreal and Kingston: McGill-Queen's University Press and John Deutsch Institute for the Study of Economic Policy, Queen's Univer-sity, pp. 55-63.

Lipset, S.M.. 1990. *Continental Divide: The Values and Institutions of the United States and Canada*. New York: Routledge.

Livingstone, D.W. 2000. "Exploring the Icebergs of Adult Learning: Findings of the First Canadian Survey of Informal Learning Practices." New Ap-proaches to Lifelong Learning, Working Paper No. 10-2000. At www.nall.ca/res/10exploring.htm.

Lucas, S.R. 1999. *Tracking Inequality: Stratification and Mobility in American High Schools*. New York: Teachers College Press.

Lyons, J.E., B.S. Randhawa and N.A. Paulson. 1991. "The Development of Vo-cational Education in Canada," *Canadian Journal of Education* 16:137-50.

Ma, X. 2001. "Stability of Socio-Economic Gaps in Mathematics and Science Achievement among Canadian Schools," *Canadian Journal of Education* 26:97-118.

Ma, X. and D.A. Klinger. 2000. "Hierarchical Linear Modelling of Student and School Effects on Academic Achievement," *Canadian Journal of Education* 25:41-55.

Mahoney, J.L. 2000. "School Extracurricular Activity Participation as a Mod-erator in the Development of Antisocial Patterns," *Child Development* 71:502-16.

Mahoney, J.L. and R.B. Cairns. 1997. "Do Extracurricular Activities Protect against Early School Dropout?" *Development Psychology* 33:241-53.

Maxwell, M.P. and J.D. Maxwell. 1995. "Going Co-Ed: Elite Private Schools in Canada," *Canadian Journal of Sociology* 20(3):333-57.

Maxwell, M.P., J.D. Maxwell and E. Krugly-Smolska. 1996. "Ethnicity, Gender, and Occupational Choice in Two Toronto Schools," *Canadian Journal of Edu-cation* 21:257-79.

McHale, S.M., A.C. Crouter and C.J. Tucker. 2001. "Free Time Activities in Mid-dle Childhood: Links with Adjustment in Early Adolescence," *Child Devel-opment* 72:1764-78.

McLauglin, N. 2004. "A Canadian Rejoinder: Sociology North and South of the Border," *American Sociologist* 35(1):80-101.

McNeal, R.B. Jr. 1999. "Parental Involvement as Social Capital: Differential Effectiveness on Science Achievement, Truancy, and Dropping Out," *Social Forces* 78(1):117-44.

Meyer, J.W., F.O. Ramirez and Y.N. Soysal. 1992. "World Expansion of Mass Education, 1870-1980," *Sociology of Education* 65:128-49.

Morgan, S.L. 2000. "Social Capital, Capital Goods, and the Production of Learning," *Journal of Socio-Economics* 29:591-95.

— 2001. "Counterfactuals, Causal Effect Heterogeneity, and the Catholic School Effect on Learning," *Sociology of Education* 74:341-74.

— 2005. *On the Edge of Commitment: Educational Attainment and Race in the United States*. Stanford, CA: Stanford University Press.

Morgan, S.L. and J. Mehta. 2004. "Beyond the Laboratory: Evaluating the Survey Evidence for the Disidentification Explanation of Black-White Differences in Achievement," *Sociology of Education* 77(1):82-101.

Morgan, S.L. and A.B. Sørensen. 1999a. "Parental Networks, Social Closure, and Mathematics Learning: A Test of Coleman's Social Capital Explanation of School Effects," *American Sociological Review* 64:661-81.

— 1999b. "Theory, Measurement, and Specification Issues in Models of Network Effects on Learning: Reply to Carbonaro and to Hallinan and Kubitschek," *American Sociological Review* 64:694-700.

Nagy, P. 1996. "International Comparisons of Student Achievement in Mathematics and Science: A Canadian Perspective," *Canadian Journal of Education* 21:396-413.

Nakhaie, M.R. and J. Curtis. 1998. "Effects of Class Positions of Parents on Educational Attainment of Daughters and Sons," *Canadian Review of Sociology and Anthropology* 35(4):483-515.

Neal, D. and W. Johnson. 1996. "The Role of Premarket Factors in Black-White Wage Differences," *Journal of Political Economy* 104(5):869-95.

Oakes, J. 1985. *Keeping Track: How Schools Structure Inequality*. New Haven: Yale University Press.

— 1994. "More than Misapplied Technology: A Normative and Political Response to Hallinan on Tracking," *Sociology of Education* 67:85-89.

Ogmundson, R. 2002. "The Canadian Case: Cornucopia of Neglected Research Opportunities," *American Sociologist* 33(1):55-78.

Orfield, G. and M.L. Kornhaber, eds. 2001. *Raising Standards or Raising Barriers? Inequality and High-Stakes Testing in Public Education*. New York: Century Foundation Press.

Parker, J.G. and S.R. Asher. 1987. "Peer Relations and Later Personal Adjustment: Are Low-Accepted Children at Risk?" *Psychological Bulletin* 102(3):357-89.

Peterson, C. 1994. "Narrative Skills and Social Class," *Canadian Journal of Education* 19(3):251-69.

Peterson, P.E. and B.C. Hassel, eds. 1998. *Learning from School Choice*. Washington, DC: The Brookings Institution Press.

Porter, J. 1965. *The Vertical Mosaic: An Analysis of Social Class and Power in Canada*. Toronto: University of Toronto Press.

Portes, A. 1998. "Social Capital: Its Origins and Applications in Modern Sociology," *Annual Review of Sociology* 22:1-24.

Quirke, L. and S. Davies. 2002. "The New Entrepreneurship in Higher Education: The Impact of Tuition Increases at an Ontario University," *Canadian Journal of Higher Education* 32(3):85-109.

Reis, S.M. and E. Diaz. 1999. "Economically Disadvantaged Urban Female Students Who Achieve in School," *Urban Review* 31(1):31-54.

Richer, S. 1974. "Programme Composition and Educational Plans," *Sociology of Education* 47(3):337-53.

Rosenbaum, J.E. 1976. *Making Inequality: The Hidden Curriculum of High School Tracking*. New York: Wiley.

— 2001. *Beyond College for All: Career Paths for the Forgotten Half*. New York: Russell Sage Foundation.

Ross, J.A., S. McKeiver and A. Hogaboam-Gray. 1997. "Fluctuations in Teacher Efficacy During Implementation of Destreaming," *Canadian Journal of Education* 22:283.

Ryan, J. 1989. "Disciplining the Innut: Normalization, Characterization, and Schooling," *Curriculum Inquiry* 19:379-403.

Sale, T. and B. Levin. 1991. "Problems in the Reform of Educational Finance: A Case Study," *Canadian Journal of Education* 16:32-48.

Sampson, R.J., J.D. Morenoff and T. Gannon-Rowley. 2002. "Assessing 'Neighborhood Effects': Social Processes and New Directions in Research," *Annual Review of Sociology* 28:443-78.

Sandefur, R.L. and E.O. Laumann. 1998. "A Paradigm for Social Capital," *Rationality and Society* 10(4):481-501.

Sayer, L.C., A.H. Gauthier and F.F. Furstenberg. 2004. "Educational Differences in Parents' Time with Children: Cross-National Variations," *Journal of Marriage and the Family* 66:1152-69.

Schugurensky, D. and K. Mündel. 2005. "Volunteer Work and Learning: Hidden Dimensions of Labour Force Training," in *International Handbook of Educational Policy*, ed. N. Bascia, A. Cumming, A. Datnow, K. Leithwood and D. Livingstone. Vol. 13 of *Springer International Handbooks of Education*. Dordrecht: Springer.

Sewell, W.H., A.O. Haller and G.W. Ohlendorf. 1970. "The Educational and Early Occupational Status Attainment Process: Replication and Revision," *American Sociological Review* 35:1014-24.

Sewell, W.H., A.O. Haller and A. Portes. 1969. "The Educational and Early Occupational Attainment Process," *American Sociological Review* 34:82-92.

Shepard, L.A. and M.L. Smith, eds. 1989. *Flunking Grades: Research and Policies on Retention*. London: Falmer Press.

Smith, M.R. 2000. "What is to be Done? And do we have any Choice?" *Canadian Journal of Sociology* 25(2):239-51.

Spenner, K.I. and D.L. Featherman. 1978. "Achievement Ambitions," *Annual Review of Sociology* 4:373-420.

Steele, C.M. 1992. "Race and the Schooling of Black Americans," *Atlantic Monthly* 269:68-78.

— 1997. "A Threat in the Air: How Stereotypes Shape Intellectual Identity and Performance," *The American Psychologist* 52:613-29.

Steele, C.M. and J. Aronson. 1995. "Stereotype Threat and the Intellectual Test Performance of African Americans," *Journal of Personality and Social Psychology* 69:797-811.

Steele, C.M., S.J. Spencer and J. Aronson. 2002. "Contending with Group Image: The Psychology of Stereotype and Social Identity Threat," in *Advances in Experimental Social Psychology*, vol. 34, ed. M.P. Zanna. Amsterdam: Academic Press.

Taylor, A. 2005. "'Re-culturing' Students and Selling Futures: School-to-work Policy in Ontario," *Journal of Education and Work* 18(3):321-40.

Tyack, D.B. 1974. *The One Best System: A History of American Urban Education*. Cambridge, MA: Harvard University Press.

Tyack, D.B. and L. Cuban. 1995. *Tinkering Toward Utopia: A Century of Public School Reform*. Cambridge, MA: Harvard University Press.

Useem, E.L. 1992. "Middle Schools and Math Groups: Parents' Involvement in Children's Placement," *Sociology of Education* 5:263-79.

Walberg, H.J., A.J. Reynolds and M.C. Wang. 2004. *Can Unlike Students Learn Together? Grade Retention, Tracking, and Grouping*. Greenwich, CT: Information Age Pub.

Wanner, R.A. 1993. "Patterns and Trends in Occupational Mobility," in *Social Inequality in Canada*, 2nd edition, ed. J. Curtis *et al.* Scarborough: Prentice-Hall, pp. 153-78.

Warren, J.R. 2002. "Reconsidering the Relationship Between Student Employment and Academic Outcomes: A New Theory and Better Data," *Youth & Society* 33(3):366-93.

Wellner, K.G. and J. Oakes. 2000. *Navigating the Politics of Detracking: Leadership Strategies*. Arlington Heights, IL: SkyLight Professional Development.

Westbury, M. 1994. "The Effect of Elementary Grade Retention on Subsequent School Achievement and Ability," *Canadian Journal of Education* 19:241-50.

Willms, J.D. 2002. *Vulnerable Children: Findings from Canada's National Longitudinal Survey of Children and Youth*. Edmonton: University of Alberta Press.

Woolcock, M. 1998. "Social Capital and Economic Development: Toward a Theoretical Synthesis and Policy Framework," *Theory and Society* 27:151-208.

Wotherspoon, T. 1998. *The Sociology of Education in Canada: Critical Perspectives*. Toronto: Oxford University Press.

— 2004. *The Sociology of Education in Canada: Critical Perspectives*, 2nd edition. Toronto: Oxford University Press.

Wotherspoon, T. and B. Schissel. 2001. "The Business of Placing Canadian Children and Youth 'at-Risk'," *Canadian Journal of Education* 26:321-39.

8

Human Capital, Civic Engagement and Political Participation: Turning Skills and Knowledge into Engagement and Action

BRENDA O'NEILL

Democracies benefit from an engaged and informed citizenry. Citizens are more likely to engage in the political and civic arenas when they possess the skills and knowledge that reduce the costs associated with that engagement. Skills and knowledge are more likely to translate into participation when combined with the motivation to engage. Education provides a significant payoff in terms of political and civic engagement by providing the cognitive skills and affective motivation behind participation. Education provides returns in the form of greater levels of and more effective participation in political and civic affairs but also greater representational gains both in the articulation of interests to and from elected representatives.

Introduction

The study of political science has recently experienced a renewed interest in the field of political behaviour, particularly as it relates to political participation. This renewed interest can be linked to two distinct sources. On the one hand, declining rates of voter turnout in a number of western democracies over the past two decades have sparked an interest in understanding how and why citizens decide whether or not to participate in politics (for comparative data on voter turnout, see International IDEA 2006). Concern for the perceived "democratic deficit" which dropping voter turnout levels appear to indicate, or at least for its weaker cousin a democratic malaise, has sparked increased interest in the field.[1] Second, the publication of Robert Putnam's *Bowling*

Alone in 2000, which argues that declining participation in social activities (hence the title) in the United States has led to a decline in social capital (consisting of social networks and norms of reciprocity), provides an intuitively pleasing and empirically testable model for examining the causes of participation decline that has since sparked a flurry of research on the topic. This paper fits squarely within this field of interest by examining political participation and the broader topic of civic engagement. At its core, it focuses on the question of what helps us to account for why some individuals are more likely to participate in politics than others, and in so doing, provides insight into possible policy responses for addressing declining rates of participation. Unlike much of existing literature, however, it approaches this question with one concept in particular in mind: human capital.

Investigating political participation and civic engagement through the lens of human capital is an approach distinct from much of existing research on the topic. The dominant approach has been to examine the socio-demographic, institutional and psychological bases for political participation to better understand how and why citizens decide to exercise their civic muscle (Dalton 1996). Research into declining voter turnout levels has concentrated specifically on investigating the various costs and benefits associated with voting with the hope of better understanding such decisions at the individual level. Defining human capital as the *set of skills and knowledge that can be drawn upon to produce outputs of value* and adopting the concept as a lens through which to examine engagement, however, brings to the examination a consideration of both the costs and benefits associated with action but additionally frames the examination within the context of a long-term investment. This notion of investment can be applied at both the individual and societal levels in an effort to better understand citizen engagement and the health of democracies.

The paper begins with a brief review of the human capital concept, and its relatively limited use within the discipline of political science. Next, the concepts of civic engagement and political participation are introduced, summarized and contrasted to provide a stronger foundation for proceeding with an examination of each through the lens of human capital. Democratic theory is briefly reviewed to provide a foundation for addressing the assumptions made about citizens in democracies, and then the concept of social capital is introduced to elaborate on the linkages between social and human capital.

The paper then addresses the various sources of the skills and knowledge that have been linked to political participation and civic engagement, including social determinants such as socio-economic status and gender, and more psychological factors such as political interest and political knowledge. The paper then moves on to a critical examination of civic engagement and political participation as "outputs of value," at both the societal and individual levels and closes with an examination of the policy implications of unequal access to human capital and suggested directions for future research in this area. Throughout the paper the focus of the discussion is concentrated on research and theory on advanced industrial democracies.

One of the key findings of the paper is that examining civic engagement and political participation from a human capital point of view makes clear the important role of education in democracies; investment in education provides substantial returns in terms of political participation and citizen engagement by increasing civic skills and political knowledge levels. The returns are likely to not only generate greater levels of and more effective involvement in politics and civil society but also greater representational gains both in the articulation of interests and from elected representatives. Another is the important role played by mobilization agencies in the private and voluntary sectors, both for the skills they engender among their members and their ability to overcome representational deficits due to participation deficits among certain groups; this role can be particularly important for those citizens for whom education cannot be expected to provide a participatory boost, that is, for those who have dropped out of the formal education system prior to earning a high-school diploma.

Concepts and Theoretical Framework

Human Capital

The use of the term "human capital" is most closely associated with the work of American economist Gary S. Becker beginning in the 1960s (Becker 1964). Becker's insight was to apply an economic model to human behaviour. In it, individual agents are assumed to act in a rational manner and in accordance with a desire to maximize the potential for achieving some outcome. In the case of the human capital model, individuals are assumed to act in such a manner as to maximize their potential for income and/or wealth. More specifically, investments in education and training are seen as costs incurred at one point in time with the expectation of reaping returns on them, in the form of monetary benefits and wealth, at a later date. The model is applied at the individual level but provides important insight into not only the social factors that can be considered to influence individual investment decisions but also the manner in which these individual level decisions influence outcomes at the aggregate, or societal, level. Outputs of value for individuals may produce positive externalities at a higher level.

One of the earliest references to human capital of consequence for the political science literature was from James Coleman, a social theorist, who argued that it consisted of "changes in persons that bring about skills and capabilities that make them able to act in new ways" (1988, 100). For Coleman, an ability to explain human actions requires more than simply an investigation of the opportunities and resources available to them; instead, as a sociologist, Coleman argued for including the social context within which such decisions were made, in light of its impact on the decision's outcome. The social context, or as he referred to it, the social capital, is a key element in the decision-making equation.[2]

One line of research that is particularly relevant to the discussion herein is that which evaluates the impact of democracy on economic growth. According to Baum and Lake, "investments in human capital are influenced in important ways by the type of regime in power" (2003, 336). Democracy has been shown to be positively related to levels of public health and education — two proxies of human capital (Lake and Baum 2001). When using indicators for public health such as life expectancy and infant mortality, and for education such as adult literacy, empirical results reveal that the "causal arrow appears to run from democracy to public health and education rather than the reverse" (Baum and Lake 2003, 335). Democracies are much more likely to invest in public services, which can lead to direct and indirect effects on the level of human capital within a state. Importantly, the political system which relies on its citizens as participants in its decision-making processes appears to be most likely to invest in them. These investments, predominantly in the form of increased education and health services, provide citizens with the skills and knowledge necessary for political participation and engagement. Whether democracies invest adequately in their citizens, however, is a question worth asking and one that will be returned to below.

Civic Engagement and Political Participation

A review of the literature on political participation and civic engagement reveals the relative fluidity and overlap between the two concepts, and a rather high level of conceptual fuzziness in their application. Maintaining conceptual distinction between the two concepts is particularly important for delineating the political from the larger civic sphere; although equally important, activities directed at the formal political arena are not the same as those directed at the civic community either for the reasons that lie behind that involvement or for the expectations tied to that participation.

Civic engagement generally is taken to represent a larger set of activities and involvement that includes political participation but extends beyond it to include activities in civil society which, according to Skocpol and Fiorina, is "the network of ties and groups through which people connect to one another and get drawn into community and political affairs" (1999, 2). For Putnam "civic engagement historically has come in many sizes and shapes" (2000, 27) and his review of civic engagement in the US includes activity in politics and public affairs, involvement in community associations ("clubs and community associations, religious bodies, and work-related organizations, such as unions and professional societies," ibid.), and informal associations and activities (ranging from bowling leagues to picnics and parties). Additionally, engagement is often distinguished from participation in that it does not restrict itself to physical activity; instead, civic engagement is normally defined to include psychological engagement in civil society. Common measures of civic engagement include such indicators as political interest, media consumption and political knowledge in that these provide a measure of the degree to which citizens are mentally participating in society. On the whole, civic engagement refers to the actions, beliefs and knowledge that link citizens to their societies and that establish the basis for cooperative behaviour.

Political participation, on the other hand, is normally restricted to conventional and unconventional activities specifically undertaken to influence political decision-making in the formal arena (Dalton 1996, chs. 2 and 3). Verba and Nie, for example, define political participation as "those activities by private citizens that are more or less directly aimed at influencing the selection of governmental personnel and/or the actions they take" (1972, 2). At its worst, political research sometimes employs voting alone as a proxy for political participation, thereby limiting a wide-ranging and multi-pronged concept to a single indicator. At its best, research taps into the multiple modes and objectives of political activity, including voting and elections, interest group and social movement activity, and protest behaviour. The recent broadening of the concept of political participation to include more civic modes of engagement, such as volunteering activities, has been criticized for having defined the concept in such an inclusive manner that the study of political participation has become in some ways "the study of everything" (van Deth 2001). Burns, Schlozman and Verba for example, in their examination of gender and political participation assess a wide range of activities that includes, but extends beyond, voting and electoral activities to include "involvement in organizations to take stands in politics, *informal efforts to address community problems; and voluntary service on local governing boards or regular attendance at meetings of such boards*" (2001, 55, italics added). This definition extends beyond influencing politics to activities such as community action, an important investigation without question, but one that clouds the distinction between civic and political activity.

Political participation should also be distinguished from the separate concept of political engagement. The latter concept importantly encompasses the psychological as well as physical dimensions of political activity, and normally addresses such elements as political interest, political knowledge, political efficacy and political cynicism. The psychological dimension of political activity provides explanatory value with respect to political participation: the more interested and knowledgeable one is about politics, the more likely one is to participate (and vice versa). But the two concepts are not one and the same thing, and maintaining the conceptual distinction is essential.

Democracy and Human Capital

Any discussion of civic engagement and political participation ought to reflect on democratic theory. The underlying assumption of much of the civic engagement literature is that democracy requires a particular level of participation by its citizens to be considered legitimate. Two questions stem from this premise: first, what assumptions does democratic theory make regarding the skills and capacity of its citizens? And second, what level of participation is required for democratic legitimacy?

Modern political democracy rests in part on the notions of democracy established in ancient Athens (Held 1996). And these notions rest firmly on the assumptions made about citizens, their duties, skills and abilities. David Held (1996) suggests that Athenian democracy was premised on an understanding that all citizens ought to participate in decision-making at the community level.[3] Although not all citizens would have equal ability, participation in public life was considered a means of developing the skills and capacity necessary to achieve the goal of the common good.

The point of citizen skills and knowledge in early democracies is also taken up by Paul Woodruff in his work, *First Democracy*. As he points out, the idea that all citizens, by virtue of being human beings, are equally capable of governing is perhaps democracy's most controversial assumption (2005, 149). As explained by Woodruff, "citizen wisdom is what the citizens in a well-run democracy ought to have. It builds on common human abilities to perceive, reason, and judge, but it requires also healthy traditions and good education for all" (ibid., 154). In political matters, trust is to be placed in the capacities of ordinary citizens rather than experts since the latter would adopt positions on issues dictated by self-interest.

Education, according to Woodruff, plays an important role in the development of citizen wisdom, as it acquaints citizens with new ideas and helps to develop tolerance. The source of citizen wisdom is quite simply common human wisdom improved by education. Not any education, however, but rather the type of education that makes for better human beings and for greater virtue. According to Woodruff this particular form of education is one that teaches about community understandings of justice and reverence: *Paideia* (ibid., ch. 9).

The benefits of education for democracy extend, one can argue, into modern representative democracies in addition to the more direct example of democracy in early Athens.[4] As noted by one researcher, "it is reasonably clear that good citizens are made, not born" (Galston 2001, 217). In representative democracies, education can provide the skills and knowledge that lower the costs associated with selecting among candidates in elections, with developing an understanding of political issues and debates, and with assessing the quality of governance. Moreover, it can assist in building the set of values upon which democracy rests, including among others, tolerance. In short, it can improve the *effectiveness* of political participation (Milligan, Moretti and Oreopoulos 2004).

The second question relates to the level of political participation required for democratic legitimacy. Two contrasting arguments can be identified: those who support increased levels of public input into political decision-making, and those whose support for political participation is more guarded. This debate has a long and distinguished history in the discipline. John Stuart Mill, for example, advocated that the best democracy is one in which as many citizens as possible voice their own interests; participation not only improves the political system, it improves its citizens as well. Schumpeter, on the other hand, argued for much more limited participation by citizens, restricted mainly to voting in general elections for the selection of political representatives and to ensure the accountability of elected officials.[5]

More recently, a Standing Committee of the American Political Science Association tasked with examining "the problem of civic engagement" (p. vii) provided a number of arguments for why robust citizen engagement is essential for American (and presumably any western) democracy (Macedo *et al.*, 2005, 4-5). Civic engagement, they argue, enhances the quality of democratic governance by providing direct and incontestable evidence of citizen preferences to decisionmakers. Second, democratic governance is only legitimate when the vast majority of citizens participate in self-rule; in line with J.S. Mill, governments are most likely to respond to the interests of those who mobilize and thus the greater the share of the population that mobilizes, the greater the number of interests that will be recognized. Third, citizen skills and knowledge are enhanced by direct participation and involvement in the political system: people learn by doing. And finally, a citizenry that is civically engaged can "provide a wide variety of goods and services that neither the state not the market can replace" leading to better lives and better communities (ibid., 5).

The argument that high levels of civic engagement and participation necessarily enhance or are required to guarantee the success of democracy is not universally held. In their classic treatment of voting behaviour in the US, Berelson, Lazarsfeld and McPhee (1954) indicate that successful democracies require a balance in the collective properties of the electorate; too much political interest, for example, can lead to extreme partisanship which can impede compromise and consensus. Almond and Verba develop a similar argument in stating that the model of democracy calling for active, informed and involved citizens neither reflects the reality of successful democracies such as the United States and Great Britain nor understands the need to mitigate political activity; the ability of democratic governments to balance responsiveness and power instead requires "that the ordinary citizen be relatively passive, uninvolved, and deferential to elites" (1963, 343). The key is to balance political activity with passivity.

In spite of such evidence, the dominant view remains that political participation and civic education are to be encouraged given the instrumental and expressive function performed by such acts. The benefits to democracy of an engaged citizenry, it is argued, outweigh whatever costs are associated with such participation.

Social Capital, Human Capital and Democracy

Much research attention has been devoted recently to an examination of social capital, in an attempt to explain declining levels of political participation.[6] Social capital theory suggests that participation in voluntary associations develops social networks that lead to increased levels of trust and cooperation within communities (Putnam 2000; Verba, Schlozman and Brady 1995). Social capital, like human capital, can be thought of in terms of an investment, but in this case an investment in networks and relationships, rather than in learning and health.

At the individual level the payoff to these kinds of investments in social networks is trust in others, the development of norms of reciprocity and the career opportunities that can result from a well-developed network of acquaintances. At a higher level, the benefits of social capital include an engaged and active citizenry that is better able to work together for mutual benefit, the very requirement of modern democracy. The social capital model in some respects parallels arguments made earlier by Almond and Verba (1963) regarding democracy's need for a "civic" culture.

The most well-known articulation of the social capital model in relation to political science is that of Robert D. Putnam in *Bowling Alone* (2000), who argues that declining levels of social capital are partly responsible for the decline in participation in the US. Participating in a weekly bowling club, as the theory argues, provides the foundation of trust, understanding and cooperation that can lead to successful democracies by providing the foundation for cooperative engagement. The theory has been challenged on a number of grounds (Adam and Roncevic 2003), including that it reflects a particularly American phenomenon, that the data simply do not support the argument of decline (Arneil 2006), that the effects of the decline in traditional social capital have been offset by growth in new forms of participation, that the returns to social capital are not equal across groups, including women and men (O'Neill and Gidengil 2006), and that democracy can sustain the decline in traditional forms of participation so long as alternative mechanisms for voicing citizen demands are in place (Stolle and Hooghe 2004). Additionally, evidence suggests that the relationship between trust and political participation is a weak one at best, and that "the causal arrows are more likely to run from trust to civic engagement than from civic engagement to trust," an assumption made by Putnam and others (Uslaner and Brown 2005, 890).

The relationship between social and human capital is important for understanding political participation and the broader topic of civic engagement. Human capital refers to the skills and knowledge that are core determinants of political participation. Education, as discussed below, can provide the cognitive skills and affective motivation for participation. Alternatively, these skills and motivation can be developed in the workplace or through volunteering. Verba, Schlozman and Brady (1995), for example, identify the various skills and knowledge that are developed through volunteering activities that can lower the costs associated with political participation. What the social capital literature brings to the discussion is an appreciation of the importance for democracy of *relational capital*. While skills and knowledge may be necessary prerequisites for political participation and civic engagement, they may not be sufficient for ensuring that citizens are motivated to engage.[7] The latter is likely to be considerable where citizens have developed the bonds of trust and norms of reciprocity that allow for cooperative action, and there is little reason to expect that these elements of social capital are distributed equally within society.[8] Where human capital is embodied in individuals, social capital exists in relationships between them. Both, it can be argued, are central to investigations of political participation and civic engagement.

Social Determinants of Human Capital and Engagement

A focus on human capital highlights the importance of understanding those factors that enhance one's likelihood of participating in the political process. Skills and knowledge, on the one hand, emphasize those cognitive elements that lie behind political participation. Yet affective elements are also important in the political participation calculus. Both are central to explanations of who participates in civil society and politics.

Socio-Economic Status

Socio-economic status, or more specifically, the combined elements of formal education, income and occupational prestige, provides significant mileage in understanding both civic engagement and political participation (Dalton 1996; Verba, Schlozman and Brady 1995; Gidengil *et al.* 2004). So well established is the link between socio-economic status and political participation that Verba and Nie refer to it as the "standard model" of political participation (as cited in Dalton 1996, 54). Their link with civic volunteerism is also well established (Verba, Schlozman and Brady 1995). Moreover, the effect of status is not limited to one generation but rather it is the case that "high-SES parents pass on advantages to their children (both political behaviour that children learn from and indirect gains through children's educational attainment)" (Plutzer 2002, 54).

Education has arguably the strongest impact on political participation of all socio-demographic variables (Verba, Schlozman and Brady 1995; Gidengil *et al.* 2004). As one element of socio-economic status, education has consistently been shown to translate into higher levels of political participation due to both the cognitive and affective changes that higher education can bring about. For one, education provides the most basic cognitive skills that are required to navigate through political information and rhetoric. Both high-school and postsecondary education have been found to have a positive impact on voting and political engagement more broadly (Dee 2004). The development of language skills, for one, that accompanies higher education appears to be linked to political participation and voter turnout (Hillygus 2005). Higher education, particularly a civic education, can provide the knowledge required for understanding and accepting basic democratic principles and basic political structures and processes (Nie and Hillygus 2001). Arguments have also been raised against limiting the discussion of learning to childhood, and in doing so emphasize the importance of learning that occurs throughout life, particularly into adulthood (Côté 2001, 30). Others highlight the importance of higher education for situating citizens within a network of politically informed and active citizens and the role that this can play in spurring political activity rather than for the particular skills that education develops (Nie, Junn and Stehlik-Barry 1996). And still others have highlighted the importance of legislative context for mediating the impact of education on political activity; differences in voter registration methods in the US and the UK translate into significantly higher returns to education in the former country (Milligan, Moretti and Oreopoulos 2004).

The better educated are not only better equipped to engage given their heightened ability to become and remain politically informed, but they are also more likely to have a desire to become politically engaged. This increase in motivation, which is the affective element of political participation, is heightened with higher education partly due to the increased sense of civic responsibility and duty that is normally part of the curriculum in institutions of advanced education (Gidengil *et al.* 2004).

Education's impact extends to voting and civic and political participation more broadly, including political knowledge and interest, and political attitudes and opinions. Research has also suggested that education can lead to positive externalities in the form of the quality of that involvement, at least in terms of voters having greater levels of political information that can be brought to bear on their political activities (Milligan, Moretti and Oreopoulos 2004). Education quite simply produces more effective citizens.

Linked to education, income provides citizens with the free time necessary to devote to political activities, as well as the resources that can be required for engagement (Verba, Schlozman and Brady 1995; Gidengil *et al.* 2004). One well-paying job, rather than several part-time jobs, for example, can make it that much easier to stay informed about politics; having sufficient income to be able to afford child care can provide one with the peace of mind and time away from family responsibilities to devote oneself to civic minded activities. And sufficient income is quite clearly required to donate to a political cause, party or campaign.

Occupation also plays a role in the development of skills that can increase the likelihood that citizens will engage in politics or civic engagement. Closely linked with income and education, one's occupation determines the types of duties that one undertakes and has direct consequences for the likelihood that one will engage in certain types of political and civic behaviour in part due to the social networks that one's occupation can offer. Importantly, it is not the fact that one works that is relevant for political participation but rather the type of occupation that one has. As noted by Verba, Schlozman and Brady, "teachers and lawyers are more likely to have opportunities to enhance civic skills — to organize meetings, make presentations, and the like — than are fast food workers or meat cutters" (1995, 315). Moreover, occupational status matters more for some types of activities than it does for others;

contacting a public official requires a set of skills that differ from that required for casting a ballot.

Generation and Life Cycle

The relationship between political participation and the skills set of citizens is one that varies across generations. Generational investigations into political attitudes and participation have revealed significant differences in political interest, knowledge, cynicism and participation (Milan 2005; O'Neill 2001; Stolle and Cruz 2005). In Canada, the evidence consistently reveals that the youngest cohort of Canadians vote less often, are less likely to be members of political parties and interest groups, and pay less attention to and are less knowledgeable about politics. The particular puzzle is that this disengagement has occurred in spite of continually increasing levels of education (Brody 1978).

According to Inglehart's post-materialism thesis, the most recent generations in western democracies place greater weight on non-material interest and concerns than material ones; human rights and the environment, for example, take precedence over balancing budgets and fighting crime (Inglehart 1990). This shift to "higher-order needs," he argues, is due to a combination of increased prosperity and security, the existence of the welfare state and increased access to physicians and hospital resources enjoyed by post-Second World War generations. Loosely based on Maslow's hierarchy of needs (1954), generations for whom security, both economic and physical, has been taken for granted, are likely to place an increased priority on self-expression needs over those of self-interest, particularly in the form of activism in social movements rather than political parties and interest groups.

Evidence for such a post-materialist shift has been employed by those seeking to explain shifts in levels of political participation across generations. Modernization theories have argued that rising educational capacities, the growth of service sector, and a rising standard of living have led to an increased capacity for and actual participation in political activities. With a Canadian focus, Neil Nevitte (1996) has examined how the shift in values across generations relates to changes in the type of political participation evident across several democratic states. Nevitte points to the importance of declining levels of deference to political and other authorities that stem from increase in skills and capacity due to rising education levels. The combination of increased cognitive skills and an increased unwillingness to defer to the authority and experience of political experts have led, he argues, to a shift away from traditional political activities (voting) toward more unconventional protest behaviour (joining boycotts or attending demonstrations). Direct action has replaced a reliance on indirect forms of political behaviour such as voting. These youngest generations have been referred to a "critical citizens" (Norris 1999). Some suggest that they are also more likely to volunteer than older Canadians, reflecting perhaps the shift away from indirect traditional mechanisms of political involvement toward more direct and outcome-driven forms of action.

Others, however, suggest that this argument is misplaced (Gidengil *et al.* 2003). Instead of a turning away from traditional forms of political activity toward more involved and hands-on engagement, political and civic engagement tends to be undertaken by the same individuals; those who vote are also very likely to be those who volunteer at the local food bank. And evidence that any shift to more direct participatory activities is due to a shift in fundamental values is limited. Among the youngest Canadians, it seems that their volunteering is occurring "in a more and more sporadic and episodic manner" and that much of the volunteering activity of youth appears to be tied to mandatory community programs in schools, as demonstrated by the drop in volunteering rates among working youth, and that it occurs for fewer hours on average than all volunteering (Stolle and Cruz 2005, 89).

Much of the recent drop in the voter turnout rate in Canada, for example, has been identified as stemming from dropping rates among one group in particular: young Canadians with less than a university education. According to Blais *et al.* (2002), turnout in the 2000 election was almost 50 points higher among university graduates born after 1970 than among those in the same age cohort who had not completed high school. Thus the positive impact of education on engagement at the individual level continues, but changes in participation rates among the less educated have led to declining turnout levels in spite of increases in education levels at the aggregate level.

Related to generational explanations for changing patterns of political participation, life-cycle explanations focus on differences in the salience and importance of politics during the various stages of life as explanations for variation in participation. If differences in participation rates and patterns are found across various age cohorts, they might not stem from the different generational forces working on each group but rather from differences in the salience of politics that stem from changing responsibilities and roles over the life cycle. Age has been found by some researchers to be as important as education in explaining political participation and importantly, may become relatively more important, for as individuals age, "experience can compensate for low levels of education" (Plutzer 2002, 42). Part of the story behind the life cycle relates to aspects of life that differ at various times: family life, including marriage and children, for example, brings with it a set of responsibilities, concerns and interests that are likely to increase the probability of voting and a number of other forms of participation, including volunteering. Home ownership, in particular, which occurs at a particular point in the life cycle, has been shown to significantly affect the likelihood of participation (Verba and Nie 1972). Importantly, however, a comparison of current differences in participation rates across age groups with those of previous generations suggests that generational effects are outpacing life-cycle ones. Participation rates among young citizens are so low, and the life-cycle boost to participation so limited that the gap will never be closed (O'Neill 2001).

Gender

Gender is also an important determinant when considering human capital in the context of civic engagement and political participation. Gender differences in levels of educational attainment, income, and occupational status translate directly into differences in levels and types of participation given variation in the skills and motivation to participate that they engender (Burns, Schlozman and Verba 2001). While the turnout gap between women and men has closed in recent years, differences in participation for such activities as running for office and in political knowledge and interest remain and in some instances are significant (Erickson and O'Neill 2002; Gidengil *et al.* 2006). Gaps in income, job segregation, discrimination and continuing primary responsibility for child care provide some purchase on explaining existing gaps in political participation and engagement. And although women's gains in education have been striking, they have not directly translated into increased political knowledge nor, as the pipeline explanation would argue, into increased levels of political representation. This puzzle remains, although some have identified gendered patterns of socialization and institutional norms as important explanatory factors (Inglehart and Norris 2003; Lawless and Fox 2005).

On some measures, however, women's participation outstrips that of men. Women, for example, are more likely to volunteer than men in spite of gender gaps in skills and knowledge (Hall, McKeown and Roberts 2001); their greater religiosity, which has been shown to relate to their propensity to participate in politics, may account for such apparent contradictions (O'Neill 2006). Women have also been linked to new forms of participation that more closely correspond with their positions are primary purchasers in the household, namely political consumerism (Stolle and Micheletti 2006). The latter, argued to be a form of political participation, is defined as "consumer choice of producers and products based on political or ethical considerations, or both" and includes both boycotts and "buycotts" of products (Stolle, Hooghe and Micheletti 2005, 246).

Quite apart from such differences, however, cultural differences regarding the appropriateness of politics for women versus men and sex roles more generally, which are likely to vary over time and across states, can also account for the weaker translation of these skills into political participation and engagement (Inglehart and Norris 2003; O'Neill 2002). Politics remains very much a "man's world." Moreover, the degree to which women and men are able to translate social capital into political participation, for example, has been shown to vary and there is little reason to believe that the same would not be true for human capital (see O'Neill and Gidengil 2006). The focus on gender makes clear that even if women and men possess the same level of skills and knowledge, the ability of each to transfer those skills and knowledge into political participation and engagement can vary significantly.

Immigrants, Visible Minority and Ethnic Groups

Given the relative importance of education, occupation and income for political participation, the barriers faced by visible minority and immigrant groups in this regard are clear and this is in addition to the added barriers resulting from racism, discrimination, settlement and a general exclusion from the dominant culture. Within the field of political science, research directed at better understanding their political participation and engagement, particularly in Canada, is extremely limited (for some exceptions see Abu-Laban 2002 and Black 2001). Focused predominantly on voting, research has found that immigration status can be generally more important for voter turnout than ethnicity, and that lower levels of turnout among immigrants are largely confined to those who are newly arrived (Black 20001). Ethnicity nevertheless matters for participation in elections, since variation in the turnout rates across a number of ethnic groups, appears linked to political activities in the countries from which individuals emigrated. Additionally, Gidengil *et al.* (2004) found that immigrants are as active in voluntary associations as other Canadians, except for those just recently arrived. Members of visible minorities, on the other hand, are less likely to be members of such associations, the exceptions being women's and environmental groups, where they are as active as other Canadians, and religious organizations and ethnic association, where their participation exceeds the average.

Research has also identified the important role played by certain agents in mobilizing members of these communities; research on ethnic groups in Winnipeg, for example, has identified the importance of political mobilization among ethnic communities for the level of descriptive political representation that they enjoy (O'Neill and Wesley forthcoming). Research on minority ethnic groups in Montreal provides similar findings for voting turnout, identifying the role played by the political culture in the community and, in particular, the normative significance attached to the voting (Lapp 1999). American research reinforces this conclusion and notes that the existence of social capital within ethnic communities does not always translate into political engagement. Citing the example of ethnically-based enclaves within major US urban centres, especially Asian-Americans, Latinos and Carribean-Americans who exhibit low levels of political engagement, Fuchs, Minnite and Shapiro (1999) argue that it is only when social capital is explicitly political that it is likely to encourage citizens to engage.

Aboriginal Status

Similar to research on the political participation and civic engagement of visible minority and immigrant groups, the political participation and civic engagement of Aboriginal Canadians have not received a significant amount of research attention. One recent investigation on traditional electoral politics reveals lower levels of turnout among Aboriginal peoples than among other Canadians, although there exists significant variation across communities (Guérin 2003). Significant barriers to electoral participation for Aboriginal people — for example, the requirement of giving up status to participate in elections was in place up until 1960 — explain part of the limited turnout levels. Socio-demographic factors are also at play, including the relatively young average age of the Aboriginal population, and their lower socio-economic status. Importantly, however, part of the explanation lies in the conscious disengagement of a number of Aboriginal Canadians from Canadian electoral politics, given questions of independent nationhood, colonialism and self-government (ibid; Ladner 2003).

Focusing exclusively on voter behaviour as an indicator of civic engagement is, however, extremely faulty methodology. In the case of Aboriginal people in particular, low voter turnout belies a community that is especially politically aware, interested and engaged; discussions with young Aboriginal leaders identified an especially politically aware group who were particularly interested in their community and band (Bishop and Preiner 2005). There is evidence, for example, that electoral turnout for band elections is in some cases significantly higher than that recorded in general elections (Bedford and Pobihushchy 1996). Others have noted that unique circumstances have required Aboriginal peoples to adopt avenues of "alternative civic engagement" such as seeking recognition and redress through the courts and in taking direct responsibility for the delivery of certain services and programs (Whittles 2005). Thus traditional definitions for concepts such as civic engagement and political participation may not "fit" for communities such as these, whose relationship to the traditional political system is unlike that of other communities.

Disability

Understanding political participation within the context of skills and motivation highlights the unique position of the disabled for taking advantage of their civic rights. Disabilities are varied and can include both physical and mental conditions. Unlike the vast majority of citizens, however, the disabled more often than not face unique barriers to political participation quite apart from their skills and motivation. These barriers are multiple and for voters can include physical barriers such as the absence of level access to polling stations, the absence of mobile polls or mail-in ballots for those unable to get to polling stations, and legislation that disallows electors from obtaining assistance when marking their ballot. For candidates, the inability to include expenses related to one's disabilities as legitimate personal expenses is similarly prohibitive.

Although academic research on the unique position of the disabled vis-à-vis political and civic engagement is especially limited, that which exists has identified the many difficulties faced by the disabled in such things as accessing elected office (D'Aubin and Steinstra 2004) and in voting (Prince 2004). The link between political efficacy and political participation in particular has been examined for persons with disabilities. Political efficacy refers to an individual's sense of their ability to effect political change, either given their own skills and knowledge (internal efficacy) or the political system's likelihood of responding to citizen demands (external efficacy). The research suggests that levels of political efficacy are significantly lower for people with disabilities than those without, and that these differences are largely explained by "disability" gaps in employment, income, education and participation in organizations (Schur, Shields and Schriner 2003). Moreover, the lower level of political efficacy explained about half the gap in political participation between people with and without disabilities. As such, policies designed to increase the educational and income opportunities for the disabled would have the additional effect of increasing their civic skills and sense of political efficacy, thereby indirectly increasing their levels of political participation. Employment in particular is likely to result in increased feelings of external efficacy, thereby additionally decreasing feelings of alienation and exclusion (ibid., 141-42).

Linking Human Capital and Participation: The Psychological Sources of Engagement

Socio-demographic factors take us some distance toward understanding why people participate in politics and civil society. There exist, however, a number of intermediary factors that mediate the relationship between socio-demographic factors and political participation more specifically, by providing in some cases the motivation and in others the ability to participate. As suggested by Verba, Schlozman and Brady, "interest, information, efficacy, and partisan intensity provide the desire, knowledge and self-assurance that impel people to be engaged by politics. But time, money, and skills provide the wherewithal without which engagement is meaningless" (1995, 354).

Political Knowledge

One element in the human capital link to political participation is political knowledge or information. It is widely understood that political knowledge is positively related to political and civic engagement: those who know more about politics are more likely to participate politically (ibid.). Political knowledge is a resource that can be drawn upon to reduce the costs associated with such participation: factual knowledge about political parties, for example, provides one with the ability to assess platforms that converge on one's own position on issues, allowing for more effective voting. Increased political knowledge has been found to lead individuals to make different political judgements than they would make without the information (Delli Carpini and Keeter 1996; Gidengil *et al.* 2004). According to Milner, "Research at the individual level ... bears out the truism that knowledge is power, that the competent, active citizen is the knowledgeable citizen" (2002, 39). For Delli Carpini and Keeter, political knowledge is "the currency of citizenship" (as cited in Gidengil *et al.* 2004, 11). Some have argued that information shortfalls can be offset by a reliance on "shortcuts" or heuristic cues (Popkin 1991). Low-information voters, for example, can overcome their information shortfalls by looking to knowledgeable friends for advice, by using party labels as clues to likely political agendas, or by evaluating candidates and leaders on the basis of their personality traits or social backgrounds. Such arguments are not without their critics (for an overview, see Gidengil *et al.* 2004, ch. 4).

Advocates of enhanced civics education have argued that the decline in participation rates in western democracies is linked to the reduced emphasis on civics courses and civic education among children and young adults. The paradox is that increased education levels over the past 50 years have not been matched by increased civic knowledge nor by dramatic increases in participation; rather the degree to which young citizens can answer questions on basic political facts has declined alongside voting turnout levels (Delli Carpini and Keeter 1996). According to this line of reasoning, a change in curriculum is partly to blame for the decline in participation. Unfortunately, the relationship between civics education and political knowledge and participation remains tremendously under-researched, particularly in Canada.

Henry Milner's research (2002) represents an important exception. He argues that levels of political knowledge, or civic literacy, help to account for variation in voter turnout levels at the aggregate level, quite apart from levels of formal education. Education's impact on political ability and knowledge has not, he suggests, been consistent across generations. Some countries, he argues, particularly the Scandinavian countries, have offset this generational trend by promoting civic literacy. Targeted largely at adults, public investments in public service television, subsidies to daily newspapers, restrictions on the use of television advertising by political parties (leading to a greater reliance on written campaign literature) and unique programs such as Sweden's study circles appear to correspond with higher rates of voter turnout at the aggregate level.

Canadian evidence suggests that Canadians are generally uninformed, rather than misinformed, about politics and that they do not live up to the "standards of traditional democratic theory" (Fournier 2002, 105). For example, while between 70 and 90 percent of Canadians at various points in time can identify their provincial premier, the numbers drop significantly when asking about specific party positions at the federal level (Gidengil *et al.* 2004). Gidengil *et al.* argue that the level of political misinformation among Canadians is such that it results in a skewing of policy preferences; they suggest that "if Canadians were not misinformed, public opinion would be more favourable to spending for Aboriginal peoples and to rehabilitating young offenders, and there would be less willingness to cut welfare spending or to trade off jobs for environmental protection" (2004, 101). Importantly, Gidengil *et al.* (2004) found that education appears to be the single most important factor in understanding varying levels of political information, although income, age and gender also add some explanatory impact; the importance of this relationship has been underscored in research conducted on the US and UK (Milligan, Moretti and Oreopoulos 2004).

Political Efficacy

As noted above, political efficacy is normally defined as the sense one has of one's capacity to influence political outcomes. The stronger one's sense of personal efficacy, the more likely one is to participate in politics. Two independent measures of political efficacy can be identified: internal efficacy and external efficacy. The former can be understood as a sense of one's own ability to understand and participate in politics, while the latter refers to a sense of one's ability to affect political outcomes through one's actions (Abramson 1983, ch. 8). Both are clearly linked to skills and knowledge; that is the greater the number of skills that one believes one possesses, the more likely it is that one will participate in politics. Moreover, the more one participates in politics, the stronger that one's sense of political efficacy is likely to be. That efficacy is a strong predictor of political participation and engagement has been confirmed in much of the literature on the subject (Verba, Schlozman and Brady 1995).

Research reveals that Canadians demonstrate very low levels of political efficacy. A survey collected in 2000 revealed that 63 percent of respondents agreed with the statement: "people like me don't have much say over what government does" and that 49 percent agreed with the statement "the major issues of the day are too complicated for most voters" (Howe and Northrup 2000, 9). Such affective predispositions play a role in determining levels of engagement, quite independently of levels of skills and knowledge more generally.

Political Interest

Interest in politics provides the motivation required to devote significant time and energy to politics (Gidengil *et al.* 2004). Political interest can be important for political participation in that it provides the motivation for acquiring political information that can assist in assessing political alternatives and governmental action. The role of political interest can be argued to have become more important for citizens' willingness to become politically informed, for although increased media communication has provided easier access to political information, it has also meant that political media content is easier to ignore (ibid.).

The concept of political interest has been operationalized in a number of ways and found to be positively linked to political activity in a number of studies (Verba, Schlozman and Brady 1995, 345-46). Gidengil *et al.* find that levels of political interest in Canada vary with age (for life-cycle rather than generational reasons), income, education and gender. The positive impact of education on political interest has also been recorded in the US and the UK (Milligan, Moretti and Oreopoulos 2004).

Political Cynicism

Like the concept of political interest, political cynicism has been operationalized in a number of ways and has been used interchangeably with concepts such as alienation and dissatisfaction. Generally, the concept refers to attitudes regarding the level of trust that one has in the competence and ethical standards of politicians and in the political system more generally and has been identified as a determinant of political participation. Increasing political cynicism has been linked to falling rates of voter turnout in popular commentary in the US and Canada, but strong evidence to support this link has yet to be found (Gidlengil *et al.* 2003; Norris 2002; O'Neill 2001). Political cynicism is generally assumed to depress political participation; those who have little faith in politicians and the political system are less willing to engage with them. But the opposite relationship can also exist in that a lack of trust in the system can provide a stimulus for mobilizing in an attempt to "fix" the system or at least increase accountability (Norris 2002, 98). Survey research conducted in Canada in 2000 revealed that 44 percent of Canadians disagree with the statement: "Given the demands made on the federal government, they generally do a good job getting things done" (Howe and Northrup 2000, 10).

Mobilizing Agencies and Engagement

Research on political participation and civic engagement has identified the important role played by mobilizing agencies, such as trade unions and religious organizations, in drawing citizens into action. Several theoretical explanations have been identified for the impact of such organizations on political activity (see Norris 2002, ch. 9). For one, membership in an organization provides citizens with social networks that build the feelings of trust and reciprocity (i.e., the social capital) that facilitate participation, particularly for those with limited cognitive and other resources. Membership also provides the possibility for learning a set of skills that can be tapped in various ways. Women's volunteering, for example, has been shown to provide them with a set of skills useful for various political activities (O'Neill 2006). Organizations are also likely to increase political participation by involving members in political discussion and, moreover, by encouraging and even mobilizing such action for their members. Finally, mobilizing agencies can provide a direct link to political parties and additionally encourage their members to volunteer and donate to various campaigns. As such, these organizations play an important role in linking citizens to the political system in democracies.

Local party associations, for example, have been argued to play an important role in mobilizing citizen involvement in urban centres in the United States (Fuchs, Minnite and Shapiro 1999). Norris' research (2002) suggests that membership in unions and religious organizations is not only positively associated with voter turnout, but with a wide range of political activities including party membership and protest activity. Moreover, she finds that their effect can help marginalized groups overcome a number of the participation barriers that they encounter. Thus mobilizing agencies both directly and indirectly affect human capital and in so doing determine engagement levels.

Civic Engagement and Political Participation
as Outputs of Value

Before proceeding to a discussion of the policy implications of the role of human capital in encouraging political participation and civic engagement, a brief discussion of the investment and payoff elements of the concept is in order. The human capital model presumes that investments are made for rational self-interest: investing in one's education now is likely to lead to the payoff of higher income and wealth at some point in the future.

How does the application of the concept to political participation and civic engagement assist in our understanding of them? Is it reasonable to presume that individuals will invest in their own human capital to improve their political and civic skills? Are political participation and civic engagement outputs of value? The question of whether voting and political participation are rational acts was first taken up by Anthony Downs (1957). Turnout, he argued, if viewed with the lens of rational choice theory, was an irrational act. The cost to voting could not be offset by the benefits, given the unlikely impact of any one vote on the election outcome. Cost-benefit calculations regarding voting, and additionally, broader forms of political participation should result in decisions to abstain. But such calculations do not adequately capture the participatory calculus given that so many people in western democracies participate in spite of the limited payoff. Clearly, there are additional forces at play. Blais (2000) has argued that part of the story behind voter turnout not captured by rational choice theory is duty. Many citizens vote quite simply because they believe it is their duty to do so as citizens. Importantly, this normative imperative has been linked to education: education not only provides the cognitive skills for active citizenship but the affective ones as well.

Beyond voting, increased skills and knowledge reduce the transaction costs associated with engagement, but the benefits to this increased engagement are neither straightforward nor guaranteed. One potential benefit includes increasing the likelihood that one's interests and values are more effectively articulated, thereby increasing the likelihood that governments will respond to them. One could consider variation in response to interest to be due to differentials in human capital investment: government responsiveness might be thought of as a premium that represents the going rate of return on past investment in human capital. But this counters the most fundamental of democratic theory's assumptions: the equality of citizens. Representative democracy ought to aspire to the effective articulation of all interests, not only those of the most skilled and knowledgeable. Moreover, it is not enough to examine the decisions made by individuals — rather the overall level of well-being additionally depends on "societal preferences and values with regard to equality of opportunities, civil liberties, distribution of resources and opportunities for further learning" (Côté 2001, 30).

At the aggregate level, government investment in human capital reaps clear benefits: increased skills and knowledge lead to increased levels of participation and engagement which are integral for the success of modern democracies. In line with the human capital model, increasing the skills and knowledge of citizens produces *general* human capital that is useful for all but one that few are willing to invest in given the diffuse nature of the benefits it produces.[9]

Governments must be kept accountable and only those that believe that citizens are attentive will respond accordingly. Additionally, investment in skills and knowledge can lead to indirect learning through political engagement; participation in politics can lead to "enlarged interests, a wide human sympathy, a sense of active responsibility for oneself, the skills needed to work with others toward goods that can only be obtained and created through collective action, and the powers of sympathetic understanding needed to build bridges of persuasive words to those with whom one must act" (Galston 2004). *À la* Tocqueville, investing in human capital can help to reduce class differences by bringing together those of various social classes to engage directly in political causes or by assisting in the development of habits of cooperative behaviour that allow for the development of functional democracies. Thus human capital can produce the social capital that assists in producing the skills, values, knowledge and action that is beneficial for public life.

Policy Implications

Policy Implications

Existing research on political participation and civic engagement reveals that no single factor can explain a significant proportion of the variation in these elements of democratic citizenship. Although socio-demographic factors provide significant explanatory power, accounting for affective factors such as political interest and political efficacy are necessary for developing a more complete model of these civic activities. Additionally, a "one-size-fits-all" model is problematic in that it can fail to adequately capture the unique political contexts within which certain groups function, including Aboriginal peoples, the disabled and women. Having said this, existing policy has an impact on citizen engagement, and future policy commitments provide a potential avenue for addressing the current democratic deficit.

K to 12 Education

A more even distribution of human capital in democracies would go some distance toward reducing the barriers that currently restrict civic engagement, and the single most effective mechanism for achieving this end is education. The skills and knowledge that result from education, particularly at the secondary and postsecondary levels, are those that directly assist citizens in managing the complexity of politics and that provide the confidence that brings with it a willingness to engage. Policies that discourage high-school students from dropping out or that help to manage the high costs associated with obtaining a postsecondary education bring with them the additional benefit of creating more effective citizens.[10] Encouraging youth to remain in high school has been singled out in particular for the positive impact this would have on declining voter turnout rates (Gidengil *et al.* 2004; Stolle and Cruz 2005). A successful effort to keep youth in school would yield additional rewards through increased income and higher status occupations, both of which are associated with higher levels of engagement.

While education alone can provide a civic boost, recent research suggests that specific curricula, including civics education and service learning, are worthy of serious attention (Galston 2001). While it is clear that not all programs are equally successful and that different types of programs encourage different kinds of engagement, organized education provides the most efficient and effective means for reaching a significant share of the population at a time when it can yield the greatest results.

While there is virtually unanimous agreement on the importance of education for democracy, agreement is likely to be harder to achieve over the particular curricula that ought to be adopted due to the lack of agreement on what modern representative democracy ought to expect of its citizens and on what makes for "good" citizens. According to Westheimer and Kahne,

> For some, a commitment to democracy is a promise to protect liberal no-
> tions of freedom, while for others democracy is primarily about equality
> or equality of opportunity. For some, civil society is the key, while for
> others free markets are the great hope for a democratic society. For some,
> good citizens in a democracy volunteer, while for others they take active
> parts in political processes by voting, protesting, and working on politi-
> cal campaigns (2004, 2).

Such differences of opinion ought not to discourage efforts to adopt civics programs given their potential democratic benefits.

Adult Education

The focus on learning in high schools and university ought not to blind policymakers to the important role that education can play in developing human capital in other forums. Importantly, adult educa-tion classes and back-to-work programs ought also to be considered essential and alternative avenues for developing the cognitive skills that are so clearly linked to engagement.

Voluntary Sector

Governments should also consider how their policies encourage and discourage the establishment and development of voluntary associa-tions, and in particular the long-term investment value of committing public resources to such organizations to assist them in their functions. In their role as mobilizing agencies, these organizations provide an important avenue for developing and employing skills and knowledge to a civic end. Such organizations as trade unions, religious organiza-tions, political parties and social movements encourage activity and engagement which develop a set of skills, a body of knowledge and the psychological dispositions that are essential for both effective citizen-ship and a successful democracy. Their importance is underscored when one considers that they offer an avenue for providing the political skills and knowledge that can encourage engagement to those young Cana-dians who drop out of school at an early age and who are unlikely to return to earn their diploma.[11]

Added Barriers for Certain Groups

Policies designed to minimize engagement barriers for particular groups ought also to be encouraged. Canada's Chief Electoral Officer has commissioned significant research on the causes of declining levels of voter turnout among youth and involved them in a number of forums addressing this question; it has followed up on this research with a set of policy changes designed to remove the barriers that are particularly restrictive for this group.[12] The permanent voters' list and the Internet and e-mail have each been the focus of these efforts. And while it remains too early to determine how well these efforts will pay off, they provide a clear model of how to formulate public policy: conduct research on the question at hand, involve the voices of the community itself in the discussion and allow both to inform the prescriptions for change. Such efforts ought to be furthered and similar efforts encouraged for groups facing barriers to participation, such as recent immigrants, women, the disabled and Aboriginal peoples.

Deliberative Instruments

Finally, investments in human capital will only reap benefits if citizens believe that their engagement is likely to be worthwhile. Modern democracies must address the current political malaise that views politics as unimportant or worse, as corrupt. While some have advocated electoral-system reform in Canada as a potential means for dealing with high levels of political cynicism (Milner 1999), the example of the British Columbia Citizens' Assembly on Electoral Reform established an important precedent in participatory or deliberative democracy. A group of randomly selected citizens from across the province participated in a year-long exercise that directed them to examine the existing electoral system and consider the possibility of reform. While its recommendation for reform (the assembly recommended a shift to a modified single transferable vote electoral system) was narrowly defeated in a provincewide referendum,[13] the exercise itself successfully demonstrated the capacity and willingness of ordinary citizens to engage in collaborative decision-making.[14] Additionally, it provided a concrete example of a government trusting the capacity of its citizens to render recommendations and a decision, something that ought to be encouraged for the potential it has for reducing levels of political cynicism, overall trust and apathy.

As such, investigations into the possibility of employing more deliberative instruments of public policy-making ought to be encouraged in
that reasoned and responsible deliberation of policy by citizens is
associated with increased political knowledge and interest, both of
which expand the probability of more engagement and participation.
Thus, quite apart from any policy benefits that might accrue from deliberative forms of policy-making, the gains to be had in terms of increased human capital, and hence engagement, would seem difficult to
overestimate.

Future Research Directions

Modelling Political and Civic Engagement

A review of the research on the development of civic and political
skills and knowledge and their impact on political participation and
civic engagement reveals the overwhelming complexity of these relationships. This complexity is assisted by a tendency for research to address narrow slices of the causal model "pie"; our knowledge of a
particular population or form of activity, for example, might be expanded but this often comes at the expense of understanding how these
relationships parallel those in other populations or those found for other
forms of activity. We would do well to step back from the tendency to
narrow our investigative focus and instead attempt to develop a more
comprehensive picture of engagement. Similarly, research would be
advanced with a commitment to improve conceptual clarity in the field;
research ought to be guided by a set of clear and well-understood concepts to allow for knowledge development.

Civics Education

Research in political science ought to continue to investigate the role
that civics education and service learning plays in the development of
participatory and civic skills and action. Linkages with researchers in
education ought to be encouraged for the obvious synergies that would
result. The evidence that has been gathered recently on this question
has advanced our understanding of the role such learning plays but
remains rather preliminary. Findings in the US suggest that service learning must "be organized in relation to an academic course or curriculum, must have clear learning objectives, and must address real

community needs over a sustained period of time" (Galston 2001, 229). Similar research ought to be encouraged in Canada, particularly longitudinal investigations, to assist in understanding how learning in the childhood and early adult years, within various contexts and with varying curricula, affects participation and engagement throughout life (Galston 2001; Gidengil *et al.* 2004).

Deliberative Democracy

The BC Citizens's Assembly on Electoral Reform provides an important example of the use of deliberative democracy in the formation of public policy. Although there exists a long history of normative treatments addressing the adoption of such mechanisms in established democracies, there is less to be found that reviews the application of such mechanisms in recent years, particularly in Canada. Case studies such as the BC example ought to be examined not only for their viability as policy-formation mechanisms, but importantly for their indirect consequences for political interest, knowledge, efficacy, participation and civic engagement more broadly. If nothing else, as educative mechanisms such instruments provide a potential opportunity for overcoming existing human capital deficits and some elements of Canada's current democratic malaise.

Women and Marginalized Groups

The political participation and engagement of marginalized groups, and to a lesser extent of women, are topics that receive far too little attention in the discipline. This lack of attention means that we understand too little about the multiplicative effects of barriers (poverty and disability, for example) and too little about the unique barriers that such groups face (our inability to explain away gender gaps in participation, for example). The examination of the political and civic engagement of Aboriginal peoples, in particular, calls attention to the manner in which conventional conceptual definitions can marginalize communities. Although a number of these groups make up a small proportion of the population, thus making it hard to capture them with large scale survey methodology, the important role that such an understanding could play in helping to break down existing barriers ought to provide sufficient motivation for adopting alternative methodologies suitable for such investigations.

Youth Engagement

The political behaviour and engagement of young Canadians demands further research attention. Contradictory claims regarding whether young people have adopted alternative forms of participation, unanswered questions regarding education's changing impact on participation among younger generations and lower levels of political knowledge in the face of rising educational levels require that additional research effort be directed at this group of Canadians. To the extent that this group might be redefining modes of political activity, research ought to be focused on them to evaluate the consequences of these shifts and their implications for Canadian political institutions such as political parties and processes such as elections.

Participation at the Subnational Level

Too little of the research focused on political participation and citizen engagement in Canada is directed at the provincial and municipal levels, reflecting in part the relative dearth of individual level data at the subnational level. Evidence of variation in voter turnout across levels of government (see Centre for Research and Information on Canada 2001) provides important evidence that similar forms of participation (e.g., voting) do not invoke similar participation calculi. There is little reason to believe that other forms of engagement and participation might not reveal similar differences and, as such, the research focus ought to extend to other levels of government.

Political Socialization

Finally, political research into the processes and agents of political socialization, and in particular the political socialization of children, ought to be revived. As noted by Verba, Schlozman and Brady (1995, 513), social structures shape participation and these structures are rooted firmly in family, schools, jobs, churches and voluntary associations. While research on the latter two has increased in recent years with the renewed interest in social capital research, our knowledge of political participation and engagement could be significantly advanced by increased research on the social and private forces behind public activity.

Conclusion

A line of democratic theory asserts that citizens possess a certain wisdom, which when refined by education, provides them with the ability to effectively engage in governance. Modern research suggests that education plays just such a role: it creates more capable, more interested and more effective citizens. Investment in human capital reaps significant returns in enhanced cognitive skills and in increased affective engagement. If citizens are made rather than born, then education "makes" citizens. What people know and what they can do explains a significant portion of the variation in engagement levels in democracies. But motivation to participate is also an important part of the picture — acquired skills and knowledge are more likely to be employed in civic pursuits in combination with a desire to do so. This desire can stem from either self-interest, a sense of duty, family, social networks and/or a political cuture that encourages political participation and engagement but does not develop in a vacuum. Thus human capital and social capital together take us much further in our understanding of civic engagement than human capital alone.

Individual investments in human capital are important, but they take place within a social and institutional context that limits the individual level benefits that derive from civic engagement. As such, government's role in human capital investment is most important. Government plays a central role in determining required levels of education and curricula, and in shaping labour market and social welfare policies; each influences skills and knowledge levels that encourage active engagement in civil society. Direct investments in human capital alone, however, are unlikely to reduce the democratic deficit. Instead, research identifies the complex interaction of skills, knowledge and affective motivation and the various mechanisms and structures that define the context within which they develop. Governments, for example, play a role in shaping the framework within which mobilizing agencies develop, and thereby indirectly shape the levels of engagement in society through their membership. Governments have also to assume leadership roles in developing and implementing policy instruments that will assist in reducing the additional and multiple barriers faced by certain communities. Finally, the actions of government can determine the skills and knowledge of citizens through their willingness to engage them directly in policy formulation (e.g., the BC Citizens' Assembly) and in political decision-making (e.g., binding referendums). Engaging the tools of participatory democracy not only increases citizens' skills and knowledge (i.e., in learning by doing) but also citizen trust in government and additionally provides an outlet for more "cognitively mobilized" citizens. A commitment by government to address the democratic deficit should begin by questioning whether their investment levels in human capital are sufficient for reaping expected levels of return.

Notes

The author wishes to thank Mary Pat Mackinnon, Ron Saunders, two anonymous reviewers and a number of colleagues in the Department of Political Science at the University of Calgary for their helpful comments on an earlier draft of this paper. Any remaining errors are my own.

1. The term "democratic deficit" normally refers to the failure of modern democracies to approach the ideal of democracy, that is in encouraging the informed, deliberative and effective participation of its citizens.
2. Note that Coleman's definition of social capital differs significantly from that employed by Robert Putnam, discussed below. Coleman sees social capital as any aspect of a social structure that facilitates the actions of actors (persons or organizations) within that structure (1988). Putnam, on the other hand, defines social capital as consisting of the networks and norms of reciprocity that facilitate collaborative action (2000).
3. An important point to remember is that citizenship in ancient Greece was limited to a small subset of the population: free adult males of Athenian descent (Held 1996, 15).
4. The use of the term "more" is very deliberate in that a number of political institutions were filled by lot from among the citizens of Athens and in this sense not all citizens participated in every aspect of public decision-making.
5. For a review of the classical debates on the appropriate level of citizen participation in representative democracies, see Held (1996).
6. The argument that levels of political participation have declined has been contested; see Norris (2002) for an argument that rather than decline, political participation has experienced a shift in the activities in which citizens engage.
7. Robert Luskin has proposed a model to assist in understanding varying effects on political behaviour: factors can be classified as influencing the ability, the motivation and/or the opportunity to participation politics. See Luskin (1990).

8.   Uslaner and Brown (2005) provide evidence that levels of trust in the United States are strongly related to economic inequality.

9.   General human capital can be contrasted to specific human capital, which provides skills and knowledge specific to a particular occupation and for which the benefits are more selective.

10.   The Ontario government recently introduced a bill that would deny a driver's licence to, and impose fines on, those who drop out of school before the age of 18 in an effort to reduce the dropout rate in the province (see Alphonso 2005).

11.   Although the drop-out rate is declining over time, it remains high among Canadians between the ages of 20 and 24. According to Statistics Canada, 9.8 percent this age group (or 212,000 Canadians) were not in school and did not possess a high-school diploma during the 2004/2005 academic year (importantly, the figure was 12.2 percent for young men and only 7.2 percent for young women). See Statistics Canada (2005).

12.   The commissioned research and the various policy and program changes can be found at www.elections.ca.

13.   To pass, at least 60 percent of valid votes had to be in favour of the referendum and majority support had to be achieved in 60 percent of electoral districts (48 of 79). Although the vote in the referendum met the latter requirement, it failed to meet the first by 2.3 percentage points (see www.elections.bc.ca/elections/ge2005/finalrefresults.htm). Such "special majorities" are often adopted in cases of fundamental policy or constitutional change to ensure that such changes are adopted with the consent of a significant portion of the population and to discourage indiscriminate and frequent tinkering.

14.   In a symposium at the 2005 Canadian Political Science Association meetings, one of the members of the assembly noted that in spite of the ultimate defeat of the recommendation, she had no regrets for having participated in the process. In spite of the frustration that accompanied trying to bring such a large group to consensus on their recommendations, she noted that the experience increased both her knowledge of political issues and the skills she possessed, and moreover, left her with a renewed appreciation for the importance of citizenship, engagement and democracy. See Carty (2005).

References

Abu-Laban, Y. 2002. "Challenging the Gendered Vertical Mosaic: Immigrants, Ethnic Minorities, Gender and Political Participation," in *Citizen Politics:*

Research and Theory in Canadian Political Behaviour, ed. J. Everitt and B. O'Neill. Toronto: Oxford University Press.

Abramson, P. 1983. *Political Attitudes in America: Formation and Change*. New York: Free Press.

Adam, F. and B. Roncevic. 2003. "Social Capital: Recent Debates and Research Trends," *Social Science Information* 42(2):155-83.

Almond, G. and S. Verba. 1963. *The Civic Culture*. Princeton, NJ: Princeton University Press.

Alphonso, C. 2005. "Ontario Plans to Deny Teen School Dropouts Right to Driver's Licence," *The Globe and Mail* (Calgary edition), 14 December, p. A4.

Arneil, B. 2006. "Just Communities: Social Capital, Gender and Culture," in *Gender and Social Capital*, ed. B. O'Neill and E. Gidengil. New York: Routledge.

Baum, M.A. and D.A. Lake. 2003. "The Political Economy of Growth," *American Journal of Political Science* 47(2):333-47.

Becker, G.S. 1964. *Human Capital: A Theoretical and Empirical Analysis, with Special Reference to Education*. New York: National Bureau of Economic Research.

Bedford, D. and S. Pobihushchy. 1996. "On-Reserve Status Indian Voter Participation in the Maritimes," *The Canadian Journal of Native Studies* 15(2):255-78.

Berelson, B.R., P. Lazarsfeld and W.N. McPhee. 1954. *Voting: a Study of Opinion Formation in a Presidential Campaign*. Chicago: The University of Chicago Press.

Bishop, G. and S. Preiner. 2005. "The Civic Engagement of Young New and Aboriginal Canadians." *The CRIC papers: Finding their Voice: Civic Engagement among Aboriginal and New Canadians*. (No. 17, July). At www.cric.ca/pdf/cahiers/cricpapers_july2005.pdf.

Black, J. 2001. "Immigrants and Ethnoracial Minorities in Canada: A Review of their Participation in Federal Electoral Politics," *Electoral Insight* 3(1): 8-13.

Blais, A. 2000. *To Vote or Not to Vote: The Merits and Limits of Rational Choice Theory*. Pittsburg, PA: Pittsburg University Press.

Blais, A. *et al.* 2002. *Anatomy of a Liberal Victory*. Peterborough, ON: Broadview.

Brody, R.A. 1978. "The Puzzle of Political Participation in America," in *The New American Political System*, ed. A. King. Washington, DC: American Enterprise Institute for Public Policy Research.

Burns, N., K.L. Schlozman and S. Verba. 2001. *The Private Roots of Public Action*. Cambridge, MA: Harvard University Press.

Carty, K. 2005. "Turning Voters into Citizens: The Citizen's Assembly and Reforming Democratic Politics," *Democracy and Freedom Series*. Kingston: Institute of Intergovernmental Relations, Queen's University. At www.iigr.ca/pdf/publications/384_Turning_Voters_into_Citi.pdf.

Centre for Research and Information on Canada (CRIC). 2001. "Voter Participation in Canada: Is Canadian Democracy in Crisis?" *The CRIC Papers*, No. 3, October. At www.cric.ca/pdf/cahiers/cricpapers_nov2001.pdf.

Coleman, J. 1988. "Social Capital in the Creation of Human Capital," *The American Journal of Sociology*, Special Issue: "Organizations and Institutions: Sociological and Economic Approaches to the Analysis of Social Structure," 94:S95-S120.

Côté, S. 2001. "The Contribution of Human and Social Capital," *ISUMA* 2(1):29-36.

D'Aubin, A. and D. Steinstra. 2004. "Access to Electoral Success: Challenges and Opportunities for Candidates with Disabilities in Canada," *Electoral Insight* 6(1):8-14.

Dalton, R.J. 1996. *Citizen Politics: Public Opinion and Political Parties in Advanced Industrial Democracies*, 2nd edition. Chatam, NJ: Chatam House.

Dee, T.S. 2004. "Are There Civic Returns to Education?" *Journal of Public Economics* 88(August):1696-1712.

Delli Carpini, M.X. and S. Keeter. 1996. *What Americans Know about Politics and Why It Matters*. New Haven: Yale University Press.

Downs, A. 1957. *An Economic Theory of Democracy*. New York: Harper & Row.

Erickson, L. and B. O'Neill. 2002."The Gender Gap and the Changing Woman Voter in Canada," *International Political Science Review* 23(4):373-92.

Fournier, P. 2002. "The Uninformed Canadian Voter," in *Citizen Politics: Research and Theory in Canadian Political Behaviour*, ed. J. Everitt and B. O'Neill. Toronto: Oxford University Press.

Fuchs, E.R., L.C. Minnite and R.Y. Shapiro. 1999. "Political Capital and Political Participation." Working Paper No. 993. New York: School of International and Public Affairs, Columbia. At www.sipa.columbia.edu/research/paper/99-3.pdf.

Galston, W.A. 2001. "Political Knowledge, Political Engagement and Civic Education," *Annual Review of Political Science* 4:217-34.

— 2004. "Civic Education and Political Participation," *PS: Political Science & Politics* (April): 263-66.

Gidengil, E., A. Blais, N. Nevitte and R. Nadeau. 2004. *Citizens*. Vancouver: UBC Press.

Gidengil, E., E. Goodyear-Grant, A. Blais and N. Nevitte. 2006. "Gender, Knowledge and Social Capital," in *Gender and Social Capital*, ed. B. O'Neill and E. Gidengil. New York: Routledge.

Gidengil, E., N. Nevitte, A. Blais and R. Nadeau. 2003. "Turned Off or Tuned Out? Youth Participation in Politics," *Electoral Insight* 5(2): 9-14.

Guérin, D. 2003. "Aboriginal Participation in Canadian Federal Elections: Trends and Implications," *Electoral Insight* 5(3):10-15.

Hall, M., L. McKeown and K. Roberts. 2001. *Caring Canadians, Involved Canadians: Highlights from the 2000 National Survey of Giving, Volunteering, and Participating*. Ottawa: Statistics Canada.

Held, D. 1996. *Models of Democracy*, 2nd edition. Stanford, CA: Stanford University Press.

Hillygus, D.S. 2005. "The Missing Link: Exploring the Relationship between Higher Education and Political Engagement," *Political Behavior* 27(1):25-47.

Howe, P. and D. Northrup. 2000. "Strengthening Canadian Democracy: The Views of Canadians," *Policy Matters* 1(5).

Inglehart, R. 1990. *Culture Shift in Advanced Industrial Democracies*. Princeton, NJ: Princeton University Press.

Inglehart, R. and P. Norris. 2003. *Rising Tide: Gender Equality and Cultural Change Around the World*. Cambridge: Cambridge University Press.

International IDEA (Institute for Democracy and Electoral Assistance). 2006. "Voter Turnout Since 1945: A Global Report." At www.idea.int/vt/index.cfm.

Ladner, K. 2003. "The Alienation of Nation: Understanding Aboriginal Electoral Participation," *Electoral Insight* 5(3):21-26.

Lake, D.A. and M.A. Baum. 2001. "The Invisible Hand of Democracy: Political Control and the Provision of Public Services," *Comparative Political Studies* 34(6):587-621.

Lapp, M. 1999. "Ethnic Group Leaders and the Mobilization of Voter Turnout: Evidence from Five Montreal Communities," *Canadian Ethnic Studies* 31(2):17-43.

Lawless, J.L. and R.L. Fox. 2005. *It Takes a Candidate: Why Women Don't Run for Office*. New York: Cambridge University Press.

Luskin, R.C. 1990. "Explaining Political Sophistication," *Political Behavior* 12(4):331-61.

Macedo, S. *et al.* 2005. *Democracy at Risk: How Political Choices Undermine Citizen Participation and What We Can Do About It*. Washington, DC: The Brookings Institution Press.

Maslow, A. 1954. *Motivation and Personality*. New York: Harper.

Milan, A. 2005. "Willing to Participate: Political Engagement of Young Adults," *Canadian Social Trends* (Winter):2-7.

Milligan, K., E. Moretti and P. Oreopoulos. 2004. "Does Education Improve Citizenship? Evidence from the United States and the United Kingdom," *Journal of Public Economics* 88:1667-95.

Milner, H., ed. 1999. *Making Every Vote Count: Reassessing Canada's Electoral System*. Peterborough, ON: Broadview Press.

Milner, H. 2002. *Civic Literacy: How Informed Citizens Make Democracy Work*. Hanover, NH: University Press of New England.

Nevitte, N. 1996. *The Decline of Deference*. Peterborough, ON: Broadview.

Nie, N.H. and D.S. Hillygus. 2001. "Education and Democratic Citizenship: Explorations into the Effects of What Happens in the Pursuit of the

Baccalaureate," in *Education and Civil Society*, ed. D. Ravitch and J. Viteritti. New Haven, CT: Yale University Press.

Nie, N.H., J. Junn and K. Stehlik-Barry. 1996. *Education and Democratic Citizenship in America*. Chicago: University of Chicago Press.

Norris, P., ed. 1999. *Critical Citizens: Global Support for Democratic Government*. Oxford: Oxford University Press.

Norris, P. 2002. *Democratic Phoenix: Reinventing Political Activism*. Cambridge: Cambridge University Press.

O'Neill, B. 2001. "Generational Patterns in the Political Opinions and Behaviour of Canadians: Separating the Wheat from the Chaff," *Policy Matters* 2(5).

— 2002. "Sugar and Spice? Political Culture and the Political Behaviour of Canadian Women," in *Citizen Politics: Research and Theory in Canadian Political Behaviour*, ed. J. Everitt and B. O'Neill. Toronto: Oxford University Press.

— 2006. "Canadian Women's Religious Volunteering: Compassion, Connections and Comparisons," in *Gender and Social Capital*, ed. B. O'Neill and E. Gidengil. New York: Routledge.

O'Neill, B. and E. Gidengil, eds. 2006. *Gender and Social Capital*. New York: Routledge.

O'Neill, B. and J. Wesley. Forthcoming. "Diversity and Political Representation in Winnipeg," in *Electing a Diverse Canada: Political Participation of Newcomers and Minorities in Canadian Cities*, ed. C. Andrew, J. Biles, M. Siemiatycki and E. Tolley. Vancouver: UBC Press.

Plutzer, E. 2002. "Becoming a Habitual Voter: Inertia, Resources, and Growth in Young Adulthood," *American Political Science Review* 96(1): 41-56.

Popkin, S. 1991. *The Reasoning Voter: Communication and Persuasion in Presidential Campaigns*. Chicago: University of Chicago Press.

Prince, M.J. 2004. "Persons with Disabilities and Canada's Electoral Systems: Gradually Advancing the Democratic Right to Vote," *Electoral Insight* 6(1):2-7.

Putnam, R. 2000. *Bowling Alone: The Collapse and Revival of American Community*. New York: Simon & Schuster.

Schur, L., T. Shields and K. Schriner. 2003. "Can I Make a Difference? Efficacy, Employment and Disability," *Political Psychology* 24(1):119-49.

Skocpol, T. and M.P. Fiorina, eds. 1999. *Civic Engagement in American Democracy*. Washington, DC: The Brookings Institution Press.

Statistics Canada. 2005. "Education Matters: Trends in Dropout Rates among the Provinces," *The Daily*, 16 December. At www.statcan.ca/Daily/English/051216/d051216c.htm.

Stolle, D. and C. Cruz. 2005. "Youth Civic Engagement in Canada: Implications for Public Policy," in *Social Capital in Action: Thematic Policy Studies*. Ottawa: Policy Research Initiative.

Stolle, D. and M. Hooghe. 2004. "Inaccurate, Exceptional, One-sided or Irrelevant? The Debate about the Alleged Decline of Social Capital and Civic Engagement in Western Societies," *British Journal of Political Science* 35:149-67.

Stolle, D. and M. Micheletti. 2006. "The Gender Gap Reversed," in *Gender and Social Capital*, ed. B. O'Neill and E. Gidengil. New York: Routledge.

Stolle, D., M. Hooghe and M. Micheletti. 2005. "Politics in the Supermarket: Political Consumerism as a Form of Political Participation," *International Political Science Review* 26(3):245-69.

Uslaner, E.M. and M. Brown. 2005. "Inequality, Trust and Civic Engagement," *American Politics Research* 33(6):868-94.

Van Deth, J.W. 2001. "Studying Political Participation: Towards a Theory of Everything?" Introductory paper prepared for delivery at the Joint Sessions of Workshops of the European Consortium for Political Research Workshop "Electronic Democracy: Mobilisation, Organisation and Participation via new ICTs," 6-11 April, Grenoble.

Verba, S. and N. Nie. 1972. *Participation in America*. New York: Harper & Row.

Verba, S., K.L. Schlozman and H.E. Brady. 1995. *Voice and Equality: Civic Voluntarism in American Politics*. Cambridge, MA: Harvard University Press.

Westheimer, J. and J. Kahne. 2004. "Educating the 'Good' Citizen: Political Choices and Pedagogical Goals," *PS: Political Science & Politics* (April):1-7.

Whittles, M. 2005. "Degree and Kind: Civic Engagement and Aboriginal Canadians." *The CRIC papers: Finding their Voice: Civic Engagement among Aboriginal and New Canadians*. (No. 17, July). At www.cric.ca/pdf/cahiers/cricpapers_july2005.pdf.

Woodruff, P. 2005. *First Democracy: The Challenge of an Ancient Idea*. New York: Oxford.

About the Authors

ROBERT CROCKER has held a number of senior positions in education in Newfoundland including Director of the Institute for Educational Research and Development, Dean of the Faculty of Education at Memorial University and Associate Deputy Minister of Education. Having recently retired from the Faculty of Education at Memorial, he is now the principal in Atlantic Evaluation and Research Consultants, a firm specializing in social policy research.

LORI J. CURTIS is an Associate Professor in Economics at the University of Waterloo and Canada Research Chair in Health Economics and Technology. Research interests include social policy, health and economic well-being. Funding has been received from SSHRC, CFI, CIHR and NHRDP and her publications appear in journals such as *Review of Income and Wealth, Health Economics, Social Science and Medicine*, and *Canadian Public Policy/Analyse de politiques*.

JACOB ETCHES is currently completing a PhD in epidemiology at the University of Toronto and is a Research Associate at the Institute for Work & Health. He has been a Junior Fellow at Massey College, a Doctoral Fellow in the Comparative Program on Health and Society at the Munk Centre for International Studies, and was awarded a Doctoral Award from the Canadian Institutes for Health Research.

JACQUELINE P. LEIGHTON is a Registered Psychologist and Associate Professor of Educational Psychology in the Centre for Research in Applied Measurement and Evaluation (CRAME) at the University of Alberta. Her research is focused on student assessment of reasoning and problem-solving skills and has been funded by the Natural Sciences and Engineering Research Council of Canada (NSERC) and the Social Sciences and Humanities Council of Canada (SSHRC).

MARK W. MCKERROW is a PhD candidate in sociology at Cornell University, Ithaca, NY. His research interests are social stratification and the sociology of education. He is currently working on his dissertation, which examines the decision to pursue postsecondary education, and the effects postsecondary education has on a range of labour-market outcomes.

STEPHEN L. MORGAN is an Associate Professor of Sociology and Director of the Center for the Study of Inequality at Cornell University. He is the author of *On the Edge of Commitment: Educational Attainment and Race in the United States* (Stanford University Press, 2005) and the co-author with Christopher Winship of *Counterfactuals and Causal Inference: Methods and Principles for Social Research* (Cambridge University Press, 2007).

CAMERON MUSTARD is a Professor in the Department of Public Health Sciences, Faculty of Medicine, University of Toronto. He is also President and Senior Scientist, Institute for Work & Health. Dr. Mustard has a background in public health sciences with research interests in the areas of work environments, labour market experiences and health, the distributional equity of publicly funded health and health-care programs in Canada and the epidemiology of socio-economic health inequalities across the human life course.

BRENDA O'NEILL is an Associate Professor in the Department of Political Science at the University of Calgary. Her research focuses on political behaviour, specifically the opinions and behaviour of women and youth. Publications include *Gender and Social Capital*, co-edited with Dr. Elisabeth Gidengil (New York: Routledge, 2006), as well as articles in *International Political Science Review, Canadian Journal of Political Science* and the *International Journal of Canadian Studies*.

GARNETT PICOT is Director-General of the Socio-Economic Analysis Branch of Statistics Canada. His labour market research interests include topics such as earnings inequality, poverty, job stability, immigrant economic assimilation, worker displacement, job creation and destruction, and he has written over 30 papers on these topics during the past decade. He has held positions at the University of British Columbia, The BC Department of Trade and Commerce, the federal Secretary of State and Canadian General Electric. He holds degrees in electrical engineering and economics.

W. Craig Riddell is Royal Bank Faculty Research Professor in the Department of Economics at the University of British Columbia. His research interests include labour economics, labour relations and public policy. Current research is focused on skill formation, education and training, unemployment and labour market dynamics, experimental and non-experimental approaches to the evaluation of social programs, unionization and collective bargaining, unemployment insurance and social assistance.

Ron Saunders has been Director of the Work Network at Canadian Policy Research Networks (CPRN) since January 2003. Before that, he was Assistant Deputy Minister of Policy, Communications and Labour Management Services at the Ontario Ministry of Labour. He has a PhD in economics from Harvard University. Ron has worked on a wide range of labour market issues, both in government and at CPRN.

Arthur Sweetman is Director of the School of Policy Studies at Queen's University, where he also holds the Stauffer-Dunning Chair in Policy Studies. Additionally, he holds cross-appointments in the Department of Economics and the Department of Community Health and Epidemiology. He has a PhD in economics, and much of his research addresses empirical issues related to the labour market and health policy.

Emile Tompa is a health and labour economist with a PhD in economics from McMaster University. He is a Scientist at the Institute for Work & Health and an Adjunct Assistant Professor at McMaster University. His research is focused on two themes: labour-market experiences and their health and human development consequences, and labour-market policies and programs that have an effect on the health of individuals and populations.

Queen's Policy Studies
Recent Publications

The Queen's Policy Studies Series is dedicated to the exploration of major public policy issues that confront governments and society in Canada and other nations.

Our books are available from good bookstores everywhere, including the Queen's University bookstore (http://www.campusbookstore.com/). McGill-Queen's University Press is the exclusive world representative and distributor of books in the series. A full catalogue and ordering information may be found on their web site (http://mqup.mcgill.ca/).

School of Policy Studies

Reinventing Canadian Defence Procurement: A View from the Inside, Alan S. Williams, 2006
Paper ISBN 0-9781693-0-1 (Published in association with Breakout Educational Network)

SARS in Context: Memory, History, Policy, Jacalyn Duffin and Arthur Sweetman (eds.), 2006
Paper ISBN 0-7735-3194-7   Cloth ISBN 0-7735-3193-9

Dreamland: How Canada's Pretend Foreign Policy has Undermined Sovereignty, Roy Rempel, 2006
Paper ISBN 1-55339-118-7   Cloth ISBN 1-55339-119-5 (Published in association with Breakout Educational Network)

Canadian and Mexican Security in the New North America: Challenges and Prospects,
Jordi Díez (ed.), 2006   Paper ISBN 1-55339-123-3 (978-1-55339-123-4)
Cloth ISBN 1-55339-122-7 (978-1-55339-122-7)

Global Networks and Local Linkages: The Paradox of Cluster Development in an Open Economy, David A. Wolfe and Matthew Lucas (eds.), 2005
Paper ISBN 1-55339-047-4 Cloth ISBN 1-55339-048-2

Choice of Force: Special Operations for Canada, David Last and Bernd Horn (eds.), 2005
Paper ISBN 1-55339-044-X Cloth ISBN 1-55339-045-8

Force of Choice: Perspectives on Special Operations, Bernd Horn, J. Paul de B. Taillon, and David Last (eds.), 2004   Paper ISBN 1-55339-042-3 Cloth 1-55339-043-1

New Missions, Old Problems, Douglas L. Bland, David Last, Franklin Pinch, and Alan Okros (eds.), 2004   Paper ISBN 1-55339-034-2 Cloth 1-55339-035-0

The North American Democratic Peace: Absence of War and Security Institution-Building in Canada-US Relations, 1867-1958, Stéphane Roussel, 2004
Paper ISBN 0-88911-937-6 Cloth 0-88911-932-2

Implementing Primary Care Reform: Barriers and Facilitators, Ruth Wilson, S.E.D. Shortt and John Dorland (eds.), 2004   Paper ISBN 1-55339-040-7 Cloth 1-55339-041-5

Social and Cultural Change, David Last, Franklin Pinch, Douglas L. Bland, and Alan Okros (eds.), 2004   Paper ISBN 1-55339-032-6 Cloth 1-55339-033-4

Clusters in a Cold Climate: Innovation Dynamics in a Diverse Economy, David A. Wolfe and Matthew Lucas (eds.), 2004   Paper ISBN 1-55339-038-5 Cloth 1-55339-039-3

Canada Without Armed Forces? Douglas L. Bland (ed.), 2004
Paper ISBN 1-55339-036-9 Cloth 1-55339-037-7

Campaigns for International Security: Canada's Defence Policy at the Turn of the Century,
Douglas L. Bland and Sean M. Maloney, 2004
Paper ISBN 0-88911-962-7 Cloth 0-88911-964-3

Institute of Intergovernmental Relations

Canada: The State of the Federation 2004, vol. 18, *Municipal-Federal-Provincial Relations in Canada,* Robert Young and Christian Leuprecht (eds.), 2006   Paper ISBN 1-55339-015-6 Cloth ISBN 1-55339-016-4

Canadian Fiscal Federalism: What Works, What Might Work Better, Harvey Lazar (ed.), 2005
Paper ISBN 1-55339-012-1 Cloth ISBN 1-55339-013-X

Canada: The State of the Federation 2003, vol. 17, *Reconfiguring Aboriginal-State Relations,*
Michael Murphy (ed.), 2005   Paper ISBN 1-55339-010-5 Cloth ISBN 1-55339-011-3

Canada: The State of the Federation 2002, vol. 16, *Reconsidering the Institutions of Canadian Federalism,* J. Peter Meekison, Hamish Telford and Harvey Lazar (eds.), 2004
Paper ISBN 1-55339-009-1 Cloth ISBN 1-55339-008-3

Federalism and Labour Market Policy: Comparing Different Governance and Employment Strategies, Alain Noël (ed.), 2004   Paper ISBN 1-55339-006-7 Cloth ISBN 1-55339-007-5

John Deutsch Institute for the Study of Economic Policy

Health Services Restructuring in Canada: New Evidence and New Directions, Charles M. Beach, Richard P. Chaykowksi, Sam Shortt, France St-Hilaire and Arthur Sweetman (eds.), 2006
Paper ISBN 1-55339-076-8   Cloth ISBN 1-55339-075-X

A Challenge for Higher Education in Ontario, Charles M. Beach (ed.), 2005
Paper ISBN 1-55339-074-1 Cloth ISBN 1-55339-073-3

Current Directions in Financial Regulation, Frank Milne and Edwin H. Neave (eds.),
Policy Forum Series no. 40, 2005   Paper ISBN 1-55339-072-5 Cloth ISBN 1-55339-071-7

Higher Education in Canada, Charles M. Beach, Robin W. Boadway and R. Marvin McInnis
(eds.), 2005   Paper ISBN 1-55339-070-9 Cloth ISBN 1-55339-069-5

Financial Services and Public Policy, Christopher Waddell (ed.), 2004
Paper ISBN 1-55339-068-7   Cloth ISBN 1-55339-067-9

The 2003 Federal Budget: Conflicting Tensions, Charles M. Beach and Thomas A. Wilson
(eds.), Policy Forum Series no. 39, 2004
Paper ISBN 0-88911-958-9 Cloth ISBN 0-88911-956-2

Our publications may be purchased at leading bookstores, including the Queen's University Bookstore (http://www.campusbookstore.com/), or can be ordered directly from: McGill-Queen's University Press, c/o Georgetown Terminal Warehouses, 34 Armstrong Avenue, Georgetown, Ontario L7G 4R9; Tel: (877) 864-8477; Fax: (877) 864-4272; E-mail: orders@gtwcanada.com

For more information about new and backlist titles from Queen's Policy Studies, visit the McGill-Queen's University Press web site at:
http://mqup.mcgill.ca/ OR to place an order, go to:
http://mqup.mcgill.ca/ordering.php